Frank Norris

A BIOGRAPHY

FRANK NORRIS

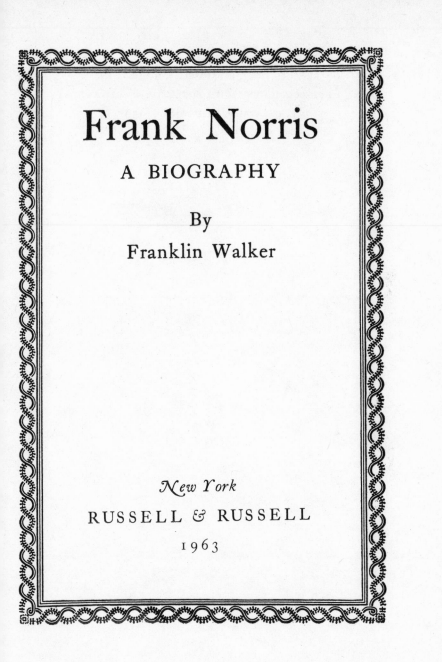

Frank Norris

A BIOGRAPHY

By

Franklin Walker

New York

RUSSELL & RUSSELL

1963

TO
LYMAN BRYSON
Friend and Counselor

TO
FRANK NORRIS

Simple and kind he lived, rich in the gracious dignity
Of labor and of love,
And knowing him our House of Life
More perfect grew, and added to its symmetry
A turret strong and bold—
A battlement within whose high serenity we dwelt
Content, as friends must ever be.
  So in his death
This splendid masonry of love's upbuilding
Has crumbled grievously to earth;
Our House of Life, more incomplete than in the days
    before his coming,
Stands strangely desolate;
Only a bird, full-throated with the melody of hope,
Sings in the empty courtyard.

—EMERY POTTLE.

Foreword

MY BROTHER died thirty years ago. Since his death I have been tempted many times to write his story, feeling that his life and struggle toward authorship would not only make interesting reading, but prove an inspiration to many another young writer. But to this temptation I have hesitated to yield, aware of my own shortcomings as a biographer, and all too conscious of my prejudiced point of view.

Mr. Walker has succeeded where I am sure I should have failed. When he first approached me regarding this work, I was impressed at once with his earnestness and conscientiousness of purpose. I gave him all the information I could, but most of this had to be drawn from memory, as all my brother's letters and diaries were destroyed in the San Francisco fire and earthquake of 1906. For over a period of two years Mr. Walker has devoted himself to gathering material, and on several occasions during that period has sought me for additional facts, to check some statement or clear up an obscurity. When at length I read the first draft of his manuscript, I was again impressed with his sincerity, but especially with his extraordinary—I can use no less forceful adjective—ability of ferreting out facts which I myself had all but forgotten, or which indeed I had never known.

In other hands the personality of my brother might have suffered. Frank's charm was unusual. Mr. Walker, who unfortunately never knew him personally, not only has not altogether failed in conveying this, but he has painted no false picture. His story—the story of a life all too short, full of early struggles and many disappointments, which knew at best but two or three years of acknowledged success—makes, I believe, absorbing reading. I am grateful to Mr. Walker for so fair and so honest a chronicle.

CHARLES G. NORRIS

May 19th, 1932
Saratoga, California

Preface

IT IS not always possible to make a first biography both definitive and interpretative. The scientific attitude necessary to the compilation of a source book and the artistic aim of the creation of a readable life are difficult to reconcile. In writing this biography of Frank Norris, however, I have attempted to present the facts of his life and to interpret those facts with unity and coherence. On the one hand, I have been freed from extensive weighing of evidence because Norris's life presents few controversial issues; he died young, his personality was singularly open to the observer, and the story of his life has not been distorted by legend. On the other hand, the details of Norris's life synthesize with ease, fitting almost automatically into the central themes of talent for story-telling and enthusiasm for experience.

Norris, in basing his novels upon the life about him, introduced much autobiography into his fiction. Thus *Blix* is frankly an account of his courtship of Jeannette Black; by removing the alloy of fictitious material, it is possible to use it as fact. To a less degree *Vandover and the Brute, The Octopus, The Pit,* and many of his short stories contain people and places of his own experience. Norris's methods in writing and views of contemporary fiction are found expressed in his essays, which have been frequently quoted. Further material for recreating his life and ideas during his formative period on the San Francisco *Wave* has been taken from the collected and fugitive writings on that journal. Finally, I have quoted at length from his accounts of experiences in South Africa and Cuba.

Manuscript sources have been limited but rich in content. Unfortunately most of Norris's letters were destroyed, either through failure to recognize their value, or through the ravages of the San Francisco fire of 1906, which burned most of the correspondence and manuscripts held by the Norris family. For letters quoted in this study I am indebted to Mr. Ernest Peixotto, Mr. Harry Wright, Miss Eleanor Davenport, and Mr. Arthur Goodrich, who have furnished copies of their correspondence, and to Miss Mildred Howells, Mr. Isaac Marcosson, and Mrs. Nellie Van de Grift Sanchez, who have permitted me to quote from letters published in *The Life in Letters of William Dean Howells*, *Adventures in Interviewing*, and *The Life of Mrs. Robert Louis Stevenson*. Mr. Charles G. Norris has turned over to me the limited amount of manuscript material in his hands: pencil drawings, notes used in writing *The Octopus*, an unpublished article on the Spanish-American War, etc. I am indebted to the University of California, Harvard University, and the Phi Delta Gamma Fraternity for giving me access to their records, and to the staff of the California State Library in Sacramento for the use of their card bibliography of Norris's writings, their indices of newspaper items, and their file of the *Wave*. By using the files of the *Wave* in the State Library, in the Stanford Library, and in the private collection loaned by Mr. Oscar Lewis of the Book Club of California, I have made an exhaustive survey of Norris's contributions to that journal. Additional information was gained by consulting newspaper files in the Bancroft Library and the San Francisco Library; from the magazine files of the University of California Library most of the background material for the biography was obtained.

The third and in some ways the most helpful source of information was the memories of Norris's friends and relatives, who went to endless trouble to give aid. In addition to those already named, I am indebted to the following for information given through interview or correspondence: Mr.. James F. J. Archibald, Mr. Gaston Ashe, Dr. Philip King Brown, Mr. Frank Gelett Burgess, Mr. Emil Carlsen, Mr. J. O'Hara Cosgrave, Mr. H. C. Chatfield-Taylor, Mrs. Dulce Bolado Davis, Mr. Charles Caldwell Dobie, Mr. Frank N. Doubleday, Mr. Theodore Dreiser, Mr. Hamlin Garland, Mr. Porter Garnett, Mr. George Gibbs, Mr. John Hays Hammond, Mr. Ralph Hathorn, Dr. Albert J. Houston, Capt. Joseph Hodgson, Mr. Henry Lanier, Prof. A. O. Leuschner, Mr. S. S. McClure, Miss Ariana Moore, Mr. George D. Moulsen, Miss Jessica Peixotto, Mr. John S. Phillips, Mr. Bruce Porter, Mr. H. W. Rhodes, Prof. Leon J. Richardson, Miss Bertha Rickoff, Miss Viola Rodgers, Mr. J. C. Rowell, Mr. Maurice V. Samuels, Mr. E. A. Selfridge, Mr. Frank L. Todd, Juliet Wilbor Tompkins, Mr. Seymour Waterhouse, Mr. Benjamin Weed, Mr. James L. White, Governor

Clement C. Young. It is difficult adequately to acknowledge the assistance of Mr. Charles G. Norris, Frank Norris's brother, and Mrs. Charles N. Black, Frank Norris's widow, who have given me freely of their time and help. Finally, I wish to thank Professors T. K. Whipple and Chauncey W. Wells, of the University of California, who have given me invaluable advice, and Mr. Lyman Bryson and Miss Imogene Bishop, who have aided in revising the manuscript.

Contents

ERRATA

p. xii, l. 29	*for* Phi Delta Gamma *read* Phi Gamma Delta
p. 10, l. 18	*for* played along *read* played alone
p. 22, l. 31	*for* astory telling *read* story telling
p. 28, l. 19	*for* to hand *read* to hang
p. 34, l. 23	*for* snd mountains *read* and mountains
p. 104, l. 1	*for* of population *read* of the population
p. 206, l. 17	*for* to a freind *read* to a friend
p. 221, l. 3	*for* prevalent code *read* prevailing code
p. 237, l. 15	*for* 1897 *read* 1896
p. 238, l. 19	*for* Stephen Graham Phillips *read* David Graham Phillips
p. 255, l. 18	same
p. 315, l. 43	same
p. 249, l. 22	*for* Tres Piños *read* Tres Pinos
p. 257, l. 21	*for* remainded so *read* remained so
p. 308, l. 19	*for* at Oakland *read* in Oakland

ADDENDUM

The notes, correspondence, and manuscripts used in preparing this biography have been deposited in the Bancroft Library, University of California, Berkeley, California, where they may be consulted by scholars.

Frank Norris

A BIOGRAPHY

Chapter 1: Chicago

THIS is the story of a boy who barely became a man before he died, but in whom the boyish qualities were the qualities which made him great. It is unfortunately true that most children spend their youth in looking forward to the time when they will grow to manhood, while most men look back longingly to the days when they were children. Occasionally a fortunate one realizes the superiority of childhood and succeeds in clinging to its advantages long after his companions have sobered down into the smug patterns of their existences. Frank Norris was one of these.

In attempting to explain the genesis of a novelist, Frank Norris wrote his spiritual autobiography. "Every healthy-minded child—no matter if he develops in later years to be a financier or bootmaker— is a story-teller. As soon as he begins to talk he tells stories. Witness the holocausts and carnage of the leaden platoons of the nursery table, the cataclysms of the Grand Transcontinental Playroom and Front-Hall Railroad system. This, though, is not real story-telling. The toys practically tell the story for him and are no stimulant to his imagination. However, the child goes beyond the toys. He dramatizes every object of his surroundings. The books of the library shelves are files of soldiers, the rugs are isles in the seaway of the floor, the easy chair is a comfortable old gentleman holding out his arms, the sofa a private brig or a Baldwin locomotive, and the child creates of his surroundings an entire and complex work of fiction of which he is at one and the same time hero, author, and public.

"Within the heart of every mature human being, not a writer of fiction, there is the withered remains of a little story-teller who died very young. And the love of good fiction and the appreciation of a fine novel in the man of the world of riper years is—I like to think—a sort of memorial tribute which he pays to his little dead playmate of so very long ago, who died very quietly with his little broken tin locomotive in his hands on the cruel day when he woke to the realization that it had outlived its usefulness and charm. . . .

"But sometimes the little story-teller does not die, but lives on and grows with the man . . . till at last he dominates the man himself, and the playroom of the old days simply widens its walls till it includes the street outside, and the street beyond, and other streets, the whole city, the whole world, and the story-teller discovers a set of new toys to play with, and new objects of a measureless environment to dramatize about, and in exactly, *exactly* the same spirit in which he trundled his tin train through the halls and shouted boarding orders from the sofa he moves now through the world's playroom, 'making up stories'; only now his heroes and his public are outside himself, and he alone may play the author.

"For him there is but little effort required. He has a *sense of fiction*. Every instant of his day he is dramatizing. The cable car has for him a distinct personality. Every window in the residence quarters is an eye to the soul of the house behind. The very lamppost on the corner, burning on through the night and through the storm, is a soldier, dutiful, vigilant in distress. A ship is Adventure; an engine a living brute; and the easy chair of his library is still the same comfortable and kindly old gentleman holding out his arms.

"The men and women of his world are not apt to be—to him—so important in themselves as in relation to the whirl of things in which he chooses to involve them. They cause events, or else events happen to them, and by an unreasoned instinct the storyteller preserves the consistencies (just as the child would not have run the lines of the hall railway across the seaway of the floor between the rugs). Much thought is not necessary to him. Production is facile, a constant pleasure. The story runs from his pen almost of itself; it takes this shape or that, he knows not why; his people do this or that, and by some blessed system of guesswork they are somehow always plausible and true to life. His work is haphazard, yet in the end and in the main tremendously probable. Devil-may-care, slipshod, melodramatic, but invincibly persuasive, he uses his heart, his senses, his emotions, every faculty but that of the intellect. He does not *know; he feels.*"

It is, then, but taking the words of Frank Norris himself to say that life for him was an adventure in which fiction-writing was his greatest pleasure. He wrote as he lived: with zest, with enthusiasm, with gusto. His successes as well as his failures were due to his intense affirmation of the creed of youth. It was his fortune to see, as few people see, at the beginning of an epoch; to impress his name ineffaceably on American fiction at a time of flux when old patterns were melting away and a new literature was taking form. This he did because he affirmed rather than denied, because he lived rather than meditated, because he saw with clarity and wrote with enthusiasm.

The retention of his youthful attitude was responsible not only for his eventful life, for his prolific writing, for the force of his books, but also for the quality which above everything else was so apparent to his contemporaries—his sincerity. It was a sincerity which sprang from artlessness, a sincerity which was as natural to him as were his daily habits. It was the code of a boy seriously intent upon playing a game as a game should be played. It reflected a faith full of prejudices, feeding upon false hopes, believing in the realization of unattainable ideals. With characteristically enthusiastic language he calls upon his fellow novelists to lead in the creation of fiction serious in its import. "Not by arrogance, nor by assumption, nor by the achievement of the world's wisdom, shall you be made worthy of the place of high command. But it will come to you, if it comes at all, because you shall have kept yourself young and humble and pure in heart, and so unspoiled and unwearied and unjaded that you shall find a joy in the mere rising of the sun, a wholesome, sane delight in the sound of the wind at night, a pleasure in the sight of the hills at evening, shall see God in a little child and a whole religion in a brooding bird."

★   ★   ★

IN THE spring of 1867 Gertrude Doggett quit the stage to marry Benjamin Franklin Norris. She did so only after a keen struggle, for from childhood she had wanted to act, and a successful career was already well begun. But stronger than the appeal of the boards was the energy of the young jewelry salesman, who, failing to heed her repeated refusals, applied the persistent tactics which had brought him success in business to the courtship of a beautiful and talented girl. The ruse with which he gained his end is a common one with romantic lovers: she was to continue her career after marriage. Necessity, however, soon cut into the romance, and the illness of Mr. Norris and the arrival of a daughter gave domesticity a complete victory. Gertrude Doggett's genuine dramatic talent and strong impulse towards self-expression, though thwarted for the present, were to be realized in full measure by her first-born son, Frank Norris.

Gertrude Doggett, daughter of a New England father and a Virginian mother, traced her ancestry to English colonists on both sides of her family. In the graveyard of Taunton, Massachusetts, the headstones record a long line of pioneer Doggetts, among whom a number were Unitarian ministers, while tradition included Priscilla Alden in the stock of the family tree. Gertrude's father, Samuel Doggett, left the homestead in Massachusetts to teach in a young

ladies' seminary in Charlestown, Virginia (now West
Virginia), where he fell in love with and married one
of his most attractive pupils, Harriet Walton, who
could remember the time when her grandfather, sea
captain and trader, had brought from Africa a little
Negro girl to be her playmate. The union in her father
and mother of warm Southern blood with strong New
England stock gave to Gertrude Doggett and her
children a romantic strain always in evidence but held
in check and guided by the best of Puritan tradition.

Gertrude was one of nine children born in Mendon,
a small New England village to which Samuel Doggett had moved on inheriting the ancestral farm from
his elder brother. She early showed a literary bent,
and, at the age of sixteen, when her brother Theophilus established a private school just outside of
Chicago, she joined him as his youngest teacher.
For a girl reared in New England, life in a sprawling
Illinois village was none too pleasant, but Chicago
near by, with its theaters and opera, offered opportunities which had long been denied her. The school
prospered, and aided by her vivid imagination and
talent for reading and story-telling, she became an
excellent teacher. But with the Civil War came a
change in fortune; Theophilus volunteered and was
killed at Shiloh, the private school was disbanded,
the family estate fell to pieces with the dispersion of
the boys to war, and Gertrude Doggett was thrown
on her own resources.

There is no record that at this time, or at any time
following, the courage of Gertrude Doggett was found
wanting. For a while she resorted to teaching in the
public schools, an occupation which, because of the

overcrowded classes and inadequate funds during the
war, was far from a pleasant one. Each morning she
faced the problem of keeping one hundred squirming
children in order while she attempted to train them
in the fundamentals of learning. As she worried,
taught, and punished, with no heart for the work, it
occurred to her that now or never was the time to put
her ambition for a stage career to the test. Her talent
won her a hearing with little trouble, and she made
her début at the McVickers Theater in Chicago,
playing the part of Emilia in *Othello*.

Other more important rôles followed. She traveled
with a stock company which produced *The Ticket of
Leave Man*, *The Lady of Lyons*, *Pizarro*, and a number
of Shakespearian plays. In spite of the arduous duties
of an undertaking which demanded that she perform
one play, rehearse another, and learn a third at the
same time, and in addition work late into the night,
making costumes which the company failed to provide, she was happy, for she was doing what she
wanted to do. She was a handsome woman and
played with grace and the grand manner of the old
school, losing herself in the melodramatic situations
of the plays of the company repertoire. Just when a
bright future seemed most assured, she met her
importunate young jeweler, who courted her in
Chicago, pursued her to Cincinnati, and caused her to
surrender to matrimony before she was aware of
capitulation.

*   *   *

BENJAMIN FRANKLIN NORRIS was the antithesis of
Gertrude Doggett in almost everything except his

abundant energy. The contrast in the personalities of his mother and father was revealed by Frank Norris when he used them as the prototypes for the leading characters in his last novel, *The Pit*. Curtis Jadwin, energetic business man who corners the world's supply of wheat, is, in his appearance, mannerisms, and tastes, an accurate picture of Mr. Norris. Jadwin's determined campaign for the hand of Laura Dearborn was similar to that of the jewelry salesman for the reluctant actress, and Laura Dearborn, in her physical charm, forceful personality, and love of the dramatic, is a faithful portrayal of Frank Norris's mother. In the novel the marriage of the talented patrician girl with the enterprising man of action, who has risen from poverty by his own efforts, is a union of naturally dissimilar personalities. "She's got a temperament, and she's artistic, and loves paintings, and poetry, and Shakespeare, and all that, and he doesn't care for those things at all." It is not surprising that Mr. Norris should have been delinquent in his taste for the fine arts, as from childhood he had been completely occupied with making his way in the world. Through his industry he was to be one of the fortunate who profited by the favorable conditions prevalent during the period between 1860 and 1900 which Charles Beard has named "The Era of Triumphant Business Enterprise." Ten years before the outbreak of the Civil War he was a penniless youth tramping the road, mending clocks; at the time of his death in 1900 he was the senior member of one of the most successful wholesale jewelry firms in Chicago.

Little is known about Benjamin Norris's forebears except that they were of British stock and long ac-

customed to the hardships of farming on a small
scale. He was born on a small farm in central Michigan where, in spite of the handicap of a chronic dis-
ease of the hip, he did his best to perform his share of
the chores, getting up during the cold winter before
daybreak to attend to the stock and running into the
stable to warm his feet in the cow fodder. When he
was fourteen, his father, realizing that he was ill-
fitted for farm life, decided to send him to a boarding
school. During a halt in the journey thither the boy
was attracted to a jeweler's window, entered and inquired if an apprentice was needed, and was given his
first job. His preference for action rather than study
was justified, for he quickly learned the trade, and
two years later he set out upon the road for New
York, peddling jewelry and repairing clocks. In New
York his zeal, expressed by his favorite phrase, "Go
get there, Eli," won him a position in a firm which
soon sent him to Chicago as their representative. At
the time he married Gertrude Doggett he had saved
enough money to start a business of his own, and the
couple, established in a room above a photographer's
shop, spent their evenings planning an ambitious
future.

★   ★   ★

FRANK NORRIS, christened Benjamin Franklin Norris, Junior, was born on the fifth of March, 1870, in a
modest house on Twenty-second Street in the South
Side of Chicago. This section, whither his parents had
moved with increase of family and fortune, was then
occupied by those who had been moderately successful; the meteoric growth of the city was to alter it for

both better and worse, bringing, after the fire of 1871, the Chicago aristocracy heretofore residing west of the river to beautify its avenues and to raise it to one of the showplaces of "the Garden City," and then, with the encroachment of business houses and influx of foreign population, to cause it to degenerate into its present state, a quarter closely packed with tenement houses and pawnshops where occasionally survives a brownstone mansion as a reminder of its more prosperous days. The material good fortune which had enabled the Norrises to move into this promising neighborhood had not been without its dark moments. Their first child, Grace, had lived three months to succumb to spinal meningitis. Their second daughter, Flora, born after Frank, died before the end of her first year in an epidemic of cholera infantum which nearly carried off Frank as well. Thus it was that Frank played along until his seventh year, when his brother Lester was born.

As the Chicago fire was checked at Polk Street, it did not reach Frank's home, but it burned his father's place of business. Fortunately, however, one of his traveling salesmen saved a good deal of the jewelry by loading it into a wheelbarrow and transporting it to a kiln, where it remained undamaged. With his diminished stock Mr. Norris started out anew, took for a partner his cashier, a young Scotch immigrant named Allister, and rode the crest of returning prosperity until B. F. Norris, Allister & Company became a wholesale jewelry house.

His father's business success meant little to Frank other than the comforts it brought him. Of more immediate importance was the fact that his father almost invariably spent his evenings at home, stretched out on the couch smoking incessantly as he listened to his talented wife read Scott and Dickens and her newly beloved Browning and Meredith. She sang to him also, particularly the songs she knew he liked best; Frank remembered they were *Beautiful Zion* and *Lord Lovell* and *Father, Oh Father, Come Home with Me Now*. Such memories help in reconstructing something of his childhood. It is not difficult to tell how he looked; a portrait taken when he was four shows him dressed for winter weather in a red overcoat trimmed with broad white bands and topped with a snow cap, standing very erect with an elbow resting on an upholstered chair and one foot negligently crossed behind the other. There is pronounced alertness in the brown eyes which gaze solemnly from a very attractive face with olive skin and dark hair, just as there is determination in the firm little chin and clean-cut lips. It is more difficult to tell what was going on inside his head, but that there was a great deal he testified later. "The first ten years of childhood are the imaginative years, the creative years, the observant years, the years of a fresh interest in life. The child 'imagines' terrors or delights, ghosts or fairies, creates a world out of his toys, and observes to an extent that adults have no idea of."

The subjects of his observation were varied by the interests of his family, to which he was more closely bound than the average boy of today. In the fall they followed the custom of the times and sat upon their stone doorsteps on the tree-lined street, cooling themselves with palm-leaf fans, while they chatted with their next-door neighbors. In the winter his

father's love for horses made it possible to go sleigh-
riding nearly every afternoon. In the summer they
usually went to Lake Geneva, where Frank dangled
his feet in the water while his father satisfied his
passion for fishing. In those days Chicago was not a
bad place in which to bring up a small boy, and we
may be sure that Frank was happy riding beside his
father, cutting capers around the iron lions in front
of Gossage's store, and watching horses with tinkling
bells upon their collars drag "bob-tailed" street
cars down Twenty-second Street.

*   *   *

EARLY in the summer of 1878 Frank made a momentous entry in the diary which he is reputed to have
begun at the age of five: "The time of departure has
now arrived. 'Is this a dream?' said I." He was
departing for Europe with his parents, who were
going abroad partly because they wished to purchase
furnishings for the new house they planned to build
on Michigan Avenue and partly because they had
always looked forward to making the grand tour as
soon as they could afford to do so. The usual visiting
of a succession of museums, art galleries, and cathe-
drals soon became tiring, however, as the Norrises
found that traveling with children was anything but
a delight. Seeking a restful haven and a familiar
language, they settled for the winter in Brighton,
where Frank had his first sight of bathing machines
and his first taste of English crumpets. The next
summer they returned to Chicago with several
treasures for the new house, among them an original
Raphael and a massive boudoir set of four pieces,

built of solid walnut and equipped with mirrors
which towered nearly to the ceiling.

The move to the new quarters was not made as
soon as the return home, for it involved much time
and trouble, and Mr. Norris's attention was completely absorbed by his rapidly expanding business.
In 1881 Charles Gilman Norris was born. Instead of
her stage career, Gertrude Doggett had had her hands
full with five children and a husband to care for.
She had lost her two daughters, but three active boys
now required intelligent supervision and education.
The talent in reading which kept her husband at
home in the evenings captured the imagination of her
children. In a breath-taking way she could make
stories live, and sometimes a thrilling tale by Scott
would absorb Frank and his mother till long after
Charles was in his crib and Lester had fallen asleep
by the fireplace. Dickens was also a favorite, and
Frank responded to his exaggerated characters; Dick
Swiveller and the Marchioness, Barkus and Uriah
Heep, Quilp, Sairy Gamp, and Bill Sykes were to
him more real than his own playmates. Later in his
novels he was to give many tributes to his mother's
reading, for Old Grannis and Miss Baker in *McTeague*
were to be products of his love for the eccentrics of
Dickens, and the romantic spirit of Scott was to take
his dentist into Death Valley.

In 1882 Mr. Norris abandoned plans for building
and bought a big house on Michigan Avenue at
Park Row, into which the family moved. This house
was quite a grand affair in the early eighties and
served Frank as the original for the mansion on
North Avenue where Laura Jadwin was nearly lost

in the art gallery equipped with a pipe organ. From
its windows Frank could see out into Lake Michigan
and watch the procession of the Great Lake steamers
from Milwaukee, far-distant Duluth, and the Sault
Sainte Marie defile majestically by. In the stable
were six fine horses and monogrammed carriages and
sleighs. There was even a coachman with varnished
boots and a cockade. Usually Mr. Norris preferred
to take the reins himself when the family joined
Chicago society in brisk drives along Michigan
Avenue to Washington Park. Michigan Avenue was
becoming "such a promenade as the world cannot
equal," and its beauty and fashionable supremacy
were unchallenged, except by its pretty neighbor,
Prairie Avenue, where were found the palatial mansions of the triumvirate of wealth and industry,
Marshall Field, George M. Pullman, and P. D. Ar-
mour. The time had come when Mr. Norris could
look upon them as fellow warriors, and Mrs. Norris
with her grand manner was not ill at ease in the
society headed by Mrs. Potter Palmer.

In religious matters the family was divided. Although Gertrude Doggett's forebears on her father's
side had been Unitarians, she had followed the High
Church Episcopalianism of her Cavalier mother,
because it more nearly suited her taste for form and
beautiful ritual. On the other hand Mr. Norris, who
had been reared in Presbyterianism on the farm in
Michigan, passed the plate in the Second Presbyterian Church. Recently a new fascination had been
added to his religion; he had found a kindred spirit
in Dwight L. Moody. Moody gave him the notion
that business principles were as good in religion as

they were on La Salle Street, and that if the church people put as much energy into the saving of souls as they did into the saving of dollars they might get somewhere. Mr. Norris took over a Sunday-school class and taught it with his usual earnestness. Here Frank may have joined in the singing of *Have Courage, My Boy, to Say No* and *Work, for the Night is Coming*, but much as he may have been fascinated by the energy of the movement sponsored by "the Sunday-school drummer," he from the first agreed with his mother about means of salvation. He became an Episcopalian and remained a member of that church, albeit an inactive one, throughout his life.

When Frank reached the age for starting his formal education, he was enrolled in a private school and began to struggle with the three *r's*, the last one of which even then gave him trouble. We may be sure that his taskmasters were not very successful in drumming into his head the essential facts of long division and compound interest; he preferred to memorize long sections of *The Lay of the Last Minstrel* and to consign his thoughts to his diary.

Of great humiliation to him was the attempt of his mother to supplement his regular schooling by sending him to Bonique's Dancing Academy, where she hoped he would acquire social poise. The jeers of his pals were annoying, especially as they were led by his boyhood favorite, young "Peely" McKay. While the fellows were at hounds and hares, Frank was forced to appear in a black velvet suit and be "nice" to simpering young ladies. His treatment of them was effective; he screwed up his face with rare ability, and they refused to dance with him a second time.

His master stroke was achieved when he secreted three kittens inside the black velvet coat and took them to the dancing school. They effectually ruined the coat, and for the time being Frank played with the gang at hounds and hares.

*   *   *

In 1883 Mr. Norris made a visit to California. The drizzly weather of Chicago had been a constant irritation to his lame hip, and he was limping badly. The sunshine of California made him walk straight and buoyed up his spirits. He decided to move West.

The other members of the family were none too eager for the change, particularly as they were wedded to the large mansion on Michigan Avenue, and Charles was barely two years old. When Mr. Norris made up his mind, however, he acted with decision. His business, returning him at least $25,000 a year, he could arrange to control from California with an occasional trip to Chicago, and as he preferred to live in the West, he bent his efforts to arousing their enthusiasm. This he did by bringing his family out to spend the winter of 1884 in a home on the shores of Lake Merritt, then on the outskirts of the village of Oakland. A year here won them over, so that they returned for good the following autumn, selling their house in Chicago and sacrificing the sleigh for more constant sunshine. A temporary stay in the Palace Hotel in San Francisco ended with the purchase of the Henry Scott residence at 1822 Sacramento Street.

San Francisco was soon to capture Frank's heart as Chicago had never done. This was not entirely due to the superior attractiveness of the Western city; but San Francisco became his home at a time when he was beginning to look for romance in his surroundings, whereas Chicago had been for him a matter of dreary weather and dancing schools. During his apprenticeship on the San Francisco *Wave* he was to write: "Realize the hopelessness of making anything out of Chicago or Buffalo, or Nashville, Tennessee. There are just three cities in the United States that are 'story cities'—New York, of course, New Orleans, and best of all, San Francisco." In the same period, speaking in the part of Condy Rivers in the autobiographical *Blix*, he often expressed his coolness towards his birthplace: "'bawn and rais' in Chicago',", always adding, "'but I couldn't help that, you know.'" As time went on, however, he decided that romance existed "not so much in things as in the point of view of the people who are things"; so that in 1901, when he returned to Chicago to collect material for *The Pit*, he found much romance on State Street.

Frank had little opportunity, however, to get acquainted with his new home at this time, for he was almost immediately sent away to school. William T. Reed, one-time president of the University of California, had just opened a boys' preparatory school on the old Ralston Place in Belmont, about an hour's ride down the peninsula on the end of which San Francisco is situated. The school had but twenty-five members, most of whom hoped by intensive study to save a year before entering Harvard. Frank threw himself with zest into the school activities and for the only time in his life "went out for a major sport."

Football was a rough-and-ready game in those days, especially as played by sixteen-year-old youngsters. An unrecorded game ended sadly for Frank. He broke his left arm in two places and was taken home to recuperate. The breaking of his arm had manifold results; it ended his secondary education, it completed his football career, and it brought with it several weeks of forced idleness during which new and far-reaching plans were to germinate.

*   *   *

Chapter 2: Lead Soldiers

WHILE the broken bone in his arm was knitting, Frank turned his attention to the exploration of the new house and its surroundings. Built in a section of San Francisco developed by the newly rich—from its windows one could see the mansions of the railroad nabobs on Nob Hill, the homes of Charles Crocker, C. P. Huntington, and Mark Hopkins—the Henry T. Scott residence[1] showed but a few touches of the bastard architecture, marked by eccentric towers and manifold gables, which prevailed among the houses of the neighborhood. It was a large frame house of two stories, the front of which was given over almost entirely to bay windows. Over the front door, between the windows of the parlor and those of the library, hung a sort of balcony which no one ever thought of using; this was a mannerism of the period, as were the wooden Corinthian columns which served the double purpose of supporting it and flanking the door. Within, the house was spacious and comfortable, and here Mrs. Norris could entertain her friends without apology.

[1]Described in detail as the home of Vandover in *Vandover and the Brute.*

19

In the yard Frank found to his delight that magnolia and banana trees grew side by side with firs and pines. He discovered eucalyptus trees and humming birds. In the back yard next door were hens and two roosters which crowed every time the cable car passed, while across the street was a vacant lot with cows in it, full of dry leaves and heaps of ashes, and surrounded by an enormous fence painted with signs of cigars, patent bitters, and soap.

The house was built near the top of a hill, at the bottom of which was Van Ness Avenue, the broadest and smoothest street in town. There Frank could watch cowboys driving in their cattle to the stockyards; there he could follow the political torchlight parades with their bands and "illuminations"; there he could stand on the curb as gayly costumed fraternal organizations drilled. But best of all he could glimpse military activities; on Van Ness the state militia, with drums and bugles, went through its maneuvers at dusk; and down it, too, went the cavalry, spurred and jingling, and even the rattling, bumping cannon from the Presidio. The pageantry of the street thrilled the lad; he could remember nothing like it in Chicago. His pulse quickened to its music, and he dreamt of uniforms and caparisoned horses.

A block farther on was Polk Street, where his mother did her marketing. It did not possess the glamour of Van Ness Avenue; the open markets were poor competitors for the drums of the parades. It was a homely street peopled with artisans and lined with cheap coffee "joints" and saloons where car conductors drank steam beer. It began suddenly and ended almost immediately—a street of no importance until Frank was to undergo a change in point of view which was still far in the future.

Of greater appeal were the lands on the other side of Polk Street. Frank discovered that Chinatown was over the next hill, and he began to imagine tales concerning dark squint-eyed orientals who slid silently in and out of their red-and-gold shops. The aroma of incense tickled his nostrils. Through Chinatown, with fleeting side glimpses into the painted vices of the Barbary Coast, past the old Plaza which had been the center of the city in the days of the gold rush, he would make his way to the waterfront and there spend the day watching the schooners and barkentines with broad-bellied sails, the steamers from Asia, Australia, and the Atlantic ports, and the paddle-wheeled river boats which plied to and from Sacramento and Vallejo. Up at the end of the waterfront were Meigg's Wharf and Fisherman's Landing, and beyond was the Presidio with gayly dressed officers on horseback and a grim red fort guarding the entrance to the Golden Gate. From the hill above the fort he watched ships disappear over the horizon on their way to the Yukon, to the islands of the Pacific, and to the Orient.

At home, also, Frank found encouragement for his fancies, for he never felt too old to join in the group when his mother found time to read to Charles and Lester in the evenings. As she read from Scott's *Ivanhoe*, Dickens's *Tale of Two Cities*, and Stevenson's *Treasure Island*, he extended the boundaries of his romantic world. He was beginning to appreciate her reading of Browning and Shakespeare, although Scott was still his favorite poet.

A new game began to absorb his attention almost
entirely. Charles and Lester were in the lead-soldier
stage. Frank felt that he had outgrown playing with
toys, for he had been away to boarding school and
had broken his arm in a manly sport. But one rainy
afternoon he watched his younger brothers marshal
their forces with even more zest than usual; after a
strenuous battle, the dead lay strewn over the field.
It was then that Frank took charge and rallied the
losing forces to a last-moment victory. The lead
puppets began to take on personality; one emerged as
Ivanhoe, another as the Black Knight, a third as
Front-de-Bœuf. The taking of Torquilstone Castle
was enacted in full detail the following day; Rebecca
threatened to throw herself off the dining-room chair
if Brian de Bois Guilbert added force to his entreaties.
The Battle of Agincourt demanded an increase in
numbers, and Lester broke the penny bank to provide
battle fodder. Incident after incident, plot after plot
developed; and the Veiled Prophet of Khorassan, the
Cid and the Khedive, Machiavelli and Corbullo the
Saxon—any heroes except the Americans, who for
Frank lacked romance—became, in defiance of historical sequence, participants in a complicated warfare that burst out of the nursery and threatened to
take the entire house by storm. By now Frank had
become a combined generalissimo and *deus ex
machina*, and the younger boys sacrificed activity to
listen and look in breathless suspense.

The directing of the campaigns heated Frank's
imagination and stirred him to astory-telling; he
started to write continuous tales and to read them
to the boys and sometimes to his mother. He even

essayed a short poem. To illustrate his campaigns
and to supplement the inadequate costumes of his
puppets, he sketched knights in armor; pleased with
his skill, he became vaguely ambitious and made
copies of the pictures in the *Home Book of Art*. His
mother began to dream that her eldest boy might
become an artist instead of a business man, and his
father grudgingly admitted that he was clever with
his hands.

It was now time to return to studies, as the arm
had been sound for some weeks and the new term
was opening at the Boys' High School. Although the
mother favored a training in art, the father looked
upon such as "thimble-head bobism" and insisted on
a business career for his son. The issue in the family
was that stated by Frank in *Novelists to Order:*
"From the very first the average intelligent American
boy is trained not with a view toward an artistic
career, but with a view to entering a business life.
The boy who is to become a business man finds, the
moment he goes to school, a whole vast machinery
of training made ready for his use, and not only is it
a matter of education to him, but the whole scheme
of modern civilization works in his behalf. No one
ever heard of obstacles thrown in the way of the
boy who announces for himself a money-making
career; while for the artist . . . education, environment, the trend of civilization are not merely indifferent, but openly hostile and inimical." His father
won a temporary victory and sent Frank to the
Boys' High School to prepare for business.

Frank had not quarreled with his earlier training in
private schools, partly because he had come into con-

tact with boys of interests similar to his own and
partly because he felt no desire to become an artist
at that time. Against this new school he rebelled.
He resented the bad manners of the sons of early
settlers and newly arrived real estate men, who joked
crudely when he talked of attending the art school to
paint from the life. His teachers objected when he
covered the fly leaves of all his books with pictures
and carved the head of the principal in chalk.
Adolescence had brought with it physical discom-
forts. His height was out of proportion to his breadth,
and his leanness offered incongruous contrast to his
great appetite; he was nicknamed "Skinny-well-fed."
His lanky figure, his complexion which remained in a
wretched state in spite of a much-hated regimen of
cod liver oil, and his unruly hair, worn in a stiff
pompadour, all combined to intensify his feeling of
awkwardness in the presence of giggling girls. Least
of all he liked the stuffy grammar lessons and the
attempts to cram him full of commercial arithmetic.
(How much money does A have? . . . If a man buys a
piece of goods at 12½ cents and sells it for fifteen,
etc., etc.)

At the end of a few weeks his misery had reached its
climax. His mother had been quietly waiting for a
break; his father changed his mind, withdrew his son,
and sent him to an art school.

*   *   *

THE school where Frank enrolled was the San Francisco Art Association, which had been founded in
1874 under the directorship of Virgil Williams, a
locally prominent artist of somewhat conservative

tastes who is remembered particularly for his friendship with Robert Louis Stevenson during the time when the latter was ill and lonely in San Francisco. The school, which under his leadership had attained a considerable reputation by helping to train several well-known artists, among whom were Alexander Harrison and Toby Rosenthal, was destined to have a notable future, for, after Williams's death in 1887, Emil Carlsen came from Denmark to take charge, shortly afterwards Mark Hopkins bequeathed to it his palatial residence on Nob Hill, and in 1893 it became affiliated with the state university under the name, the California School of Fine Arts—its status today. Frank found a score of students at work in the roomy, light studios above the California market, among whom were Eric Pape, Helen Hyde, Guy Rose, and Ernest Peixotto. Rose and especially Peixotto became his close friends and spent much time with him both here and in Paris where they later studied together.

Frank's enthusiasm for action and color was hardly satisfied by the conventional exercises which he was asked to do in the studio. He became impatient with constant drilling in drawing from the antique and in making still-life studies. He wanted to do things on a grand scale; then, as later, in both art and literature, he hankered after the dramatic subject and the wide canvas, and was impatient with the meticulous practice and revision required in an orthodox training. He preferred to spend his days with Ernest Peixotto at the Presidio, where the boys studied the horses of the cavalry barracks, making sketches of legs, rumps, hoofs, and heads.

In those days boys who desired to become artists
did not remain in San Francisco but looked always
towards Paris, to the Julien atelier and the Beaux-
Arts. It soon became Frank's ambition to go abroad
to study. With his mother favoring the idea and his
father hesitating, unforeseen circumstances came to
the boy's aid—Dwight L. Moody arrived to conduct
a campaign for souls in "the wickedest city in
America" and brought with him one of his choir
masters, Mr. George C. Stebbins. Mr. Moody was
pleased with the Sunday-school class which Mr.
Norris was teaching at the First Presbyterian Church;
and Mr. Stebbins, who, as a friend of long standing,
was a guest in the home for a fortnight, was impressed
by Frank's enthusiasm and surprised them all by
heartily endorsing a European training. There followed in his footsteps a friend from London who
recommended the Kensington School of Art as a
good place to go. They discussed the move at length.
Mr. Norris's desire that his son might receive the
best training possible was reinforced by a wish to
travel, engendered by the restlessness which had
followed his partial retirement from business. They
decided that Frank and his father should go to
London and Mrs. Norris remain in San Francisco
with the two boys and her niece, seventeen-year-old
Ida Carlton.

On June 10, 1887, the journey of the two pilgrims
was arrested in Chicago by the arrival of a wire
bringing the news that Lester, taken suddenly ill
with diphtheria, had died after a bitter struggle.
Mrs. Norris was heartbroken; she could stay no
longer in San Francisco, and with Charles and Ida

she joined her husband and oldest son in Chicago. Late that month they sailed for Southampton. The stay at Morley's Hotel in Trafalgar Square lasted only a month, for friends advised them to seek better instruction in Paris. The Julien atelier had drawn them like a lodestone, and by the middle of August the family was established on Boulevard Haussmann in an apartment house with rear windows looking out upon the Paris Opéra. Frank had become a student in the land of George Moore and Du Maurier.

*   *   *

ONE late afternoon the Norris family, fresh from hearing Gounod conduct *Faust* at a special matinee, paused on the steps of the Grand Opera House. The boulevards converging on the Place de l'Opéra were crowded with evening strollers, artisans returning from work, the audience pouring out of the theater. It was a gala occasion for Paris, and forty mounted cuirassiers with burnished coats of mail and brilliantly plumed helmets were controlling the crowds. Suddenly the raucous horn of a passing omnibus sounded clear above the noises of the street so that the frightened horse of a cuirassier reared and nearly threw his rider. In all good faith Frank exclaimed, "He hears the call to battle." In the world of his mind at that time there was nothing incongruous about the remark. He was daily concerned with romance and battles; although he had come to Paris to study art, he had, instead, become absorbed in chivalry; the pageantry of the opera was to influence him more than the Atelier Julien.

Frank enrolled as a *nouveau* in the Bouguereau studio of the original Julien Academy, "the old place over the smelly feather-cleaning establishment in the smelly court off the smelly Rue de Faubourg Saint-Denis." There he would go each morning and make his *esquisse* of the life model, working patiently on composition and line in the accepted manner. Like most of the Paris art schools, Julien's was in reality an association of students working together in order to obtain suitable studio space, models, and professional criticism. They had no regular instructor, but various well-known artists came frequently to comment on their work. Those Frank saw most often were the handsome Tony Robert Fleury, the debonair Lefebvre, and particularly Bouguereau, then at the height of his fame. Every Wednesday and Saturday Bouguereau would come to correct the sketches and to select outstanding ones to hand on the line. "He looked more like a well-to-do butcher than like the painter of Aphrodites and Cupids, very fat, very red as to the face, very loud as to the breath, very wheezy as to the voice." On taking Frank's drawing up with his delicately kept hands, he invariably prefaced his criticism with, "'*Eh, eh, pas trop mal.*'" But skill in sketching pictures of horses and men in armor did not help him in drawing nudes, and Frank never became one of the favorite ten to sit on the tabourets in the front row just below the model. At home he did a picture of his mother's black cat perched upon a cushion; to his delight it pleased the master and was chosen as one of the week's best. But even this was not enough to qualify him to enter the Beaux Arts, and his interest began to flag and his absences from the atelier to become frequent.

Participation in studio life proved more fascinating than work, as Julien's was the "true undefiled well of bohemianism." Consider the Monday mornings when the *massier* auctioned off the models before the hundred students; forty naked maidens offered with a, "*Qui est-ce qui en veut?*" Then there was almost always a row about retention of the front tabourets, and the students loved to turn the rows into riots. Perhaps Frank did not see Gilet spin around and catch Haushaulder on the tip of his chin with a move in the *savate*, causing him to slice off his tongue, but he did see some rough fights and hear some challenges —enough to prompt *This Animal of a Buldy Jones*,[1] the story of an ex-baseball pitcher from Yale, who, as a result of an argument for place, fought a duel with baseballs.

Features of studio life which appealed to Frank appear in a fugitive article on student life in Paris.[2] "And then [after a row over seats], just after everything has quieted down again, and the two men have arranged their difficulties by the drawing of straws, and the atelier has settled to its work, some 'light-complected' Englishman, who wears clean linen and disdains a blouse, pipes up from his high stool in the very back row:

"'Eh modail toornay la tait pahr es-cy seel vou plai!'

[1] Published in the *Wave*, July 17, 1897, and republished in *The Third Circle*.

[2] *Collier's Weekly*, May 12, 1900. Quoted by permission of the publishers.

"And twenty voices, in frantic execration, reply:
"'*Ah non à la fin!*'
"'*Elle est bien comme ça la modèle!*'
"'*A la porte l'anglais!*'
"'Gode tsaif se Quveene; oh yais Goddam!'
"And the row starts up again as vigorous as ever."

At another time, "A student is *flânant* among his comrades in the atelier. . . . For *blague* one addresses him in *récitatif*—
"'*Va donc, va donc!*
As-tu encore vu,
As-tu encore vu,
As-tu encore vu le Salon, Triquet?'

And Triquet, not for one moment at a loss, responds in kind. He proceeds from this point, he elaborates, he versifies, finding rhymes Heaven knows how. An anecdote occurs to him apropos; promptly it runs off his tongue in rhymed couplets set to music. A little song is the result, always funny, sometimes risqué, but invariably of an astonishing cleverness. The song becomes part of the repertoire of the atelier. It is sung years after the anecdote is forgotten. It is a matter for wonder and great interest, all this. The whole evolution of ballad poetry exemplified before your eyes and ears. An entire phase of literature developed in miniature while you wait."

On still another morning a student in the Bouguereau studio starts humming the opening bars of an act of *Faust*. "Two more join in, then three, five, ten, thirty, the whole atelier; some singing the orchestration, others the soprano parts, others the bass, or contralto, and so on. The neighboring Lefebvre atelier joins in, then the Gérôme atelier, then, far off in a remote corner, the sculptors, and before the end is reached the whole eight hundred go thundering off into—

> "'*Joie immortelle de nous aïeux*
> *Soyons fidèles, mourons comme eux.*'

"Then, reacting from the almost sublime to the wholly ridiculous, someone proposes that the common fund of all the ateliers—some two hundred dollars perhaps—be devoted to the immediate purchase of bazoos. The idea has a tremendous success. A committee is sent out, returning in an hour with four handcarts loaded with trumpets of pasteboard. These are distributed among the eight hundred. Each man arranges his shirt outside his trousers, a line is formed—'*Allons marchons!*'—'*On va descendre dans les rues!*'—'*Houp-là!*'—'*A la Bastille!*'—'*A bas la République!*'—the entire number of students debouches into the street, the eight hundred bazoos intoning Marguerite's prayer, and all work is over for that day."

Of still more importance to Norris's later work, the ateliers were full of characters—eccentrics who would have delighted Dickens. An American named Octavius appeared each day in naught for clothing but shoes, trousers, a fez, and an overcoat which reached to his shoe-tops. A compatriot called Tiger attended the atelier for nine years, drew tigers that took away the breath of the Salon judges, disappeared from the face of the earth. A Texan carried a bowie knife in his boot, danced clog dances in sabots on the posing platform, and fell dead of apoplexy on the corner of the boulevard. An Italian prototype for Svengali hypnotized the model till she fell off the throne.

Choubersky the Russian, when funds were short, danced Cossack dances in the street and passed the hat. He appears in the Buldy Jones stories along with Camme, and "Horse" Wilson, and the studio orphan model, Juliana. Eventually, a mute Frenchman named Slush-slush, who could talk only when half drunk, was to become, with a touch of horror, Dummy in *Vandover and the Brute*.

Frank spent only his mornings at Julien's. In the afternoons he had intended to paint in the apartment on the Boulevard Haussmann, and sometimes he did get around to doing some work. Animals were at first his subjects and prompted trips across the Seine— up the river—to the Jardin des Plantes, where he found all the wild life he could desire. For a long time he remembered the sound which he heard the boa constrictor make at feeding time—a sound which made him feel "as though some cold slime had been poured down the hollow of his bones where the marrow should be," and the impression of the camels chewing their cud as they dozed, "the breed brand, shorn into their necks, moving slowly up and down in unison with the motion of their jaws."

In spite of study at the art school and visits to the zoo, Frank's activities were at sixes and sevens during this first year in Paris. Although he was seventeen years old, he had found not one goal but a dozen to aim toward. Each new event was a distraction, and there was no paternal pressure to keep him at a task, for soon after their arrival in Paris, Mr. Norris had grown disgusted with the poor cooking of the American food which he demanded and had returned to Chicago. Later in the fall his mother had taken

Frank to Florence and Rome, but, though he enjoyed
the art galleries and was deeply impressed on hearing
the *Miserere* sung in the Sistine Chapel, he returned
with no added zest for studio routine. His ambitious
mother began to worry about his future. He was
absent-minded and unkempt; he wanted to do everything he wasn't supposed to do. As constant oiling
had failed to clear up the bad complexion, she called
in a French doctor with indifferent success. Worst of
all, she considered the *argot* which he picked up at
the studio to be corrupting his French, and, driven
to desperate measures, she read long passages from
Télémaque to him each night, hoping to develop in
him a feeling for correct idiom. In spite of his hatred
for this procedure he absorbed enough of the language
to prompt him to further reading. As his understanding increased, he found it opened up to him the
storehouse of a foreign literature; paradoxically, he
passed the stalls filled with Balzac, Flaubert, and
Zola, the proper food for one who was to become a
naturalist, and plunged unhesitatingly into the romantic Middle Ages. It was not Zola's *L'Assommoir*
nor Flaubert's *Madame Bovary* which won his heart,
but Froissart's *Chronicles*. He lived and dreamed
his favorite book; for the rest of his stay in Paris
his companions were Philip of Valois and the King
of Navarre, and his thoughts were concerned with
events which had happened five hundred years ago.
As he extended his reading in the field, learning the
early French vocabulary as he proceeded, his lin-
guistic zeal culminated in an ambition to read the
Chanson de Roland in the original.

Other stimulus for his enthusiasm was close at

hand. The Norris apartment belonged to a collector who had assembled swords, daggers, cuirasses, and coats of mail. At first Frank had delighted in playing with them; he now began the scientific task of classifying them as he found them used in his reading. Six-year-old Charles watched his brother measure the casques and make notes, but he wanted more exciting activity. The death of Lester had left him to play alone, and Frank, eleven years his senior, sympathized and joined in until once more the lead-soldier campaign became all-absorbing, and more elaborate and detailed than ever. Frank was seized with a desire for verisimilitude—although he had not yet reached the stage where he would eschew historical anachronisms—and gave to many of the participants the names of Froissart's characters. While Charles collected jam jars to exchange for sous to buy more boxes full of lead soldiers, Frank spent hours fashioning wonderful cannon out of the thick handles of paint brushes and the sides of cigar boxes. He drew maps of the two countries continually at war, dividing them into provinces, carefully marking the rivers snd mountains, roads and railways. Certain characters in the *mêlée* developed continuity and prominence; villainous Gaston le Fox, after Froissart's Gaston Phœbus de Foix; the wily Duke of Burgundy, and his nephew, the hero, Charles Gilman Norris in fourteenth-century accouterments. Frank became so engrossed in the story that he forgot it was a game; the story-teller had lived on, widening the nursery and finding a new set of toys to play with.

Just when Gaston le Fox had banished Charles into Saxony for getting drunk and killing a man and

he didn't see how he was going to get out of the
country in the allotted time, Mrs. Norris decided to
go home to California. It seemed that by now Frank
knew Paris well enough to get on alone; so just before
Easter in 1888 Charles and his mother sailed for
America, leaving Frank to continue his studies. The
episodes of the cycle of *Gaston le Fox* were to be
continued by mail, finding their way into manuscripts, carefully tied with loops of blue and red
string in the upper left-hand corner, rolled up inside
French newspapers to save postage stamps.

*   *   *

THE *pension* where Frank lived during his following
year in Paris still stands at Number 1, Rue de Lille.
The large house near the left bank of the Seine was
the home of M. Quatremain and his wife; the former
had been a frescoer of some note until he had fallen
from a scaffolding and had been forced to give up
painting and to take lodgers. The family offered an
environment genteel as well as art-loving, for
Madame Quatremain had at one time been the
governess of the young Czarina of Russia. There were
of course other members of the *pension*, among them
a Madame Desseau and her black-eyed daughter,
Marguerite. As Frank had outgrown the awkwardness and physical blemishes of adolescence, the other
sex now found him attractive, and when Marguerite
responded to his attentions, he was more delighted
than disturbed. During the year alone in Paris he
was to acquire an "Old World manner," and surely
love for a French maiden was one of the first requi-
sites.

Although his *pension* was nearer to the Hôtel des Invalides than to the Boulevard Saint-Michel, students who lived in garrets were his companions, and he saw much of the Latin Quarter without experiencing any of its inconveniences. Chief among his friends was Ernest Peixotto, who had drawn horses with him at the Presidio in San Francisco and who was now working in earnest at the ateliers. Together they visited the cafés of the Boul' Mich', made longer trips to St. Cloud and Versailles, basked in the sun in the Luxembourg Gardens, and sketched the animals in the Jardin des Plantes. But the most alluring attraction was close at hand. Not far from Frank's *pension* was the long line of bookstalls along the left bank of the Seine where one could find anything and everything from a paper of nasturtium seeds to a cuirassier's helmet—"the line of scum thrown up against the rampart of the Quai by the tide of reckless life that beats all day between the Luxembourg and the Beaux-Arts." Here the boys played at beach-combing, and many were the finds they made. Frank thrilled over the discovery of a skeleton hand with the manacle still attached, of bronze medals stamped with portraits of the French kings from Hugh Capet to Louis XIV, of a *livre d' heures*, "Black Letter, of course," containing the Litany in which he found the words:

> "*From battle, murder, the sudden death,*
> *And from the fury of the Norsemen,*
> *Good Lord, deliver us!*"

Two other student pastimes fitted in well with Frank's search for dramatic action. He bought some foils, a mask, and long black tights, and learned how to fence; he was back in the Middle Ages, sword to sword with Gaston de Foix or answering the call of Roland at Roncesvaux. The Opéra also continued to heat his imagination. Although he could afford a fauteuil at twenty francs as frequently as he pleased, he chose to join the *claque* with his student friends and thus become an organic part of the opera drama. When they were given the signal the members of the *claque* applauded and things happened. "The *chef de claque* gives the note to the *claque*, the *claque* gives the note to the audience, the audience gives the note to Paris, and Paris gives the note to the world." Later in a short story he pictured Buldy Jones gaining control of that drama, with interesting results.

Such were the games which Frank played in Paris; he seems to have been untouched by the contemporary movements in French literature. He who twelve years later was to introduce the methods of Zola into America was probably at the time of his arrival in Paris unaware that Zola existed, although he came at a time when the influence of naturalism on French fiction hung in the balance. The hardy school of French realism, given impetus by Stendhal and Balzac, had increased its emphasis on scientific verity and extensive documentation until it had culminated in the naturalistic novels of Flaubert, the Goncourts, Daudet, De Maupassant, and Zola, who had had things almost entirely their own way throughout the seventies and for the first half of the eighties. In 1887, when Frank entered the Julien atelier, Jules Goncourt had been dead for seventeen years, Flaubert for seven, and De Maupassant was going mad. Zola had been turning out the novels of the *Rougon-Macquart* series for sixteen years, and, during the decade following the enormous success of *L'Assommoir* (1877), he had been the ruling power in French letters. Early in 1887 he published *La Terre*—a fearful book which, according to Matthew Josephson, marks "the full tide of the Naturalistic manner and the Zola genius." It became the most discussed novel of the year and was reviled, damned, and praised. The reaction to Zolaism was about to begin; the appearance of the most outspoken, the most thoroughly naturalistic of his novels brought on a storm which was precipitated when it was called "the irremediable, morbid depravity of a chaste man" in *Le Manifeste de Cinque*, which appeared in bold type in the *Figaro* just a few weeks before Frank's arrival in Paris. It is fairly safe to assume that during his two years' sojourn Frank was little concerned with the discussion aroused by Zola's novels, or, for that matter, with the novels themselves. As the record of his enthusiasm for the French naturalist is so emphatic when it finally emerges some five years later, it is difficult to grant that he first read him in Paris and was so little impressed as to fail to reflect the discovery in his writings or activities. Moreover, his absorption with lead soldiers, battle pictures, and medievalism seems to preclude any strong sympathy with contemporaneous realism. Paradoxically enough, he was to become a convert to Zola in California and introduce naturalism into American fiction after its period of greatest activity had passed in France.

In his "studio" on the fourth floor of the *pension*, Frank worked on his weekly composition with more enthusiasm than usual. His lead soldiers had grown to canvas size, and there was energy and color in the picture of Philip the Bold fleeing in the rout at Granson. Bouguereau praised it. A great idea came to Frank—he would do something big and grand, a huge picture of the Battle of Crécy for the Salon. He bought a canvas which completely covered one end of his room and began to outline his composition with charcoal. He had long ago read Froissart's account of the battle, and he and Charles had acted out the whole from the advance of the Genoway archers in face of the arrows from the English cross-bows, "so thick, that it seemed snow," to the carnage of the French cavalry by "certain rascals that went afoot with great knives."

He wanted the details to be correct and so he, like Zola, started making notes, not, however, of the slum life of Paris but of the armor in the Musée d'Artillerie of the Hôtel des Invalides. Among the few of Frank Norris's documents which survived the San Francisco fire is a sheaf of these notes. The pages bear testimony to the careful study he made of the types of armor which he found in the museums. Each page is furnished with a complete sketch: "salade de guerre," "bacinet," or "great helm." The parts, "crest, timbre, vue, ventail, bavière, gorgerin" are illustrated and discussed. "This casque was only employed when fighting on horseback—as the head could not turn either to right or to left," etc. The notes also indicate that he was still busy in his research on the 20th of June, 1889. Frank had obtained a special permit to allow him and Ernest to go to the Musée de Cluny when it was not open to the general public. There the boys lifted the jousting helmets, tested the spears and lances, and, on measuring the suits of armor, were surprised to find that the most of the warriors had been small in build. When Frank donned a suit, brandished a sword, and became a very fierce and terrible soldier of the fourteenth century, he stopped to think that the predicament of a modern encased inextricably in such a suit would make a good story.

While Frank made continuous trips to the museums, the great battle picture grew colder and colder, and the interest in historical local color became a passion. Frank went further and made a close study of the Bayeux tapestry; in the manuscript Bible of Charles the Bold he found an armored knight of the ninth century; "lorica," "broigne," "trelised coat," and the "gambison" he added to the jargon which he was to use in his first poems and short stories. He wrote and illustrated an article, *Clothes of Steel*, which was a review of the development of armor from its use by the conquerors of Rome to its disuse because of the employment of gunpowder in the seventeenth century. He sent the article to his mother, and it appeared as his first published work, unsigned, in the San Francisco *Chronicle*, March 31, 1889. Frank wrote with the assurance of an expert: "I doubt whether a third of the readers of *Ivanhoe* ever pictured that gallant knight in the costume given in figure three. Scott, it is true, gives quite a different description, but with all respects to the greatest of all novelists, Sir Walter was wrong."

In the meantime the canvas at the end of the room stared down at him in its blankness and seemed ever to increase in size. One evening Ernest Peixotto and

Guy Rose tried to encourage him, but he felt that he
could never succeed with such a big picture. The
more they talked the more he felt that it could not
be done, and he finally ended by exclaiming, "If you
fellows want the canvas, take it home with you!"
His friends saw that further argument was useless,
and the big piece of canvas looked very good to them.
With ropes they carefully lowered it out of the French
windows and down into the court. It was a windy
night, and the tall Guy Rose and the short Ernest
Peixotto tacked home like a ship in a storm, with the
big sheet blowing like a sail, hurling them around the
narrow street corners. They cut it into small sections
and divided it between them; thus ended Frank's
plan and, with it, flickered out his desire for an artist's
career.

It was during this period that Frank, by means of a
gradual transition, turned from a career of painting
to one of writing. Within him enthusiasm and creative
imagination formed a common factor uniting the
two arts; they were alternate roads in passing from
the play of the nursery to more mature story-telling.
His method of making the change was unusual; as
the subjects of his drawings always involved action,
created as they were by his absorption in the life of
the Middle Ages, he found that it enhanced them to
connect them with the aid of a story. For long, the
pictures dictated the erratic movement of the story,
but in time they lost their control and the story began
to determine the subjects of the pictures. This transition had resulted in a "novel" called *Robert d'Artois*,
which was a further step in the narrative direction
than the lead-soldier epic, *Gaston le Fox*, which was

being mailed home to Charles weekly. What improvement there may have been in plot structure was offset by the rubbish which it contained. Now, instead of manipulating the action to include a certain picture, he wrote a whole chapter to be able to use a final phrase which pleased his fancy. The characters of Froissart failed to live with any warmth in its pages, and the plot was still occasionally forced to make turns in order to accommodate the illustrations. It did, however, contain a great many technical terms and utilized almost all of the types of armor which Frank had been studying. Meanwhile, in the epic cycle of the "pewter platoons," the hero had escaped into Saxony, accompanied by a detective with a glass hat, who interrupted the narrative to tell Stockton's story of the lady and the tiger. The hero was locked in a signal tower and the heroine tied to a switch, when Mr. Norris discovered the manuscript. He had sent his boy to Paris to study art, and good money was not to be used in such idleness; he cabled Frank to come home, and Frank was none too reluctant to do so. He packed up his curios, his foils, and his Froissart, and sailed for America. When his mother met him in New York, she was startled at the change wrought in her son since she had left him in Paris. He was dressed as a boulevard Parisian in silk hat, frock coat, spats, a walking stick—and he was wearing side-burns. He would have preferred to return in full armor, but he had begun to suspect that the romantic and picturesque was not confined to the fourteenth century.

*   *   *

THE two years after Frank's return from Paris, one spent at home, the other in college, make up the third and final canto of the lead-soldier epic. Although a trip of six thousand miles removed him from historic ground, he could live in the Middle Ages in San Francisco almost as conveniently as in Paris. He had brought home side-burns, a walking stick, and an old-world manner; he had in his trunks fencing foils, a fourteenth-century casque, and *black-letter* books; he held as not the least of his treasures the manuscript of *Robert d'Artois*, profusely illustrated in the manner of its period. It is probable that he found it very pleasant to be at home with his beautiful mother and successful father; it is certain that Charles welcomed him with the enthusiasm and tribute worthy of a hero of romance. But he felt vaguely homesick, and San Francisco appeared to him a provincial town and its Chinatown and waterfront barely interesting. He was not yet able to see a story in the purlieus of Polk Street, or to rub elbows with romance among plumbers' apprentices and shopgirls. Rather, he was all for "taking romance a weary journey across the water—ages and the flood of years—and haling her into the fuzzy, worm-eaten, moth-riddled, rust-corroded 'Grandes Salles' of the Middle Ages and the Renaissance." He was not now, however, aware of the worms, moths, or rust, for he was but nineteen and was consumed with a passion for the far-away and long-ago.

★ ★ ★

LIKE every youth who wanders from the hearthstone and opens his eyes, nineteen-year-old Frank discovered his parents on his return home. He found his mother to be a very handsome woman, who, with her abundant white hair, imposing profile, and patrician bearing, impressed all who met her with the force of her personality. As of her children only Charles now needed her care, home-making no longer absorbed the greater part of her energy. The growth of her freedom had coincided with a change in American society during which many women, relieved of their heavier duties in the home, turned their liberated energy to the furthering of activities and "movements" in the realms of education, politics, and culture. Impressed by the widening sphere of the "New Woman," Frank Norris later suggested that women should write the best novels because they had the time and the literary training to do so. Perhaps this thought developed as he watched his mother, for she had both the energy and the ability for intellectual activities. It was the heyday of Browning Clubs, and Mrs. Norris, as permanent leader of the local society, used her stage experience and talent for reading dramatic poetry to such good account that her fame in San Francisco has lasted to the present day. She also gave much attention to the Lester Norris Memorial Kindergarten, established by the Norrises in 1888 as a memorial to their second son. In these ways she found both happiness and independence.

Mr. Norris's hair and long mustache were now quite white. Of more than medium height, heavy-set with broad shoulders, he walked with a noticeable limp. In spite of this handicap his energy was sufficient for two men; Charles Norris remembers that at one time, impatient with a delay in the delivery of a heavy cornice for one of the houses which he was building, he went to fetch it, returning with it on his shoulder. He was determined rather than choleric, for his manner was evenly straightforward and he was never known to swear.

Frank's father was not as well satisfied with his life in California as he had hoped to be. His prospering Chicago business, together with his skill in conducting it at long distance, made it possible for him to spend almost all of his time in San Francisco. Listening to his wife read, teaching his Sunday-school class, and indulging his hobby for fishing failed to keep him happy. Time hung heavy on his hands, for he missed the drama of business. In spite of trying his hand at real estate, building a number of cheap flats financed by successive mortgages, he remained restless and chafed at the comparative inaction of his life.

Impatient at Frank's failure to make anything of his opportunities to become an artist, annoyed by his incessant scribbling of childish stories, he returned to his former conviction that his eldest boy should prepare to take over his wholesale jewelry business. The most obvious thing to do was to put him for his next four years in the University of California, to obtain the conventional Bachelor's degree. Such was his decision, and it was left to Frank to adjust himself to a future which attracted him not at all. To fit back into the pattern of this orthodox education, Frank had to start in where he had left off at Belmont, in some way cover the work usually done in the four years of high school, and pass the entrance examinations to the university. This he planned to do by private tutoring and by attendance at a coaching school. During the winter before his examinations he set about acquiring the necessary smatterings of Latin, history, English, and mathematics, but, as might be expected, he failed to apply himself diligently.

It suited Frank at this time to pose as a dilettante. He had in no sense found himself; his interest in painting had ended in a *cul-de-sac* and he had not yet begun to realize any power in writing. His recalcitrant attitude towards a college career was accentuated as he discovered that the students whom he met in San Francisco were so provincial that he felt completely out of sympathy with them. Instead of making him rebellious, his disappointment accentuated an attitude of languor and indifference which well fortified the "Old World manner" he loved to assume. He played at things—at sketching horses, writing poetry, studying algebra, and making love to pretty girls in a courtly way. These girls found him fascinating, for he was now good-looking, and the side-burns and sallow complexion gave him a foreign air. Although he could imagine himself in love with a different belle each day, no girl aroused his enthusiasm as did horses, which he called "the most noble conquest of man." He learned all he could about them, attended races, acquired the jargon, and prided himself that he could "talk horse." "There are three things every man, by virtue of his sex, must know all about, and must never under any circumstances be afraid of; these are firearms, women, and horses." Remembering the military pageantry of Van Ness Avenue and the mounted cuirassiers before the Paris Opéra, he decided to join the state militia. The step proved to be a dreary mistake; reality demanded forced drills with a dummy gun and no horse. It was the beginning of his disillusionment with military life; modern soldiers were not romantic.

Frank was still trying to wed the arts by making his stories vehicles for his illustrations. He played with both the pen and the brush in the manner of a young Thackeray, but now the writing was beginning to gain the upper hand. *Robert d'Artois* seemed sorry stuff and was laid aside for good. A new venture of greater sweep began to take form, a three-canto narrative poem in the style of Scott, a free and flowing fancy of the days of knight-errantry, with valor and love and horses and armor. He became more and more interested in it, worked steadily on it throughout the winter, and probably added many touches to it during his first year at the university. Its publication during his sophomore year will be considered in its place, but here it is well to stop and note indications in it of a maturing talent for writing.

Yvernelle must be read as the attempt of a nineteen-year-old boy in love with the spirit of feudalism to bring back the "day of romance, quaint and old." Its jingling octosyllabic verse can hardly be called poetry, for obviously the enthusiast had little ear for melody. But plot construction it has, and unity and movement. One reviewer noted, "In narrative poetry one generally finds a prolixity of words and paucity of

action, but *Yvernelle* is full of life, color, and incident."
In it is found that same enthusiasm which had put
life into the lead soldiers, the inborn talent to tell
stories. It starts pretentiously with a quotation from
Virgil, an acknowledgment to Goethe, and a para-
phrase of Shakespeare, but it moves along with a
swing to the third canto which is a mad race ahorse-
back to save the heroine from a convent cell. Even
in this early and ill-fitted form it is easy to recognize
the hand which was to describe Dyke's dash for safety
in *The Octopus.*

Yvernelle and the militia having absorbed too much
of Frank's energy, he took his entrance examinations
for the university in half stride, with the result that
he failed his mathematics test and entered Berkeley
in the fall of 1890 as a student of limited status. To
him there was nothing of the dramatic about algebra;
he detested it with all his heart. Each semester he was
to plan to attack it anew, but after much shuffling
of papers and scowling at problems he always came
to the conclusion that he did not have a "mathe-
matical mind." Even the shift of learning by heart the
equations written on sheets of paper pasted about
the room failed to get results. Perhaps he planned to
combat the effort to thrust him into business by
refusing to learn its *abracadabra;* at any rate, because
of his failure to learn mathematics, he was to remain
a student of limited status throughout his four years
at Berkeley and to leave without a degree.

The lingering embers of his residence abroad
smouldered well throughout his first year in the
university. When he moved over to his lodgings in
University Avenue near Oxford Street, he took with

him his curios garnered on the left bank of the Seine
and decorated his room with the pair of fencing foils,
the fifteenth-century casque, the skeleton hand to
which the manacle was still attached, and sketches
of still life and of the nude from the Paris art school.
He was most courtly in manner, and his side-burns
and mustache, his somewhat striking clothes—occasionally he even wore a "Sherlock Holmes" cap—
and his dignified bearing gave his classmates the idea
that he was surely a man of vast experience and
aristocratic background. His reserve added to this
impression, so that opinion was divided as to whether
he was queer or talented; it was not until sometime
later that the attempt to make him into a "regular
fellow" was to get under way. Most of this first year
he spent with two attractive young Jews, Myron
Wolf and Maurice V. Samuels, and the three were
known as "The Three Guardsmen," for Frank was
every inch Athos, Myron had the warm heart and
portly figure of Porthos, and Maurice completed
the group as Aramis.

Frank made the transition from medieval to modern adventure by throwing himself whole-heartedly
into the hazing and pranks of the Western college,
in which there was more than one hint of the dramatic struggles he had loved to invent and enact for
himself and his younger brother. He joined in the
open warfare when the members of the entering class
were always subject to attack and shifty wits were
as valuable as physical strength; he took part in
carefully planned pranks such as the expedition made
with a handful of his classmen to steal the huge white
elephant which stood as an advertisement near the

Sixteenth Street Station and to place it in full view of those attending the Sophomore Hop as a symbol of its failure; he shared in the drama of a whole student body moving together, as when they went to the Tivoli Theater across the bay, where the big Market Street telescope was brought into the house and trained upon the chorus girls gaily sporting in gowns and mortar boards.

The high moment came when, late in his freshman year, he was appointed one of the orators at the Bourdon Burial, a ceremony of long standing, the greatest event of the year. Annually, a grotesquely dressed multitude of freshmen paraded a large coffin through the Berkeley streets, made eloquent speeches over it when they had brought it to the campus, and consummated the holocaust by burning copies of their most obnoxious texts, Bourdon's *Algebra* and Minto's *Manual of English Prose*. This year Frank was to wreak his vengeance on mathematics. "Dirae Preces; Bourdonis Damnator.—B. F. Norrysus." The sophomores, however, planned to break up the ceremony, and, the night before the date set, kidnaped Frank and took him to a barn in Oakland, where they held him prisoner until it was too late to deliver his speech. It was almost as exciting as if Gaston le Fox had locked him in a tower.

Likewise, as Frank continued his writing, the romantic themes of the lead-soldier days still predominated. The student paper carried three poems by "Norrys"; *At Damieta, A. D. 1250*, tells of Margaret of Champagne's resolute stand against the Saracens; *Brunhilda* narrates the dragging to death of the Austrasian queen at the heels of her horse; *Les*

Enerves de Jumièges pictures the half-mythical sons of Clovis, whose father had punished them for revolt by cutting the tendons of their legs and arms and setting them adrift in a barge on the Seine.

> *"For they were lifeless, sodden, numb,*
> *Their ears are deaf—their tongues are dumb.*
> *With leaden-lidded fishy eye*
> *And open palms they lifeless lie."*

Only once more was he to use his *Yvernelle* manner—in the short story, *The Jongleur of Taillebois*, published during his second year.

At last Frank's thralldom to the Middle Ages was coming to a close. Paradoxically enough, the printing of his first book marked the end of the interests which had created it; his mother, ever ready to encourage him, had been enthusiastic about *Yvernelle* and with his pen-and-ink sketches she had sent it to Lippincott. They accepted the poem but rejected the drawings, preferring to tickle the holiday trade with engravings and full-page pictures in color by Will Low, Church, and Deilman. Mrs. Norris advanced four hundred dollars towards the expense of publication. By the time the book appeared in handsome make-up, however, priced at $3.50 and $5.00 for the Christmas trade of 1891, Frank was ready to deny it as his child. New influences had come into his life. The members of the Phi Gamma Delta fraternity, having at last come to the conclusion that he was no Jew and could be made into "a regular fellow," had pledged him. His growing conviction that "an hour's experience is worth ten years of study" was causing him to transfer his interests from French medievalism to modern college life. But of most importance to his future work, Rudyard Kipling had come out of the East and had captured America; Frank learned that romance was much closer at hand than he had supposed, and began whole-heartedly "to dance to the little spectacled colonial's piping."

Chapter 3: College High Jinks

IN SPITE of his reluctance about entering college, Frank spent five years of his life as a student. During four of these, 1890–94, he attended the University of California; leaving Berkeley without graduating, he passed the following year at Harvard, where he specialized in writing. In Frank's opinion his four years at Berkeley brought very meager results, whereas during the year at Harvard he learned more than at any other period of his life. But the record of low grades at Berkeley does not tell the whole story. While he was failing in mathematics he was observing life in Berkeley and San Francisco; while he was neglecting Macaulay and Carlyle he was discovering Kipling and Zola; while he was at odds with the English department he was writing acceptable stories for San Francisco journals. As he gradually but surely fixed upon contemporary life as the subject for his fiction, he reduced college to an orientation course which led him away from books. Thus in his freshman year he finished *Yvernelle;* in his senior year he started *McTeague*. He left Berkeley without a degree but with a perspective.

* * *

As HE was not interested in an ordinary college training, Frank entered the University of California under protest. He hoped, however, to receive aid and encouragement in his writing, but, early disappointed by the English department, he developed an antagonism towards all things academic. The symbol of his university work came to be the word *Fustian* scrawled by the instructor across the face of an enthusiastically written theme. No doubt part of the difficulty resulted from Frank's recalcitrance, but the burden of blame must be laid upon the system. He had become an unwilling unit in an organization which demanded that he conform to its rules in order to receive its recognition; instead of a course in creative writing he was told to be satisfied with the composition of a series of compulsory themes and exercises, devised to "raise the level" of student expression and looked upon by the majority of students as a trial and a nuisance. The subjects of these themes were of the usual type, reflections after reading Macaulay, Carlyle, De Quincey, *et hoc genus omne*. His individuality in the treatment of his paper on Thomas-à-Becket resulted in the *Fustian* reproval; in another of his papers he departed so far from the assignment as to give a detailed description of the moon rising, only to have his paper read to the class as an example of what not to do. Paper after paper he turned in to the exacting professor, each time to be informed that his work lacked unity or syntactical perfection. The professor's view speaks for itself: "Student essays are seldom very good or very bad, but about twelve years ago I received one that was

both. [Frank's first theme.] The descriptions in it
were so vivid that the thousands of student papers I
have since read have not effaced them from my memory; but the style was marred by mannerisms and
affectations, the essay as a whole lacked unity and
consecutiveness, and the last passage in it was an
echo of the famous apostrophe by De Quincey, whose
work the class was studying at the time. . . . I had
hoped the crudities in his style would disappear. But
not so. By no means ignorant of his own ability, he
was self-sufficient and impatient of criticism, and
almost to the end of the chapter each of his papers,
no matter what the subject, proved to be a string of
unconnected pictures, each excellent in itself, but
the whole not forming an adequate treatment of the
topic. It was not until he submitted an original short
story that he attained the highest grade."

If the fault lay with the system, it also lay with the
professor. The help which he was prepared to give
Frank was in reality negative; his corrections were
based on the common denominator of the acade-
mician: "Does it meet the assignment?" The result
was that Frank attempted to find salvation by reading and imitating contemporary authors, and by
contributing to student papers and San Francisco
journals. As time went on, his attitude spread from
resentment towards his English professor to scorn
for all attention to style. "What pleased me most in
your review of *McTeague* was 'disdaining all pretensions to style.' It is precisely what I try most to
avoid. I detest 'fine writing,' 'rhetoric,' 'elegant
English'—tommyrot. Who cares for fine style! Tell

your yarn and let your style go to the devil. We don't
want literature, we want life."[1]

What little interest he had aroused for an academic
training having thus met a check, he failed to exert
himself in his other studies. Hopes that the literature
courses would be of value died quickly when he found
them distorted by their emphasis on rhetoric; he
asked for an approach which appealed to the emotions, and instead he found one which emphasized
analysis. His distaste for abstract thought had been
partly responsible for his failure in mathematics; now
it minimized his pleasure in literature courses. "In
the announcement of courses published annually by
the faculty of the University of California the reader
cannot fail to be impressed with the number and
scope of the hours devoted by the students to reci-
tations and lectures upon the subject of 'literature.'
Be pleased for a moment to consider these 'literary
courses.' They comprise 'themes' written by the
student, the subject chosen by the instructor and the
matter found in textbooks and encyclopedias. They
further include lectures, delivered by associate professors, who, in their turn, have taken their information from textbooks and manuals written by other
professors in other colleges. The student is taught to
'classify.' 'Classification' is the one thing desirable
in the eyes of the professors of 'literature' in the
University of California. The young sophomore, with
his new, fresh mind, his active brain and vivid imagination, with ideas of his own, crude, perhaps, but

[1]Letter to Isaac Marcosson written March 14, 1899. *Adventures in Interviewing* by Isaac Marcosson, John Lane, 1919,
p. 235.

first-hand, is taught to 'classify,' is set to work count-. ing the metaphors in a given passage. In his junior and senior years he takes up the study of Milton, of Browning, of the drama of the seventeenth and eighteenth centuries, English comedy, of advanced rhetoric, and of æsthetics. Here the 'classification' goes on as before. . . . The conclusion of the whole matter is that the literary courses of the University of California do not develop literary instincts among the students who attend them. The best way to study literature is to try to produce literature. It is the original work that counts, not the everlasting compiling of facts, not the tabulating of metaphors, nor the rehashing of textbooks and encyclopedia articles."[1]

The records of the University of California show that Frank Norris did not do well in his literature courses, showing ability in only one, a study of medieval English poetry, which may have introduced him to the Germanic and Scandinavian sagas, Viking women, and the predatory traits of the Anglo-Saxons. In his other studies, "barely passing" was the prevailing grade. Occasionally history struck his fancy, and his indifferent translations of Horace were enhanced by illustrations drawn in the margins of his text, but it was only in French that he did really good work. As a matter of expediency, he enrolled in all of the French courses which were offered, partly because its literature interested him more than the English, partly because he liked the professor, but chiefly because, with the knowledge of the language he had gained in Paris, he could meet the requirements without much work. As he read much French litera-

[1]Editorial in the *Wave* (unsigned) November 28, 1896.

ture, his knowledge of the language improved, and the French influence on his writing, always stronger than the English, became more and more important. Thus when the time came when he was to lead in American fiction, his impulse sprang from French rather than English soil.

He avoided philosophy and economics and learned only as much science as was to be found in the popular courses in zoölogy and geology given under Professor Joseph Le Conte, who was noted for his liberal teachings in evolution. Although the members of the Oakland pulpit were attacking Le Conte as one of the devils in a godless university, Frank seems to have been little disturbed in his own Episcopalian orthodoxy. It was rather the elements of drama in the teaching of Le Conte which elicited his enthusiasms. "Professor Joe has one favorite lecture on glaciers that comes early in the Geology course. It is a masterpiece of scientific analysis, exquisitely blended with veritable eloquence. At its termination the class invariably bursts into enthusiastic applause." The most significant product of his exposure to Le Conte's classes was the dramatization of evolution in the short story *Lauth*, written at the time; thus his principal reaction to scientific thought was to find another story subject.

Frank never outgrew his early attitude towards collegiate training. Just before his death he protested against the sin of a boy's spending nine years to win the Townsend Prize at Yale. "Nine years—think of it—the best, the most important of a boy's life given to devoted study!—not of Men, not of Life, not of Realities, but of the books of other people, mere fatuous, unreasoned, pig-headed absorption of ideas at second hand.... And the result? Not a well-ordered mind, not a well-regulated reasoning machine, not a power of appreciation, not an ability to create. None of these, but . . . a Townsend Prize. . . . The student in the literary course does not—no, not once in a thousand instances—graduate a literary man. He spends the four years of his life over a little Greek, a little Latin, a little mathematics, a little literature, a little history, a little 'theme' writing. . . . I do not think I shall ever forget the spectacle and impression of a student in my own Alma Mater—a little lass of seventeen—with her hair still down her back and her shoes yet innocent of heels, rising in her place in the classroom to read before a half-hundred of raw boys and undeveloped girls a solemn and quite unintelligible 'theme' on 'The Insincerity of Thomas Babington Macaulay.'"

* * *

"The natural bent of his genius is observation, imagination, intensity, not thought, not intellect." This statement made by Walter Morris Hart about Kipling applies equally well to the young Frank Norris. If Norris had been primarily of the intellectual type, he would have become a rebel; he would have left the university, or, realizing the puerility of his attitude, would have sought out from books and sympathetic companions speculative bones to gnaw upon. Instead of looking for bones, be satisfied himself with cakes and ale; he joined a fraternity and supported student activities. His disappointments merely accentuated an indolence of body and mind—

an indolence frequently relieved by bursts of enthusiasm for acting, poker, fencing, or dog fights. For in "affirming" his environment, thrusting himself into student rigmarole and horseplay, indulging in fraternity stunts, or shouting at football heroes from the sidelines, Norris retained a detachment which marked him off from his fellows. "Life" of a sort can be found in college; it was this "life" which Norris wished to experience and at the same time retain the rights of a spectator. Believing that one must live stories in order to write them, he drained his environment of all the drama which it held. After the first year of adjustment to the Western college scene, he transferred his interests from the fourteenth to the nineteenth century, from medieval battles to hazing, from armor to battered "plug" hats, and from chivalric knights to football players.

His first step was to assume the rôle of "the regular fellow," which he described as follows: "Well, to begin with, he is a good fellow, but by that I do not mean to say he is *good*. He is not good in that sense. In that sense I am very much afraid to say he is a sorry case. He loves his pipe and his glass and is given over to late hours and riotous homecomings with a great noise of shouting, his pockets stuffed with spoons and beer glasses and individual salt cellars and small tradesmen's signs which he hangs up in his room as souvenirs. He wears either a cloth cap or a battered 'plug,' he smokes a briar pipe, he owns a dog, he carries a cane, and he believes that the captain of the football team can do no wrong. If he wears moderately good clothes, 'joshes' about everything and everybody, never talks about himself, and understands athletics, he is voted 'on to himself,' and is popular and joins a fraternity."

By the end of his freshman year, Norris was voted "on to himself" by the members of the local chapter of the Phi Gamma Delta fraternity, known popularly as the "Fijis." After he joined their group, doubters who had objected to his foreign appearance and literary bent were completely reconciled. Soon the relics from Paris were installed in a front room in the "house" on Dana Street, where Norris delighted to take unsuspecting freshmen to startle them with unusual questions and accusations concerning their private lives. Here he and his roommate returned one evening after a fishing trip, to find "Sloop," a sauce specialized in by the cook, spread in their beds as a practical joke. Norris enjoyed this sort of humor, but his roommate was enraged and left the house for a week, an incident which was later used in *The Octopus* just as it occurred. And here in this same room he wrote the ritual for the first "pig" dinner, which has been celebrated annually ever since as "The Norris" by all "Fijis" throughout the country.

His companions found in Norris that quality which is best described as lovable. He was different from them but in a way that in no way alienated them, for his sincerity and ingenuous enthusiasms made him popular with all. To the stranger he seemed to be a likable fellow of patrician blood, living in a Continental rather than American atmosphere, bohemian in inclinations. Those close to him found him enthusiastic, responsive to the beautiful in art and life, and fond of any lark which appealed to a story-teller's sense of fun. He played the banjo, befriended the fraternity dog, acted in the "Skull and Keys" plays, invented nicknames for his brothers, joined readily in a game of poker, and went on occasional "binges." He was not given to excess, but seemed to get much fun out of a little stimulation. In poker he lost continually; he played for the excitement rather than the stakes. A little drink made him merry, but he was most careful to avoid drinking in women's company. One of the show-points in Berkeley was the back room of Hagearty's Saloon, the walls of which were covered with Norris's drawings, many of them of girls in deshabille. Toward the co-eds on the campus he was scrupulously polite and would tolerate no disrespect among his companions. Always immaculately dressed, he would treat them with his "Old World manner"; one of his friends remembers that when he met her on the campus while he was smoking a pipe, he put it lighted in his pocket with disastrous results. His respect for women of his own class went deeper than manners; his best friends remember that he applauded the independence of the girls who led the movement to shorten dresses to the level of their shoe-tops.

Norris's absent-mindedness and boyishness added to the general impression that he was irresponsible. He was careless about keeping appointments, always permitting his momentary enthusiasms to determine his conduct. So undependable was he that at times it took considerable patience to put up with him, but so pleasing was his personality that forgiveness was always forthcoming. Always independent in means, he had no capacity for keeping money, and the house treasurer insisted that his bills be paid before the month's allowance had disappeared, for debts might easily be forgotten.

They were a very congenial and more than usually capable set of youths—those California "Fijis" of Norris's day, and their fellowship offered more than distraction from his studies. They gave him little in the way of literary criticism, but their various interests opened up to him, eager as he was for experience, for knowledge of widely diverse fields. No later friends were closer to him than these college chums who made deep impressions on his thought, and through his thought on his novels. He frequently turned to them for technical advice as well as companionship. Bert Houston, whom he befriended and treated like a younger brother, became a doctor and furnished medical information; Harry Wright, who took up school teaching and then turned lawyer and judge, was consulted *en re* injunctions in *The Octopus;* Harry Rhodes went in for navigation and helped with many a detail in *Moran;* Eddie Selfridge and Fred Juilliard were to be his closest companions during his lean days in New York. Two of the "Fijis" he transported directly into fiction. Jimmy White, several years older than Norris, was one of his heroes; the former football star who kept fit by running five miles every morning frequently amused his brothers by the ease with which he could throw them about the room as if they were children, or crack a walnut in the hollow of his arm. In many ways he suggested McTeague. Seymour Waterhouse, prototype of Annixter, was noted for his gruffness because of his scorn of "female girls," and *legend* has it that at one time he was forced to live in a shed in the back yard when he refused to

stop smoking his stogies. Norris greatly admired him,
as he was able to superintend a mine and attend college at the same time, and frequently accompanied
him to the Big Dipper Mine in the High Sierras near
Colfax, where they would fish, ride horses, and practice pistol shooting. The mine was to figure promi-
nently in his fiction.

It was in his attitude towards college sports that
Norris's ardor waxed strongest. His admiration for
the "red-blooded he-man" became a form of hero
worship. In no sense an athlete, he was not a weakling
for in his hobbies, fencing, horseback-riding, and
fishing, he was a fair amateur. It would be hardly
justifiable to assume that his emphasis on physical
strength in his novels was a compensation for physical
weakness in himself, for his flabby muscles seem to
have been due to physical laziness (more pronounced
at this time than later) rather than to any congenital
inability. In fencing, for instance, he was fairly skill-
ful, and some of his companions took part in bouts
in his rooms, where he took down the foils from the
walls and displayed with effect the training which he
had received in Paris. For his required course in physical training he wore black tights, and his attempts
to perform on the parallel bars reminded his fellows
of a huge spider. Toward the required two years of
military training he was openly antagonistic and
absented himself from drill so often that at one time
he was suspended from the university. His only consolation was that in his junior year he would be able
to sit on the front steps of North Hall and "watch
the lower classmen toiling through military drill,
with proper exultation and fitting ridicule."

A football game was to him a dramatic struggle where two teams, like armies, faced each other and shed blood in noble strife, and captains constantly met situations demanding quick decisions and shrewd thinking. With his fraternity brothers he stood on the top of a stagecoach drawn up on the sidelines at the first California-Stanford "big game" in 1892 and lost himself in cheering and in imprecations which shocked the ladies in the vicinity. He mastered the details of football so that his later reports of games combined technical skill and dramatic interest. Here he finds red-blooded activity. "That dogged, stubborn spirit that shuts its teeth and eyes; that fights at full steam every minute of the thirty-five; that absolutely refuses to be defeated; that does not know when it is beaten, and that asks for the last ditch to die in, and dies there, if needs be, beaten and broken, perhaps, but doing its best to the very last." The clasp of the hand of one particularly massive player convinced him of the presence of a superman. "He is so big that he ceases to be broad and tall—you feel like speaking of him as wide and high, as though he were the steeple of a clock tower—and he has an enormous bell-toned voice and a fist that your hand loses itself inside."

Likewise he saw that the "primordial instincts" held sway in the warfare between freshmen and sophomores, which assumed such proportions that the faculty intervened and suspended it for some years to come. During his sophomore year for weeks he hobbled about the campus on a sprained ankle— the result of the active part he played in the scrap which provided the subject for his contribution as class historian for the yearbook. He tells how, after being besieged in the gymnasium all night by a band of freshmen, a handful of sophomores decided to make a quick attack on their enemy grouped about the baseball back-stop. "Well, sir, we 'cooked the goose' of those freshmen that morning in as pretty a rush as the present chronicler ever saw or ever hopes to see. There were but seventeen of '94, but there was no resisting that rush, as, locking arms, they went in, heads down, and making the very windows of North Hall rattle with their ''94, '94, wah, hoo, wah!' It was all over in a few minutes. The eight prisoners, being cut loose, joined their classmates, and soon every freshman was bound and either led or carried away captive. We returned from the campus covered with blood, dust, and glory."

Kipling's enthusiasm for the aggressiveness of the Anglo-Saxons appears pale beside Frank's support of hazing. "If the boys of our universities want to fight, let them fight, and consider it a thing to be thankful for. They are only true to the instincts of their race. We Anglo-Saxons are a fighting race; have fought our way from the swamps of Holland to the shores of the Pacific Coast at the expense of worse things than smashed faces and twisted knees. One good fight will do more for a boy than a year of schooling. If he loses, he has at least had an experience which can be made profitable; if he wins, it gives him a self-confidence and a self-reliance that cannot be instilled into him by any amount of encouragement or boosting on the part of his 'parents, pastors, or masters'; it wakes in him that fine, reckless arrogance, that splendid, brutal, bullying spirit that is the Anglo-

Saxon's birthright; that got for us this whole mid-ocean country from under the guns of England; that got Texas and New Mexico and the whole Southwest for us, and California and the northern boundary."

★   ★   ★

THAT Norris's energy was not entirely absorbed by his college activities is made clear by his published writings which reveal his development between the period of the composition of *Yvernelle* and the time late in his university career when he started an ambitious program of novel-writing under the spur of Zola. During his four years at Berkeley he contributed three poems, four sketches, a play, and two short stories to student magazines, and, after abandoning that field, published one poem and twelve short stories in the San Francisco *Argonaut*, the *Overland Monthly*, and the San Francisco *Wave*. As many of the stories were patently experimental and all of them were to some degree imitative, they disclose his literary enthusiasms. The medievalists are gradually displaced by vital contemporary writers, the chief of whom are Rudyard Kipling, Richard Harding Davis, and Emile Zola. Of the three, Davis was an ephemeral model, Zola was chiefly responsible for turning Norris to the novel, as will be shown in the next chapter, while Kipling remained paramount in his influence on his short stories, and even antedated Zola in making Norris aware of modern life as the vital source for his fiction.

Kipling, who was discovered by Americans in 1890, became Norris's new literary idol late in his freshman year, and, from the moment of the Anglo-

Indian's apotheosis, he remained his "adored and venerated author." It is most natural that Frank Norris should have been attracted to Kipling, for the latter expressed those talents and ideas closest to his own nature. Here was a writer only five years older than Norris, wedding romance and realism, turning out stories of his own locale, proclaiming the attractiveness of the machine age, spreading the doctrine of the indomitable fighting spirit of the Anglo-Saxon. Here was a man who radiated energy, who wrote with intensity, and whose philosophy of life accepted rather than rejected. Here was a writer who gained his effects by objective portrayal of life "in the raw." To the reader wearied of American fiction, with its triple streams of historical novels, sentimental romances, and local-color vignettes, the freshness and vitality of Kipling's portrayal of the life about him acted like a tonic. This experienced young journalist had known familiarly all races and castes of India, had interviewed priests and fakirs, had explored Chinese opium dens, had absorbed the jargon of popular sports, and had insisted on writing of the brutal, the crude, and the virile.

Because of the light which they throw on the genesis of Norris's most characteristic ideas, it is of value to comment at some length on his early stories. Of the writing for student papers little need be said. In addition to the three poems already mentioned,[1] two stories appeared in the *Occident* during his freshman year. *The Coverfield Sweepstakes*, a racing story

[1]These three poems and *Yvernelle* comprise all of Norris's verse with the exception of *Crepusculum*, a short poem on death which appeared in the *Overland Monthly*, April, 1892.

overloaded with technical phrases, is notable for an animated description of a horse running at full speed, while *The Finding of Lieutenant Outhwaite*, a negligible sketch of mistaken identity among the *chasseurs d'Afrique*, introduces a character named Vandover, who acts as the raconteur. In the following year Norris helped to edit a short-lived humorous journal called *Smiles*, which published a number of his drawings and *The Great Szarratar Opal*, a dismal hodge-podge of nonsense done in the biblical style. His reputation as a humorist suffered least when he wrote parodies, such as those on De Quincey, Carlyle, and Macaulay which appeared in the *Occident*.

His classmates, wishing to adapt his literary talent to practical purposes, insisted that he be their historian, and for two years he wrote accounts for the yearbook, stressing in one the war around the baseball back-stop and in the other the most famous of all badger fights which took place in the rear of "Hagearty's" in 1893. But the real opportunity to achieve campus fame came with the Junior Farce of '94. Two years before, the farce had been a "scorcher," and its personal attacks had put the faculty on its guard, with the result that the following year the class resorted to Ben Jonson's *Alchemist*. Thus the *Occident* reported their failure: "Under the combined weight of the Faculty and Ben Jonson the life of '93's Junior day was crushed out of it." The class of '94 had a reputation for originality, and writers were busy throughout the summer preparing farces. Norris wrote a farce of domestic intrigue called *Two Pair*, and it was accepted with acclaim and prepared with much publicity. However, the marriage of French sophistication and college wit proved a little too much for his audience, and the ever-present frontier Puritanism came to the fore. The *Occident* condemned it with self-righteousness, stating that it contained "vulgarisms and innuendos" and that its morality was not in keeping with "the higher collegiate spirit."

The farce was poor stuff, but the attitude of the reviewer was typical; in truth, Norris's literary aspirations received little encouragement from his fellow students. Their bantering, which he labeled "wit about as delicate as a brickbat," was felt on more than one occasion; they were particularly given to twitting him about *Yvernelle*. In the '92 annual appeared the comment, "B.F. N-rr-s, 'I bridle in my struggling muse with pain'"; in the '93 annual, "'Tis pleasant sure to see one's name in print. A book's a book although there's nothing in it"; and in the '94 annual, "Old Favorites by New Authors— 'Lay of the Last Minstrel,' by B. F. Norris." These lampoons represented a general attitude toward literary endeavor, and even in his fraternity house Norris faced continual *razzing* about his artistic ventures. Not only was *Yvernelle* disowned, but he became increasingly reserved about his other writing. His college fellows today remember much about the pranks in which he took part but little about the stories which he was writing for the San Francisco journals or the novel which he was planning.

He was less reticent about his drawing, which he still worked at sporadically, although he was much joshed about it as well. As a follower of Gibson, he drew statuesque men and women, which always turned out to be wooden and lacking in proportion, a fact which did not seem to bother him, although it amused his friends. He was at his best in sketching in backgrounds for the scenes illustrating his medieval poems and stories, and in his designing, of which the cover of the *Berkeleyan*, founded in 1893, is his best example. Despite the refusal of his illustrations by Lippincott, he continued illustrating his stories for the *Overland Monthly* until after he left college.

In the end he gave up hope of finding an appreciative audience in the college. The majority of his fellows sniggered over Zola surreptitiously and satisfied their literary urges by attending the lemon sociables of the Longfellow Society and writing poems such as *When the Freshie Came to Town* and *The Perambulating Encyclopedia*. His first real encouragement other than that given by a few of the more discerning students and one or two faculty members came with the publication of *The Son of the Sheik* in the *Argonaut* on June 1, 1891. This story sprang directly from Kipling in both subject and method. In *On the City Wall*, Kipling had included a minor incident in which a youthful cynic, who pretended to scorn his native religion, broke through his Western veneer during a religious struggle and plunged into the thick of the fight, shouting, "Ya Hasan! Ya Hussain!" Norris took the germ of an idea from this minor incident, expanded it, transferred the action to North Africa, and, with the use of effective detail, produced the story which is explained in the subtitle, "How a Parisianized Arab found that blood was thicker than water."

He returned to his medieval *milieu* in *Le Jongleur de Taillebois*, an ambitious but somewhat puerile

attempt at the horror tale. His emphasis on the cruel
and gruesome in this story may have been partly
due to the influence of Bierce, as it was contributed
to the San Francisco *Wave*, which was then publishing
the latter's stories; on the other hand, the youthful
zest for brutality may have been the first result of a
growing interest in the novels of Zola. At any rate
the story had its desired effect in shocking the readers
of the *Wave*. Norris's father was much disturbed when
one of his friends, meeting him on Montgomery
Street, stopped to declare: "If I had a son who wrote
a story like that, I'd have him put out of the world
in a lethal chamber."

The Way of the World, which followed six months
later, is the tale of a youth who considers himself
hopelessly in love with a *bouffe* actress until his friends
(among them, Vandover) disillusion him by arranging to have him discover her in an intrigue with his
father. Its flippantly humorous manner, illustrated
by the closing phrase, "It was all very pitiful," was
borrowed from Richard Harding Davis, who had but
recently published his tales concerning Gallegher
and Van Bibber. Davis's portrayal of the doings of
the "Four Hundred," his creation of the sentimental
Van Bibber, and his discovery of the drama in report-
ing had gained him great popularity, and Norris, as
he puts it in *Blix*, "suffered an almost fatal attack
of Harding Davis." One result of this attack was a
flippancy and affectation of *savoir-faire* to be found
in several of Norris's society tales, of which *The Finding of Lieutenant Outhwaite* and *The Way of the
World* are examples. And, in so far as the Vandover
who appears in these sketches is of much the same

type as Van Bibber, it is not unreasonable to assume
that Vandover is Van Bibber's offspring, at least in
name.

In *Lauth*, the sole product of his junior year, he
used an idea possibly suggested by Kipling's *Mark of
the Beast*, in which a man temporarily became a beast
as the result of insulting a native idol. *Lauth*, however,
makes only a peripheral contact with Kipling's story,
and, as an example of Norris's method and ideas, is
the most significant of his experiments at this stage
of his development. The tale is in two parts, of which
the first is a vivid account of an attack on the Châte-
let in medieval Paris in which Lauth, a young student,
takes part. In the thick of the fray Lauth kills a man
with his arbalist. "At the sight of blood shed by his
own hands all the animal savagery latent in every
human being awoke within him. *He could kill.* In the
twinkling of an eye the pale, highly cultivated scholar,
whose life had been passed in the study of science
and abstruse questions of philosophy, sank back to
the level of his savage Celtic ancestors. His eyes glit-
tered, he moistened his lips with the tip of his tongue,
and his whole frame quivered with the eagerness and
craving of a panther in sight of his prey." Here appears a favorite theme to be used from *Vandover
and the Brute* to *The Octopus*—the presence of the
brute beneath the veneer of civilization. It is to be
the cause of the deterioration of Vandover, the spirit
which animates the fight between Wilbur and Moran,
the source of the virility of Bennett in his war with
the Arctic ice, and the essence of the brutal life of
McTeague.

Lauth is mortally wounded in the fight, and the

first part ends. The second opens with Jacquemart de Chavennes, Doctor of Medicine and closest friend of Lauth, speculating upon the nature of death. What is "this mysterious, dreadful force that has brought him to this state?" Chavennes, who does not believe in a soul, decides that the life is still in the body, and with the aid of Anselm, a reluctant divinity student, determines to make it active once more. Together they work over the body, pumping blood into the veins, air into the lungs, and adding stimulants to the tongue. Slowly, surely, Lauth returns to life and his former self; but one day he cries out, "This is not I; where am I?" After which he falls upon the floor, foaming and wallowing. The cry is the beginning of a steady decline. "From this time on the process of decay became rapidly more apparent; what little lustre yet lurked in the eye went out, leaving it dull and fish-like; the expression of the face lost all resemblance to humanity; the hair grew out long and coarse and fell matted before the eyes. The nails became claws, the teeth fangs, and one morning, upon entering the room assigned to Lauth, Chavennes and Anselm found him stripped, groveling on all fours in one corner of the room, making a low monotonous growling sound, his teeth rattling and snapping together." The process continues until Lauth becomes "a horrible shapeless mass lying upon the floor. It lived, but lived not as do the animals or the trees, but as the protozoa, the jelly-fish, and those strange lowest forms of existence wherein the line between vegetable and animal cannot be drawn." Finally the thing dies and decomposition sets in.

"'Now, what does it all mean?' asked Anselm.

'For a time Lauth lived, but the soul being taken away, the whole body with the life it contained began successively to drop back to the lower forms of existence. At first, he existed merely as a dull and imbruted man; soon he fell to the stage of those unfortunates whose minds are impaired or wholly gone; he became an idiot. At the time when he so savagely bit and snarled at you he had reached the level of the ape; from that stage he fell to that of a lower animal, walking upon all fours, savage, untameable; thence he passed into those lowest known forms of life such as possessed by the sponge and the polyp, and thence to the second and final death. The *soul* of man is the chiefest energy of his existence; take that away and he is no longer a man.'"

Thus Norris used Kipling, Zola, and the teachings of evolution received from Professor Le Conte in expanding his conception of the brute nature in man; the degeneration of Lauth is an exercise on the central theme of *Vandover and the Brute*.

The eight remaining stories of this period show him experimenting freely with the techniques of his literary models, aiming to create atmosphere by the use of realistic detail, which he came more and more to select from his own experience, and preferring subjects which involved brutality, violence, or at least adventure. In *Unequally Yoked* and its sequel, *A Caged Lion*, he presented an explorer who sacrificed his career to marry a society-loving girl (the reverse of the theme of *A Man's Woman*), and in *Travis Hallett's Half-Back* he eulogized football by having the hero use his knowledge of the flying wedge to extricate himself from a burning theater with his girl tucked neatly under his arm. In the series which he entitled *Visible Signs* (a phrase from *The Phantom 'Rickshaw*), *She and the Other Fellow*, influenced by Davis, tells how Desfield helped his friend retrieve his girl by diverting his rival's attention to a dog fight; *The Most Noble Conquest of Man* concerns the downfall on the Berkeley campus of one Taggart, who did not know his horses; *Thoroughbred* couples blue blood in men and dogs and shows how it triumphs over Chinamen enflamed by a tong war; *After Strange Gods* uses the Chicago World's Fair and San Francisco's Chinatown as locales and is very imitative of Kipling, as is *Outside the Zenana*, which is laid in India and strewn thick with borrowed phrases. Although not uniformly successful, these stories were effective and mature enough to establish Norris's reputation in the Bay Region as a promising writer.

Norris's allegiance to Davis and Kipling carried with it far more significance than is evinced in negligible details of imitation, such as the spirit of *savoir-faire* which he temporarily absorbed from the former or the occasional phrases he borrowed from the latter. He owed more to Kipling than the model furnished by his narrative method, which taught him to introduce the colloquial tone into his stories, to lighten his action with effective dialogue, to rely on objective methods in portraying his characters and building up his climaxes, and to concentrate and intensify his action. The fact of utmost importance was that, in transferring his allegiance from Scott and Froissart to these portrayers of contemporaneous life, he was made aware of the wealth of story material which lay around him. His talent was focused permanently on what he was able to observe; he had discovered the source of his strength. Under the tutelage of Davis and Kipling he had shifted his locale from medieval France to modern San Francisco —the setting which he was to use in five of his seven novels.

The time had not yet arrived, however, when Norris was ready to apply all of his industry and determination to realization on the assets of his new point of view. In spite of the considerable output during his university days, the high jinks of college life received more of his attention than did the writing of stories. But the new force was gathering, and in time he was to attempt by his own example to answer the question which he put to the readers of the *Wave:* "Who shall be our Kipling? Where is the man that shall get at the heart of us, that shall go a-gunning for stories up and down our streets and into our houses and parlors and lodging houses and saloons and secretest chambers of our homes as well as our hearts? . . . The tales are here. The public is here. A hundred clashing presses are hungry for you, future young story-writer of San Francisco, whoever you may be. Strike but the right note and strike it with all your might, strike it with the iron instead of velvet, and the clang of it shall go the round of the nations.

"*A qui le tour*, who shall be our Kipling?"

Chapter 4: Naturalism

But what of Frank Norris the realist? Those whose acquaintance with him began with the reading of *McTeague*, ruthless study in poverty and violent death, will ask this question as they mark his strong predilection for the romantic in literature and life. Was he actually a realist at heart? Or did he, as Vernon L. Parrington suggests, begin as a romantic and work out of it slowly? Or did he, as others maintain, write romances side by side with his more serious work as a means of achieving popular success? It is clear that no writer has been entirely romantic or entirely realistic; likewise it is obvious that a great many of the acknowledged realists may be labeled romanticists if one is allowed to define his own terms. In fact, good fiction is usually elusive enough to escape from the unnatural boundaries set for it by such terms; who will satisfactorily pigeonhole the works of Balzac, of Dickens, of Kipling, of Flaubert, of Conrad, of Zola? Call Frank Norris realist and ignore *Moran of the Lady Letty;* call him romanticist and ignore *McTeague;* call him a romantic realist and escape by begging the question. Probably the most satisfactory answer can be made by stating as clearly as possible Norris's attitude on the subject and allowing each reader to apply it for himself.

In *A Plea for Romantic Fiction*, written after he had been recognized as a leader in the realistic school, Frank Norris attempted to clarify the principle which had guided him from the beginning of his career. "Why should it be that so soon as the novelist addresses himself—seriously—to the consideration of contemporary life, he must abandon Romance and take up the harsh, loveless, colorless, blunt tool called Realism? Now let us understand at once what is meant by Romance and what by Realism. Romance, I take it, is the kind of fiction that takes cognizance of the variations from the type of normal life. Realism is the kind of fiction that confines itself to the type of normal life. According to this definition, then, Romance may even treat of the sordid, the unlovely— as, for instance, the novels of M. Zola. (Zola has been dubbed as a Realist, but he is on the contrary, the very head of the Romanticists.) Also, Realism, used as it sometimes is as a term of reproach, need not be in the remotest sense or degree offensive, but on the other hand respectable as a church and proper as a deacon—as, for instance, the novels of Mr. Howells.

"The reason why one claims so much for Romance, and quarrels so pointedly with Realism, is that Realism stultifies itself. It notes only the surface of things. For it, Beauty is not even skin deep, but only a geometrical plane, without dimensions and depth, a mere outside. Realism is very excellent so far as it goes, but it goes no further than the Realist himself can actually see, or actually hear. Realism is minute;

it is the drama of a broken teacup, the tragedy of a walk down the block, the excitement of an afternoon call, the adventure of an invitation to dinner. . . . But to Romance belongs the wide world for range, and the unplumbed depths of the human heart, and the mystery of sex, and the problems of life, and the black, unsearched penetralia of the soul of man. . . . Romance and Realism are constant qualities of every age, day, and hour. They are here today. They existed in the time of Job. They will continue to exist until the end of time, not so much in things as in point of view of the people who see things."

By his definition, then, Frank Norris is a romanticist because of the "point of view" with which he sees things. His retina absorbs the unusual, the violent, the adventuresome, "the variations from the type of normal life." He is not concerned with the drama of the broken teacup, because such dramas do not exist for him. And yet the broken china does not escape his glance; his attention is held, however, only when there is a great deal of china broken at once, and he prefers heavy restaurant ware and thick clay pitchers to Royal Copenhagen demi-tasses and Haviland plates.

Moreover, Norris's crockery must be genuine crockery; he admits no fairy urns or pseudo-antique dishes. His distinction between romanticism and realism is a distinction between two methods of looking upon actuality and takes no cognizance of the older appurtenances of romance—fantasy, magic, and poetry. Moreover, when he portrays a large and preferably ungainly pot—thick, coarse, and rugged— he describes it with realistic detail, pointing out the flaws, delving into the cracks, and showing the grime upon its unwashed surface. And, above all, he insists on putting it to the purpose for which it was intended, refusing to romanticize a pickle jar into a flower vase. His slogan is, "Tell the Truth."

If the distinction made by Norris between romanticism and realism—that the one deals with the unusual and the other the normal in life—is too arbitrary to be accepted by his critics, it at least serves to explain his own procedure. As one would expect in the case of a novelist who was creative rather than analytical, his definitions appear after his method has developed, a method empirical rather than deductive. From the beginning his temperament merged the romantic and the realistic, selecting the unusual subject and presenting it with verisimilitude. When he wrote *Yvernelle*, he became absorbed in the details of medieval armor; when he wrote *McTeague* he "got up" the particulars of dentistry. The method was the same; the formula alone was different; and it was the discovery of this formula which so completely changed the nature of his writing. The change came as the result of an interest in Zola and French naturalism. Thus it is of primary importance to an understanding of Norris's literary theory to trace the genesis and development of the influence of Zola upon him and to determine to what extent he followed the method and adopted the point of view of his chief literary model.

It is almost impossible to determine just when Norris discovered Zola. As has been pointed out, his interests in Paris do not reflect any contact with the turmoil which was centering about French naturalism while he was there. On the other hand many of his friends testify that while he was at Berkeley he was frequently seen about the campus with a French paper edition of Zola under his arm and was always ready to stop and defend the novelist, who to him embodied strength and truth but to most of them was of interest chiefly because of his obscenity. It is certain that he did not learn of Zola in his French courses, for in the only one in which that author should have been considered—a senior course in "Recent Realistic Fiction in France"—he was carefully avoided as unfit for co-educational ears. The probability is that, as he browsed about in French literature during his early days at the University of California, he came upon a copy of *Nana* or *L'Assommoir*, after reading which he devoured all of the series of the *Rougon-Macquart* obtainable. Suggestions of Zola appear in some of the short stories which he wrote at this time, particularly in *Lauth*, but it was not until he started to write *McTeague*, probably in his senior year, that the French naturalist's influence became dominant.

The transition in literary models from Froissart and Scott through Kipling and Davis to Zola did not, in Norris's opinion, involve any *volte-face*. The acceptance of Zola was the logical conclusion of his search for a writer treating the unusual in contemporary life. According to his definition of the term Zola was a romanticist. In an editorial in the *Wave* written soon after he left the university, he discussed this attitude towards Zola. "It is curious to note how persistently M. Zola is misunderstood. . . . Naturalism, as understood by Zola, is but a form of romanticism after

all. That Zola should be quoted as a realist, and as a
realist of realists, is a strange perversion. . . . To be
noted by M. Zola, we must leave the rank and file;
. . . we must separate ourselves; we must become
individual, unique. The naturalist takes no note of
common people, common in so far as their interests,
their lives, and the things that occur in them are
common, are ordinary. Terrible things must happen to
the characters of the naturalistic tale. They must be
twisted from the ordinary, wrenched from the quiet,
uneventful round of everyday life and flung into the
throes of a vast and terrible drama that works itself
out in unleashed passions, in blood, and in sudden
death. The world of M. Zola is a world of big things;
the enormous, the formidable, the terrible, is what
counts; no teacup tragedies here. Here Nana holds
her monstrous orgies, and dies horribly, her face
distorted to a frightful mask; Etienne Lantier, carried
away by the strike of coal miners of *Le Voreux*, is
involved in the vast and fearful catastrophe that
comes as a climax of the great drama; Claude Lantier, disappointed, disillusioned, acknowledging the
futility of his art after a life of effort, hangs himself
to his huge easel; Jacques Lantier, haunted by
hereditary insanity, all his natural desires hideously
distorted, cuts the throat of the girl he loves, and is
ground to pieces under the wheels of his own locomotive; Jean Macquart passes through the terrible
scenes of Sedan and the Siege of Paris, only to
bayonet to death his truest friend and sworn brother-
at-arms in the streets of the burning capital.

"Everything is extraordinary, imaginative, grotesque even, with a vague note of terror quivering

throughout like the vibration of an ominous and low-pitched diapason. It is all romantic, at times unmistakably so, as in *Le Rêve* or *Rome*, closely resembling the work of the greatest of all modern romanticists, Hugo. We have the same huge dramas, the same enormous scenic effects, the same love of the extraordinary, the vast, the monstrous and the tragic. . . . Naturalism is a form of romanticism, not an inner circle of realism. . . . That Zola's work is not purely romantic as was Hugo's, lies chiefly in the choice of *milieu*. . . . It is a school by itself, unique, somber, powerful beyond words."[1]

Thus, Norris, in identifying himself with the naturalists, revealed a more profound understanding of Zola than he did of naturalism itself. Just as he missed its underlying mood, he failed to accept in its entirety the philosophy back of naturalism. Naturalism in France was as much the product of a popular disillusion as the expression of a faith in science. It was, if carried to its logical conclusion, the application to fiction of the philosophy of determinism. It involved a "realism of environment that conceived of the individual as a pawn on the chessboard of society," and necessitated the ultimate acceptance of scientific tenets which, denying the individual all power of will, conceived of him as a plaything of the laws of heredity and environment. Norris's model, Zola, although he had given both name and popularity to the school, had failed to carry his thought through to these conclusions; his appli-

[1]An unsigned editorial on *Zola as a Romantic Writer* appeared in the *Wave* on June 21, 1896. There is little question that it was written by Frank Norris.

cation of the ideas of Claude Bernard to the conception of a scientific or "experimental" novel was to a considerable degree but the rationalization of a taste for the portrayal of sociological extremes. Norris had grasped the strength of Zola's story-telling, had sensed the timeliness of its theme, had seen how much more penetrating and contemporaneous it was than the methods of his fellow novelists in America. His enthusiasm was for Zola, "the man with the iron pen," who defied the strictures of society and wrote heated pæans to "Truth." Norris in turn became a militant naturalist, and attempted, like Zola in his later years, to make an optimistic thesis out of a world-weary philosophy.

Norris accepted determinism only in so far as it appealed to his dramatic sense. (How could anyone be enthusiastic about determinism if he applied it to himself, particularly if he were as naturally optimistic as Norris?) He followed Zola because the latter, in presenting man as the victim of external laws, allowed for big forces and hence big conflicts, and, in order to make the battle more spectacular, Norris endowed his characters with the best equipment for the fight against nature—brutal, primitive strength and the intuition of the animal. It was the display of energy, the apotheosis of force. Frank Norris, child of an unusually energetic father and an unusually forceful mother, threw himself into the creation of strong novels built upon the naturalistic scheme. It is this apotheosis of force which is the residue when the naturalistic amalgam is melted away.

★   ★   ★

It is not surprising that finally the superabundance of energy in the Norris family resulted in trouble. For some time Mr. Norris's nerves had been in a state resembling internal combustion; the restlessness which had appeared soon after his move to California increased with his absence from Chicago, despite the outlets provided by his real estate ventures, his driving of horses and his fishing, his Sunday-school class, and his quiet evenings at home with his family. Possibly Mrs. Norris's growing independence and self-expression gave him a feeling of inadequacy. The undercurrents which brought on the crisis are unknown and irrelevant to this study; the warning of trouble came in the form of an insistence on the part of Mr. Norris that the family make a tour of the world, a desire which was strenuously opposed by his wife, who preferred to remain in the city where the family was established and with which her interests had become identified. Accordingly, on May 25, 1892, Mr. Norris embarked by himself on the trip around the world, apparently leaving San Francisco with no intention of returning to his family. Soon after his return to Chicago, he filed a divorce suit against Mrs. Norris in order to bring her to action. She filed a countersuit and obtained a divorce in 1894. As Mr. Norris remarried, the estrangement from his first wife and his children was complete. Frank, who was twenty-two when his father left home, did not see him again before his death in 1900.

As might be expected, such a radical change in Frank Norris's family environment had a far-reaching effect on his life. One may state with some surety the material results, but his inner reaction is much

more difficult to ascertain, particularly as he kept
his thoughts on the subject to himself. In so far as he
never failed to grasp the dramatic import of an event
no matter how close to him it might be, it is probable
that the unexpected defection of his father, whom he
had always known as a quiet, home-loving man with
markedly orthodox ideas, struck him as coinciding
forcibly with the themes of the realistic novels which
he was reading. His genuine emotion at what was
practically the loss of his father was somewhat light-
ened by the fact that he had always felt more closely
bound to his mother than to him, and was ready to
accept her view of the matter. Although the separation of his parents did not touch him deeply enough
to make him bitter, it thrust a serious element into
a life heretofore given largely to play—a serious
element which may be partly responsible for the tone
of the novels which were written during the years
immediately following the event.

Whatever may have been his innermost reactions
to his father's departure, the most apparent material
result was the loss of the prospects of inheriting a
considerable fortune. The size of his father's income
at the time of the separation is indicated by the fact
that Mrs. Norris sued for a monthly stipend of eight
hundred dollars to support herself and Charles;
Frank, who was of age, was in a position to ask for
additional help, but he seems to have made no move
to do so, and by the end of his year at Harvard he was
determined to refuse any help from his father. That
his father felt no further obligation towards his elder
son was shown when he left his entire fortune of
nearly a million dollars to his second wife. Thus it was

through the separation of his parents that Frank Norris lost the privileges of the elder son of a wealthy father, privileges which had done much to encourage his dilettante attitude at the University of California. Furthermore, although he was never in any sense poverty-stricken, he gained a widened sympathy for those who were. Up to this point his ideas on society had been those of a moneyed youth; in his early years at college he had shown little sympathy for labor problems, openly despising the *"canaille"* and frequently voicing the desire to see all radicals "drowned on one raft." Now, as he grew older and faced the prospects of supporting himself with his writing, his opinions changed, and he began to appreciate his mother's familiar quotation from Daudet's *Jack*: *"La vie n'est pas un roman."* It was as a whole quite fortunate for Norris, the novelist, that he suffered a change in fortune.

His father's departure also brought the permanent abandonment of attempts to force him into the jewelry business, and he was now free to turn his attentions toward a literary career. This was an ambition which his mother had long furthered in opposition to her husband, and now she began again to spur him on persistently and indefatigably. She encouraged him to spend his week-ends at home, knowing that he could work more diligently in the attic room which she turned into a studio than he could in the fraternity house. She was ready to further his interests in any field which he might choose, and, although many aspects of Zola's novels made them alien to her conservative tastes, she joined in Frank's admiration for the virility and force of the French-

man's writing and approved of his desire to try his
hand at a naturalistic novel. Frank responded slowly,
content with his college high jinks, but as it became
clear that his father did not intend to return, the opportunity to write, the encouragement of his mother,
and the enthusiasm for Zola combined to act as a
stimulus. His first step was to acquaint himself
thoroughly with San Francisco; Polk Street would
be an excellent *milieu* for his new venture. He studied
its life, watching its men and women as they went
about their work. He noted the habits and listened
to the conversation of the drunkards and prostitutes
in the saloons and brothels of the Barbary Coast. He
spent afternoons at the Mechanics Fair, impressing
on his memory the dress and behavior of the crowds
of working people who attended it. He now held
"that no one could be a writer, until he could regard
life and people, and the world in general, from the
objective point of view—until he could remain detached, outside, maintain the unswerving attitude
of the observer."

Here was the groundwork of the novel which
finally emerged in 1899 as *McTeague*. It has been
suggested that the sordid murder of a charwoman in
a school near his home was the starting point; it is not
unlikely. Other supporting ideas presented themselves: the murderer was to be a burly, ignorant
dentist—there was an upstairs office at the corner of
Polk and California which would serve as his office
and bedroom; the Lester Norris Memorial Kindergarten could be used as the locale for the murder; his
characters might picnic at Scheutzen Park in Oakland, where artisans flocked on Sundays and holidays;

he could include a walk to the Cliff House, an evening
at the Orpheum, a bourgeois wedding supper *à la Zola*
with Polk Street cuisine and table manners. . . . He
found the tone of his book when he noted the view
from the windows of the suburban train which
brought him to the ferry on his way home from
college. "Across the railroad tracks, to the seaward,
one saw the long stretch of black mud bank left bare
by the tide, which was far out, nearly half a mile.
Clouds of sea-gulls were forever rising and settling
upon this mud bank; a wretched and abandoned
wharf crawled over it on tottering legs; close in, an
old sailboat lay canted on her bilge. But further on,
across the yellow waters of the bay, beyond Goat
Island, lay San Francisco, a blue line of hills, rugged
with roofs and spires. Far to the westward loomed the
Golden Gate, a bleak cutting in the sandhills, through
which one caught a glimpse of the open Pacific."

It was just the first ideas of a novel which Norris
had in mind when he finished his fourth year at
Berkeley. Now, probably for the first time, he felt
the need of an adequate training in writing in order
to proceed with his ambitious task. He was entirely
free to do as he pleased in seeking such a training;
the legal separation of his parents had at last fixed
his mother's income and she was ready to further his
plans. Accordingly they decided that the best move
was to go to Cambridge, where Frank could enroll
in one of the courses in creative writing for which
Harvard had become famous through the work of
Barrett Wendell and his assistants. In the early fall
of 1894 Mrs. Norris and her two sons arrived in
Cambridge, where she rented rooms for herself and

Charles near the college, while Frank, wishing to work without interruption, went into residence in 47 Gray's Hall.

★   ★   ★

DURING his year at Harvard, Norris gave practically all of his time and energy to the writing of two naturalistic novels, *Vandover and the Brute* and *McTeague*. As he worked, he transferred into fiction the impressions he had been collecting during the five years since his return from Paris. For five years his experiences and reading had been thrown together, shaken, and stirred like liquids in a test tube, until, now under the proper conditions, they crystallized in a moment.

Of these advantageous conditions not the least important was the absence of the diversions which had occupied Norris's time at Berkeley. Gone were the days of hearty companionship, of fraternity parties, and of college activities. He found in Harvard a collegiate society which encouraged individuality but minimized handshaking, a society which applied its critical strictures to men as well as to books, a society where one's next door neighbor never offered more than a nodding acquaintanceship, and friendships were formed only after years of contact. To a stranger from the West, unused to its code, Harvard appeared cold and inimical; Norris's only consolation in his lonely moments was that they were common to many of his fellow students, particularly to those who had not been acclimated during their undergraduate years. Thus, when asked how he liked Harvard life, he would answer that he agreed with

Flandrau's presentation of it in *Harvard Episodes*, or perhaps would state the objections of his fellow Californian, who wrote for the Berkeley student paper a typical protest: "In Harvard you will find a different life entirely from what you have been accustomed to. People here call it culture. It's none the more desirable for its name. To hear the nice modulation of the conversational voice which carefully eliminates all personal passion and emphasis; to see the attempt to avoid any appearance of energy, any inclination to push, to make things move; to listen to the polished indifference of the lecture platform; these are things a Californian does not like. . . . You seldom or never hear a real hearty laugh in the college yard, such as is so often heard on the Berkeley grounds. . . . Even we 'cowboy' Californians, as the Harvard graduate is pleased to call us, have to keep our spirits to ourselves. . . . The voice of the freshman or his antagonist is annihilated in the Nirvana of Harvard." Much as he disliked the coldly intellectual atmosphere, Norris realized that he could now work rather than play.

At Gray's Hall, Norris moved into living quarters of rigorous simplicity; they consisted of a cubicle study room some sixteen feet square, with a small alcove for a bed. The stone building promised to be cold during the winter, for there was little window space for sunlight, and the sole heating device was a fireplace; furthermore, the rooms were bare of furniture. This time Norris did not unpack his relics, but, instead, obtained a bed, a good work table, and a couple of straight-backed chairs. He went out for his meals, taking part of them with his mother at her

boarding house but most of them in the commons at
Memorial Hall. As Harvard club life was not open
to a newcomer, his chief recreation was association
with men whom he had known at California. Occasionally they would drop in and persuade him to
join in a "sing fest"—his banjo remains with a record
of their favorite songs on its head, "Oh Honey, Mah
Honey," "Ef the Night Would Only Las'," and a
half-dozen more; at other times he would go with
them to Locke's, across the river, where they drank
quantities of a temperance beverage which Norris had
invented. Occasionally the theater in Boston tempted
him from his writing; Charles Norris remembers how
thrilled he was at the premier performance of *Trilby*,
which reminded him of his Paris days.

At Harvard, Norris applied himself for the first
time to his college assignments. Outside of three
courses in French, which kept him reading in that
language, he was enrolled in but one class, English 22
—Sophomore Composition. As this course met all
of his demands, he devoted his time to it unstintingly,
using it as a laboratory to experiment with his writing. He attributed the merit of the course to the
system and the instructor. He describes the system
thus: "The literary student at Cambridge has but
little to do with lectures, almost nothing at all with
textbooks. He is sent away from the lecture room
and told to look about him and think a little. Each
day he writes a theme, a page if necessary, a single
line of a dozen words if he likes; anything, so it is
original, something he has seen or thought, not read
of, not picked up at second hand. Once every two
weeks he writes a longer theme, and during the last six

weeks of the year, a still longer one, in six weekly instalments. Not a single suggestion is offered as to subject. The result of the system is a keenness of interest that draws three hundred men to the course and that fills the benches at every session of the class. The classroom work consists merely in the reading, by the instructor, of the best work done, together with his few critical comments upon it by the instructor in charge. The character of the themes produced under this system is of such a high order that it is not rare to come across one of them in the pages of the first-class magazines of the day." In this class Norris received criticism on a number of passages from his short stories already in print and on large portions of *McTeague* and *Vandover*.

Thus Norris's receptive attitude, his maturing interest in naturalism, the absence of vitiating diversions, and an adequate system of instruction were all favoring conditions. To these was added a talented and sympathetic teacher. Norris often stated that he learned more about writing from Professor Lewis E. Gates than from any other man, and he expressed his gratitude in the dedication of *McTeague*. Gates was just ten years Norris's senior, reserved, even austere, to those who did not know him well. Underneath the reserve burned an enthusiasm which a writer in the *Critic* likened to that of an express train—"jolt, jar, whiz, and hold fast." His enthusiasm was founded on thorough scholarship and tempered by a critical sense which came near to genius in the faculty of appreciation. His taste and sympathies were very catholic, for, in spite of his own standards, which favored delicacy and beauty in style as well as subtlety in thought, he was able to recognize Zola's talent and willing to encourage Norris in the method to which he seemed best fitted. As there is no evidence that his friendship with Norris went any further than the classroom, he must have marked his student's ability early in the course and followed his papers with special attention.

Norris was now a writing man in earnest. He studied the dictionary for words and the obituary notices for striking names, he kept a large black notebook in which he jotted down well-turned phrases, potential subjects for novels, and effective titles, and he worked his material over and over for his classes. Although his stories were still appearing in the *Overland Monthly* in San Francisco, his only publication in Harvard was *The End of the Act*, the opening of Chapter XIV of *Vandover*, which appeared in the *Harvard Advocate*. Chiefly, he worked on his novels.

Norris's reasons for dividing his attention between two novels at this time are not clear. *McTeague* he seems to have laid aside after reaching the point at which the dentist murders his wife. This early draft of the novel elicited from Gates a good deal of detailed criticism, the preponderant part of which was devoted to increasing the crispness of the descriptions in the book and to retaining the objective point of view. Norris was specially impressed when his instructor pointed out that in order to retain his objectivity, the cat which witnessed the murder of Trina should not be represented as having thoughts of her own, but should exist only as she would appear to an observer. Probably a desire to use the Harvard *milieu* and a college student as his chief character caused him to drop *McTeague* in order to concentrate on *Vandover and the Brute*, which was entirely a product of his year at Harvard.

*   *   *

In *Vandover and the Brute*, Frank Norris followed the Zolaistic formula more closely than in any of his later novels. Impressed by Zola's portrayal of the degeneration of Gervaise and Jacques Coupeau in *L'Assommoir*, of Claude Lantier in *L'Œuvre*, and of Jacques Lantier in *La Bête humaine*, he wrote a story which centered about a character from his own world, Vandover, telling his life from birth to disaster, picturing the gradual physical and moral decay of his too pliable, sensitive nature, subjecting him to misfortunes of circumstances which pile one upon another. In this book the conception of his principal character is much more imitative than is *McTeague*, for Vandover is the victim of inherent weakness of will and constant misfortune—a common naturalistic type— whereas the brutish McTeague in his rise and fall of fortune is original in conception and portrayal.

To say that *Vandover* is imitative, however, is to tell only a small part of the truth. Norris donned Zolaistic spectacles to look through, but the life which he saw was his own immediate environment. He wisely fixed upon a *milieu* and characters as close to his experience as possible. For the former he used Harvard and San Francisco, putting into his vivid descriptions the observations which he had been making for some years. He turned to his college life to find his characters and fixed upon himself as the subject for Vandover—not himself as he really was

but as he imagined he could develop. In this connection Charles Norris states that Vandover was
"inspired, to a large degree, by the unmorality of the
undergraduates with whose lives he was familiar."
There is no indication that Frank Norris was unduly
worried about the laxity of morals at Harvard or
California, but there were two factors in his own
nature which made him feel that the excesses of
college life could easily lead to a tragic dénouement.
One must not lose sight of the fact that Norris inherited a strong puritanical strain from his mother,
and that, as he remained under her control, this
heritage was accentuated by training. It is true that
he did not conduct himself as a puritan, but no doubt
his laxity frequently seemed to him to be an indication of grave weakness, particularly when he took
his mother's point of view. Of even more importance
in the creation of Vandover, however, was his tendency to dramatize on his own petty vices; he was, in
fact, not at all likely to become a slave to gambling,
drinking, or lechery, but it was one of his favorite
games to imagine himself a victim of excess. It
amused him to speculate on his potentialities in vice,
and it was thus that Vandover evolved from within
him.

Choosing the tendency to take the line of least
resistance as Vandover's chief trait, he portrays his
subject's initial weaknesses in college and allows
them to develop after his return to San Francisco.
Vandover, like Norris a dilettante in art, fails to use
his talent and drifts with the current of gay life. In
matters of chance, the operating principle of determinism, the pennies invariably fall the wrong side

up—Vandover's luck is uniformly bad; an unfortunate alliance with a "fast" girl leads to her suicide, Vandover is ostracized from his social group, his father dies just when he is about to help his son out of his difficulty, he loses his ability to paint, he gambles away his fortune, he forfeits his self-esteem, and ultimately he develops *lycanthropy* as a result of his drinking and irregular living. Reduced to poverty, with all pride and initiative gone, he last appears cleaning out the refuse from beneath the kitchen sink in a house which his friend, Charlie Geary, has stolen from him. Where Vandover is weak, Geary is strong; he stays on top because of his dominant will and ruthless egotism. He is the big fish that swallows the little fish. The story's strength lies in the vivid portrayal of the successive steps in Vandover's degeneration; the action is interlocked, and the time sequence, always a problem to the naturalist, is well handled. Rarely does the focus of attention shift from Vandover in his downward movement, although occasionally, in an incident such as the shipwreck or the venereal misfortune of Dolly Haight, the writer succumbs to the temptation to digress in order to include a vivid scene suggestive of Zola or Ibsen.

The main flaw in the book is the insufficient motivation of Vandover's downfall; the weaknesses within himself which Norris dramatized, exaggerated, and transferred to his leading character were not sufficient to account for radical degeneration; and the reader is inclined to look upon Vandover as a normal individual strangely succumbing to a series of lamentable misfortunes. The difficulty was magnified by Norris's failure to retain the necessary amoral attitude throughout the book; he might have succeeded in making Vandover's collapse appear credible in the light of an exceptionally pliable nature defeated by a malignant fortune had he adhered to a deterministic presentation. He gives Vandover freedom of choice, however, and condemns him when he does wrong. As the book stands, Norris does not escape from the idea that "undoing follows hard upon unrighteousness," and his limited experience of twenty-five years gives him the wrong perspective. Thus he identifies his sympathies with Vandover and at the same time condemns him to a fate which he does not deserve. By the time he had finished *McTeague* he was to learn more thoroughly the need of a completely detached attitude.

The drama of degeneration was carried to the limit in presenting Vandover as a victim of *lycanthropy*, a dementation which causes him to discard his clothes, paddle up and down the room on hands and feet, and bark and snarl like a dog. No doubt Norris considered it no more of an excess than Zola's portrayal of Coupeau's *delirium tremens* in *L'Assommoir*. As we have seen, he had in *Lauth* first used the idea that man becomes a beast when the soul is removed. This theme had not been entirely discarded when he wrote *Vandover*, although he must have realized that to the naturalist a soul apart from the organism is an impossibility. Vandover's dual nature is not that of a Dr. Jekyll, but that of a human being composed of a soul and a beast; as the soul deteriorates the beast becomes dominant. But now Norris uses an uncommon derangement in order to retain a favorite

dramatic situation. Thus Vandover, in becoming a
wolf, illustrated Norris's theme of the brute beneath
the civilized man. As he learned more about writing,
he tempered his presentation of this theme in the light
of reality, but he nevertheless continued to use the
atavistic as a source for drama.

It is probable that when Norris left Harvard
Vandover and the Brute was as nearly complete as he
was to make it. At any rate, perhaps because of its
outspoken theme, he put it aside for the more promising *McTeague*. After the publication of *McTeague*
in 1899, he submitted *Vandover* to the Doubleday,
McClure Company for whom he then was working.
John S. Phillips remembers that he and his associates
were forcibly impressed by the novel but doubted the
advisability of publishing it. Phillips then sent the
manuscript to William Heinemann, hoping that the
Continental-minded English publisher would bring
it out; but the latter, although he dared print Dreiser's
Sister Carrie after its abortive American issue a year
later, did not feel that the British public would
stomach Norris's *Brute*. That Norris despaired of
publication is indicated by the use of sections of the
book in later writings, such as the description of Ida
Wade's parlor, which he transferred to *Blix*.

Vandover and the Brute was published in 1914,
twelve years after Norris's death. Even at that time
it was necessary for Charles Norris to cut out a number of expressions and omit an entire chapter to make
it acceptable to the publisher. That Norris in his
later fiction avoided much of the frank detail of the
French naturalists may quite possibly be due to
the writing of *Vandover;* the obvious unmarketability

of the novel in America must have been impressed
upon him at the time. In order to complete the book
for publication, Charles Norris added about five
thousand words to the manuscript, which however
did not alter any essential feature of it. As a whole,
its publication was well-advised. Although at the
time many critics declared that it was a mistake
to publish the novel unrevised by its author, it is now
generally agreed that *Vandover* is a valuable addition
to Norris's writings. The strength of the novel far
outweighs its weaknesses. In realistic portrayal of
college life, it is the first of a *genre* in American fiction,
the crispness of the descriptions is not excelled in
any of his other books, many of the episodes have
great dramatic strength, and the conclusion is the
most effective and the most logical of all of the endings of his novels.

Chapter 5: South African Adventure

THE first article in Frank Norris's credo was, "Life is better than literature"; the best preparation for writing stories is living them. "Of all the difficult things that enter into the learning of a most difficult profession, the most difficult of all for the intended novelist to acquire is the fact that life is better than literature. The amateur will say this with conviction, will preach it in public and practise the exact reverse in private. But it still remains true that all the temperament, all the sensitiveness to impressions, all the education in the world will not help one little, little bit in the writing of the novel if life itself, the crude, the raw, the vulgar, if you will, is not studied. An hour's experience is worth ten years of study." In truth, experience contained more than ordinary value for Frank Norris because, as he moved from the nursery to "the world's playroom," he retained the vivid imagination of a boy, dramatizing everything about him. Now that he was back in San Francisco after his year at Harvard, he chose between writing and action; instead of setting about to complete either of the novels upon which he had worked during the previous winter, he left them untouched to seek experience in Africa.

Norris characteristically chose the most romantic
and adventuresome of continents to explore first.
His plans were very ambitious; he hoped to reach the
very inmost mysteries of Africa in a trip to start at
Cape Town and end at Cairo. From Cape Colony
he would go by rail to Kimberley, double back to
Johannesburg, and there join a wagon train going
north to Bulawayo, in the heart of "that mysterious
wilderness of South Africa known indiscriminately
as 'up country,' or Charterland, or Matabeleland."
(The exotic names pleased him.) From Bulawayo he
thought that a determined traveler could make his
way northward to the headlands of the Nile, down
which he would journey to the Mediterranean. The
scheme was too ambitious to talk about openly; he
confided the extent of it to Charles Norris, but to his
mother and his friends in San Francisco he went no
further than to speak of a visit to South Africa with
an excursion into Rhodesia on a bullock wagon.

It was chance and not foresight which led Norris
directly into an exciting adventure. Instead of trying
to trek across the heart of Africa, he walked into an
armed camp and took part in a bloodless revolution,
for fate provided that he should arrive in Johannesburg on the eve of the Jameson Raid. Before he left
San Francisco, the stage was set (unknown to him)
for that most spectacular and disastrous raid, which,
had it succeeded, would have changed the history
of South Africa and which made the Boer war inevitable by its failure.

It is necessary here to give a brief and arbitrary
statement of that raid in order to present Norris's
part in the drama. The Uitlanders, or foreigners, who

made up a large majority of population of Johannesburg, mining town in the heart of the Transvaal, had for some time resented the reactionary policy of the Boer government, headed by President Kruger. Their unrest culminated in a scheme by which they would receive external support in case they should revolt in a demand for their rights. Cecil Rhodes, then prime minister of British Cape Colony and head of the company which owned Rhodesia, was to allow his lieutenant, Dr. Jameson, with a force of men assembled on the Transvaal border, to invade Boer territory simultaneously with an insurrection in Johannesburg. The plan resulted in a fiasco when the Uitlanders failed to rise on the date agreed upon, and the importunate Jameson marched into the Transvaal to relieve a city which had not yet revolted. The Boers withdrew from Johannesburg, surrounded and defeated Jameson, and taking advantage of the uncertain position of the Uitlanders, recaptured the city without resistance. The results of the illegal raid were disastrous; Jameson and the Uitlander leaders were imprisoned, Rhodes was thoroughly discredited, and the world looked upon the event as an unjustifiable attempt on the part of the British to add the Transvaal to their fast-growing South African empire. And Norris, in the process of becoming one of the revolting Uitlanders, saw his favorite tenet of aggressive Anglo-Saxon empire-building put to the test.

The journey to South Africa was partly the result of a return of "the attack of Harding Davis." Lured by the romance of newspaper-corresponding, convinced that the journalist came in closer contact with *raw* experience than other writers, he was eager to cast in his lot with the number of young men emulating the example of Davis, who had popularized the trade by his unprecedented travels in remote parts of the world. After angling for a contract with *Harper's Weekly*, Norris made an arrangement with the San Francisco *Chronicle* to publish his letters. These letters are the notes of a novelist in the making; because he threw himself into the adventure with zeal, recording his impressions with vivid detail, they remain as truly representative of his creative nature as are the novels to which they are corollary.

★   ★   ★

ON THE night of the seventh of December, Norris stood upon the deck of the *Norham Castle* watching the lights of Cape Town. In his desire to reach Africa as soon as possible, he had left his transatlantic steamer at Southampton in a tugboat in order to catch the *Berlin*, which was already in the stream on its way to Madeira. When he was picked up by the *Norham Castle* at Madeira, he found four hundred young Englishmen aboard who were on their way to join Dr. Jameson at Pitsani Potlugo, on the Transvaal border. Although they had been informed that they were to be used for policing duty, it was clear that there was a momentous secret in the air. As Norris gazed at Africa, he was keyed up for adventure. "For three weeks the *Norham Castle* had perseveringly screwed her way southward through an empty sea. Upon the equator she had slid through still, oily waters, blue as indigo, level as a cathedral floor, broken only by the quick flash and flight of hundreds of flying fish. . . . But since these three or four perfect days that she had met and passed on either side of the line, she had butted her nose into persistent northerly trades. All at once . . . the weather grew warmer and warmer, and the poor old cow that for twenty-one days had been cooped in her portable stall by the hoisting engine on the forward deck began to low excitedly and blew with her nostrils through the cracks of her box because she smelt the earth once more and caught the odor of the fields and growing trees. . . . The night was very dark, and the inky black prow went on describing jagged and serrated patterns against the sky and heaving itself against a very faint blur of golden light about a certain point on the horizon. . . . It grew stronger and brighter with every roll of the great ship, and then, all at once, right at its core a light flashed out and disappeared and flashed again, and everyone cried out at the same time, and you felt, as it were, a little thrill down in your throat, for that was a light on the land that you had come so far to see. It was Africa, the great 'Dark Continent,' stretching out there behind the horizon for so many miles of pathless forest and nameless desert."

His three-day stay in Cape Town was devoted to making notes on its provinciality, to sketching Englishmen, Malays, and Kaffirs, and to visiting the suburbs at the foot of Table Mountain. Table Mountain itself reminded him of a truncated life, a career disappointed in mid-course and relegated to failure. He found time to attend a native circus with Major Goold-Adams, a member of the ill-fated Wilson party, who became enthusiastic with him over a presentation of the Matabele war—"Matabeleland and a two-months' war in a forty-foot sawdust ring in an hour and a half." Norris's activities even included a visit to a tattooer, who decorated one arm with his fraternity seal and favorite girl's initials and the other with a snake bracelet, but in his absorption with native life he forgot his promise to cable his mother of his arrival. As a result, soon after his departure from Cape Town frantic demands for news of his whereabouts began to harass his bankers, who were unable to reply satisfactorily.

Meanwhile, after his train had rolled for two nights and a day through a "baked and sun-cracked desert in the midst of mirages, sand spouts, ostriches, and things," Norris had reached Kimberley. The mining town gave him an impression of incipient decay— "a hideousness, a rampart shrieking deformity, an ugliness beyond words," with never so much as a geranium growing in a tomato can to relieve it. He visited the combine which imprisoned eight hundred Kaffirs; gazed into the *kopje* or diamond pit, "the biggest hole in the ground in the world," whose variegated sands he compared to the colors blended on the bitumen end of an artist's palette; and descended to the diamond mine where the velvet darkness, dripping rocks, and queer-tasting atmosphere reminded him of the Big Dipper Mine at Colfax, California. He saw a Kaffir, mortally wounded by a rock which had "come punzie" upon him, endure his misery with a savage's fortitude. The stay in Kimberley depressed him, but his enthusiasm returned as his train moved through the green rolling veldt and hundreds of chimney stacks along the Rand, which told him that he was nearing Johannesburg. Fate, or the intuition which he called "the sixth sense," had timed his approach well.

*   *   *

DURING the ten days following Norris's arrival in Johannesburg on the 15th of December, 1895, he had a period of quiet in which to become acquainted with the theater of the action which was to precipitate itself at the end of that time. From his fellow lodgers at Long's Hotel he received many varied explanations for the spirit of unrest and tension which he found so noticeable in the frontier city. There were rumors of plots and counterplots, wrongs unredressed, machinations of subtle politicians and empire-builders; but it was quite impossible for him to get an accurate idea of the extraordinary network of plans which were to become so badly entangled in the days to follow, for he was an outsider—a young traveler from America seeing the country and hoping to pick up information which would make good articles for a San Francisco newspaper. He did not even have the privileges of a cable correspondent but was forced to be satisfied with visiting the mines on the Rand and sketching the bullock wagons in the Market Place.

He found Johannesburg to be a city which had grown like a mushroom in the center of the Witwatersrand reef. Only ten years before his arrival, the discovery of gold in the conglomerate of this reef, which extended for fifty miles through the center of the Transvaal, had caused President Kruger of the South African Free State to invite foreign capitalists to develop the mines and recoup the fortunes of a bankrupt state. As the wealth of the mineral deposits proved greater than had been dreamed, foreign capitalists, engineers, miners, and their families poured into the extensive operations so that in 1895, of the 250,000 non-native population of the Transvaal, 75,000 alone were Boers; the remaining number were Uitlanders, mostly English. In Johannesburg, the Uitlanders, who outnumbered the Boers three to one and paid nine tenths of the taxes, were denied franchise. They lived in a city inadequately governed and policed by unsympathetic Boer reactionaries, their children were provided no schooling in their native tongues, and their living quarters were made continually hazardous by miserable sanitary conditions. Those in control of the mining industry, forced because of the nature of the deposits to operate on a large scale, were hampered by government monopolies, excessive import duties, and exorbitant freight rates. As the demands of the newcomers became imperative, the Boers grew recalcitrant, realizing that the granting of them would imperil their own control of the country.

It is not surprising that Norris, a stranger to the country, found all of his sympathies with the Uitlanders, a considerable number of whom were Americans. The failure to use modern methods in cultivating the veldt, the primitive means of transportation, the unimaginative nature of the "Zarps" or Dutch policemen, together with many other evidences of a people non-progressive in the American sense, made him call the natives "the sluggish, unambitious, unenergetic, unspeakably stupid Boers. . . . Give the Boer his four or five farm buildings of mud and corrugated iron, his Transvaal tobacco—the strangest tasting stuff ever put in a pipe—his rifle, with which he is wonderfully expert, and his bullock wagon, and the world may roll as it will. The Arab to his camel, the Eskimo to his dogs, the Sioux to his pony, and the Boer of the Transvaal to his bullocks. The two are admirably adapted to each other; by long association they have grown to be exactly alike: slow, placid, content, stupid." In the revolt of the Uitlanders he saw a righteous stand for independence. "It is very curious to see the old, indomitable Anglo-Saxon spirit rousing up again in this far-away corner of the world as it roused itself in the Puritan colonies in the days of 1776 over the identical question of taxation without representation."

In Johannesburg the situation was tense. Norris felt that he was sitting over a powder barrel, and there is little doubt but that he wanted it to explode. He knew nothing of the parleys of Cecil Rhodes, Dr. Jameson, and John Hays Hammond under the stars in Mashonaland the summer before, when it was first suggested that external aid could be sent in case of an uprising in the city; he did not know that only the previous month Dr. Jameson had departed from Johannesburg with an invitation from the five leaders of the Reform Committee to march in to their aid on a day tentatively set late in December; he did not know that at the very time in which he was wandering about the streets of the mining city, the members of the Reform Committee were cultivating the seeds of their own destruction by squabbling over whether the insurrectionists were to raise the Transvaal or the British flag. He did have, however, an inkling of the presence of Jameson on the Bechuanaland border with his six hundred men under the employ of the British South African Company, for he had come to South Africa on the *Norham Castle* with a group of young soldiers on their way to Pitsani Potlugo. And, of course, he was aware of the omniscient Rhodes, who was to him the unseen force controlling the drama. "There is a big fish somewhere in these troubled waters. One never sees him, but one feels his presence at every moment. Poor, old, purblind, stupid, obstinate 'Oom Paul,' with Majuba Hill still in his mind; poor, little, stupid Zarps, hardly able to read a newspaper; oxlike, placid, country Boers, content to grow only such produce as will keep them from starvation, are so much small fry almost within the jaws of the fish already. The big fish is never seen and is but little talked of; he lives down yonder in Cape Town and his name is Cecil Rhodes. What part he is to play in the coming struggle is not yet discernible, but it would not be at all surprising if within the course of the next ten years a United States of South Africa, embracing everything between the Cape of Good Hope and the Zambesi River, should spring into existence with the Honorable Cecil as its president." He even gave full credit to the rumors that Rhodes was responsible for the crippling of the steamer *Scott* on the Spanish coast so that guns would not reach the Boers, and that he had seen to it that such Maxims as the Boers did receive should lack the "breech-piece" "without which a Maxim is about as effective as a bow without a bowstring." He was the man "who had conceived the idea, had prepared these tremendous effects, and was even now carrying them into execution."

On Christmas day Norris dined at the home of John Hays Hammond. He had many mutual friends with Mr. and Mrs. Hammond, for before this successful engineer had been brought out to South Africa as consulting engineer for Barnato Brothers, he had been a resident of San Francisco. Hammond, after leaving Barnato to work for Rhodes, had made his reputation in exploring the mineral resources of Mashonaland; he was now the consulting engineer for the Consolidated Gold Fields Company, the "combine" of all the mines on the Rand. He was probably the most powerful member of the committee which was planning the insurrection in Johannesburg. Norris found his pretty bungalow at New Doornfontein to be one of the few habitable homes in the Transvaal. He marveled at the complete self-command of his host, who was able to entertain his guests with the light commonplaces of dinner-table talk while he was keeping his grip "upon the vast and complicated forces of a great political uprising that was to disorganize the machinery of an entire empire." . . . "Think of it, while Mr. Hammond sat there at the head of his dining table chatting easily over his black coffee and cigarettes, Jameson and his six hundred with their Maxims and Lee-Mitfords were straining at the leash, away up there in Pitsani on the Bechuanaland border, waiting and listening for the word from him to precipitate an insurrection, a crisis whose shock would be felt around the world." Mr. Hammond's calmness may have been partly due to the fact that on that very day messengers had departed for Cape Town with instructions to stop Jameson's march as the Uitlanders had decided not to resort to an armed insurrection. And Mr. Hammond doubtless would have had more difficulty with his coffee and cigarettes if he had known that Dr. Jameson intended to invade the Transvaal whether he was asked to or not.

After the publication the following day of the Uitlanders' manifesto to Kruger which demanded equitable franchise, a new constitution, equality of languages, free trade, and other rights, the drama developed very rapidly. Andrew Trimble perfected his organization of a secret police a thousand strong to take over control of the city. Colonel Bettington gathered together his nucleus of officers who were to direct the only serviceable corps of riflemen in Johannesburg. The conspirators laid elaborate plans for the taking of the Pretoria fort at the first sign of trouble. Norris heard rumors of 15,000 Martini rifles smuggled in from Mafeking as baking powder, of 6,000 horses requisitioned in Swaziland and Basutoland for special service, of 2,000 men about the streets of the city, in the pay of "some mysterious committee," holding themselves in instant readiness. He edged himself over towards the fuse in the barrel of gunpowder.

Sunday morning, Norris found the English church crowded and noted the emphasis with which the prayer for the Queen's majesty was intoned, and the vigor of the congregational response. On Monday evening, when he came to supper in his hotel, the man who sat opposite him cried out, "The fat is in the fire now! The BBP have crossed the border, and are on the march to Johannesburg." As he was speaking, the half-naked Zulu who delivered the evening papers on a tricycle brought in the stop-press edition of the *Star*. The headlines screamed out: "Crossed the Border—Forces Making for Johannesburg—Conflict Lamentably Imminent—Suspense at an End—Immeasurable Gravity of the Situation." At 7:30 the evening before, Dr. Jameson and his six hundred men had started on their ride of a hundred and sixty miles through Boer territory to interfere in an insurrection which had not yet taken place!

In writing his account of what followed, Norris divided the action into the five phases of the classical drama: the start, the rise, the pause, the height, and the close. Tuesday morning saw the action on the rise, with Jameson making steady progress, the Reform Committee wondering what to do, the Boer police retiring from the city, leaving the Uitlanders in control, and great masses of the population stampeding to get out of the city. Norris, still an onlooker, took notes as the plot tightened. The red-faced Englishmen who yesterday had trotted up and down Commissioner Street on their little Basuto polo ponies were now wearing khakee outfits instead of whipcord breeches and carrying rifles instead of crops. The bullock carts which yesterday had creaked at snail's pace in and out of the public square were now crowding the streets of the town, piled high with mattresses, bedsteads, chairs, and tables, fleeing from the city which everyone believed would soon echo with the rattle of Maxims. ("Precisely as the war novelists have told us.") The Kaffir who yesterday in his sacking shirt and ostrich plume had scraped the dirt from the street-car tracks in front of the hotel had now discarded the sackcloth and was having a

little native war dance all by himself between the
tracks, stamping his feet, shaking his fists, and
chanting in a low voice.

Norris saw life, raw, crude, terrible, as he looked
out from his hotel window on the endless stream of
humanity surging towards the railroad station. With
the gayety of a group of actresses from a variety
theatre fleeing in a carriage piled high with theatrical
luggage, he contrasted the dejection of the women
of the poorer classes, going they knew not where,
their arms loaded with enormous bundles, stunned
by the clamor and hurry and frightened by the vague
feeling of danger that ran in the air like the sense of
a coming storm—panic-stricken, dazed, their children
weeping into the folds of their skirts. He saw scores
of Cornishmen, sullen and chafing under the execra-
tions of a whole city, hated because they fled before
the issue of a cause which was not their own. . . . The
procession streamed on incessantly; men and women,
jaded horses, weeping children, scared dogs dragged
about by leashes of rope, Kaffirs with wide rolling
eyes, overworked porters, even occasional Hindoos.
As he pushed his way towards the station he came
upon a heap of furniture—black walnut bedsteads,
an empty parrot cage, smoke-blackened kitchen tins
done up in red counterpanes—which parted the crowd
to right and left as a stranded snag would part a
current. Sitting in the midst of this ruin was a little
child, a girl of ten years, benumbed and dazed with
the hurrying multitude, the confusion, and the noise.
She rolled her eyes wildly and answered never a word
to the questions put to her. . . . The confusion of the
marching thousands mingled together into a vast

clamor; the plaint of an entire people, the lamentation
of a tribal migration. . . .

When he reached the railroad station, he witnessed
a dreadful struggle. Men and women grappled on the
platforms, on the steps of the carriages, and even in
the carriages themselves; lost children, frantic with
terror, screamed in the press; . . . trunks were abandoned and plundered by the Kaffirs; a woman was
struck on the temple by a Cornish miner and was
seized with hysteria, hiccoughing and shouting, wav-
ing her arms, her hair about her eyes and her bonnet all
awry; a window glass in a carriage was smashed . . .
and a man's bloody hand and wrist emerged. The
report spread that he had fought with a Kaffir and
his throat was cut. . . . Norris saw an incoming train
disgorge its passengers. In an instant two multitudes
had mingled, one fighting to get out of the city and
the other fighting to get in, and both alike lashed on
by a blind fear—the brute terror of mobs and herds
of cattle, the terror that shuts its eyes and ears. . . .
Women and children crowded into cattle cars, open
pens enclosed merely by breast-high slats. . . . The
day grew cold. . . . Norris heard later that it was here
in one of these open cattle cars, hurried along at full
steam through the barren veldt in the biting wind
and under a driving rain, that a poor Swedish woman,
the keeper of a little newsstand in Rissek street, gave
birth to a child. He also learned that one of the overladen trains which he had seen leave the station that
day was thrown from the track at Glencoe Junction
a few hours later, killing twenty and injuring thirty
of the people who had fled.

Norris returned to the center of the city to find

another crowd milling about the Goldfields Building. He saw that each of the men emerging from the improvised recruiting station carried a Lee-Mitford rifle, "the gun that kills at 1,000 yards." Around the corner he noted the cavalry headquarters, where groups of horsemen, equipped with revolver, rifle, haversack, and blanket, continually came and went. The rifles were still wrapped in the waste of their packing cases; the saddles and bridles showed violently yellow against the bay of the horses' flanks and cheeks; the horses themselves were fresh, sturdy, just off the veldt. Norris, ignorant that there were only 3,000 guns for 20,000 men, felt that the stage manager had done his work well.

During that Tuesday he had seen a bloodless revolution take place. The Boers had withdrawn without a shot, and Kruger at Pretoria thought that Johannesburg was in the hands of 20,000 armed Uitlanders. As Norris believed that the Uitlanders had won their independence, it seemed to him ironical that in the middle of the afternoon the Transvaal flag was flown over John Hays Hammond's office in the Goldfields Building. The altercation as to their allegiance among the unwilling leaders of the insurrection had been settled when Mr. Hammond had offered to shoot anyone who objected to the Boer colors. Thus it was that the Reform Committee, uncertain of its stand and wishing to keep one foot in either manger, swore allegiance to the Transvaal within their office and sent a member out on the balcony to encourage the populace with the good news of Jameson's approach. When Norris went to bed, he decided that the crisis had been reached.

The next day he would get a horse and a gun and join in the defense of the city. Meanwhile Johannesburg slept on its arms, confident that Jameson would soon be with them, while the Reform Committee entertained a delegation from Kruger, who, far more crafty than the members of the irresolute committee, was tying their hands with an armistice. If he could be certain that Jameson, now within a few miles of the city, would receive no aid from the insurrectionists, Kruger felt sure that he could surround him with his Boer marksmen and force his surrender.

★   ★   ★

NEW YEAR'S DAY brought to Johannesburg a strong wave of enthusiasm. The inhabitants, who had been slow to react to the abortive revolt, began to sense their strength now that the city was in their hands. As they were ignorant of the small number of guns at their disposal, they felt sure of success both for themselves and Jameson in spite of the cordon of Boers around the city. Nearly every able-bodied man in the city enrolled, the women established two hospital bases, the committee became confident that Jameson would fight his way through to them. The people prepared food and flowers for a grand reception, and the buildings and hills behind the city were lined with watchers, hoping to get the first sight of the approaching column. On arising, Norris found the streets filled with companies of soldiers drilling with sticks for rifles. As they went round and round the city blocks, they reminded him of the supers at the Paris Opéra, appearing and reappearing in simulation of a great army.

Norris determined to get a rifle and horse so that he could join in the battle which, rumor put it, was taking place not far outside the city. Five times he tried to get through the complicated approach to the headquarters in the Goldfields Building in order to see Mr. Hammond. He knew the watchword, "Maxim," but the sentinels posted at each turn of the stairway shouted up his message with no success. Undismayed by his failure, he tried another ruse, and by evening he had enrolled in a mounted defense corps under Andrew Trimble, the acting chief of police. He and two young Englishmen whom he had met at the hotel expected to be given rifles and horses and to be sent to help bring in Jameson. They were disappointed; the chief set all three to work dividing a map of the city into a thousand "beats" to be patrolled by the police. It was slow business, for the flame of their single candle sputtered and danced, and the shed in which they worked was miserably cold and drafty. As they thought of the fighting which might be taking place out on the veldt, they grew impatient. About midnight Norris and one of the Englishmen, Solz, stole out of their prison, leaving their companion assiduously sticking pins in the map.

They walked the streets until dawn, when their repeated efforts got them two horses from a livery stable on Fox Street, freshly shod ponies from Basutoland, fitted out with new saddles, saddle pockets, and combination headstalls and halters. They then rode to Trimble's office for rifles, but the guns had long since given out. Fortunately Solz produced two hunting rifles, which he had brought from Kimberley, and, thus mounted and armed, they dashed across the city to join "Bettington's Horse," the crack cavalry unit of the defenders. They arrived too late, however, for Bettington had just made a last futile effort to persuade the Reform Committee to let him go to Jameson's support. At almost the moment when Norris had succeeded in gaining the status of a soldier, the battle was over; Jameson, checkmated by Kruger, had, that morning at nine-fifteen, surrendered to the Boers, who had surrounded and outfought him at Doornkop, thirteen miles from Johannesburg.

*   *   *

WITH the collapse of Jameson's venture, the Johannesburg insurrectionists found that the coal which they had unwillingly seized was too hot to hold, and yet they knew not how to drop it. The populace, now thoroughly aroused, was in favor of fighting to retain their control of the city from which the Boers had retired. The news of Jameson's surrender did not reach them till late in the day, but when the crowds learned the truth, their mood was a very ugly one. They considered themselves betrayed; Jameson had been defeated within earshot of the city while they had been given no opportunity to ride to his rescue. Success had turned to disaster. When Norris rode past the Goldfields Building, he found a mob beside itself with wrath. Again and again members of the committee appeared at the windows, explaining, reasoning, expostulating, but the crowd would listen to nothing, refused to see anything except that Jameson had been sacrificed within a few hours' march of twenty thousand men. Stones began to

fly; men spoke of lynching. The speaker's voice was
drowned in a roar of indignation. "Why did you not
send us to join him?" "If you made an armistice
with the Boer government, why did you not include
Jameson in it?" "It is a revolution of capitalists—
a money-grabbing scheme of Rhodes and Barnato."
The depression and resentment were so intense that
no one slept that night, and civil war threatened to
take the place of revolution.

As the city remained in revolt, Norris still looked
forward to participating in some actual fighting.
He was again to be disappointed, because the Boers
preferred to win by strategy rather than force. The
astute Kruger informed the Uitlanders that, unless
they surrendered their arms and control of the city,
he would deliver Jameson and his men to a firing
squad. This tense situation continued for a week,
while parleys were held and the eternal question,
"Why was Jameson not included in the armistice?"
was shouted across the bars by voices husky with
alcohol, to an accompaniment of red clenched fists
banging upon the counter.

The greatest danger of all was the possibility of
riot among the thousands of Kaffirs, thrown idle by
the closing down of the mines. Norris was put to
work helping to shut up such miners' canteens as
attempted to keep open in spite of the stringent
commands from headquarters; it was imperative that
the Kaffirs should obtain no liquor. When, as he
approached the Geldenhuis Deep, Norris witnessed
five hundred Zulus dance their war dance, working
themselves into a frenzy of hatred and lust for blood,
he realized what havoc would result should the na-

tives obtain liquor and get out of control. "The effect
was amazing, almost terrible. . . . They held their
assegais by the butts, sometimes pointing them high
in the air, sometimes thrusting them point downward
toward the earth, sometimes catching by the middle
and brandishing them as if about to throw. . . . As
the five hundred feet came down together with each
line of the chant, the sound was tremendous, and the
earth trembled at the shock as if at the passage of a
heavily loaded train. . . . Occasionally one or another,
driven to a frenzy, would start from the ranks and
bound into the center of the circle in one or two
springless leaps, yelling shrilly, brandishing his shield
and weapons, sounding his weird and hideous war
whistle. . . . The circle narrowed more and more, as
the pressure against shoulder and flank increased a
number of men were thrust to the front forming a
second rank, then a third rank was formed in the
same way; next every assegai was raised high in the
air and with a wild medley of yells and shouts the
circle of dancers . . . rushed altogether to the center
till they formed a solid jam. . . . One might have
been in Uganda, Barotseland, or in the very heart of
the Dark Continent itself—the thing could not have
been wilder or more savage."

During this time Norris twice came near to real
action—first, by carrying a dispatch, and second,
by being shot at. The dispatch proved disappointing;
although it was carried in the proper style, it turned
out to be merely a demand on the part of the officer
in charge of the camp at Yoeville for an English-
speaking Kaffir "boy" to act as assistant to the
overworked camp cook. The shooting was of more

consequence. On the evening of the fourth of January the party of canteen closers was riding back to town, anxious to remove their storm-drenched clothes. As they passed the head-gear of the Wemmer mine, close to Johannesburg, a party of horsemen came into sight through the mist of the driving rain, riding along an embankment which paralleled their road. At a distance of fifteen hundred yards Norris could make out that they were Boers because of their broad hatbrims. Both groups pulled up, and the Uitlanders sat for a moment watching to see what the Boers would do. Suddenly the Boers fired on them. As the thin wreath of smoke cleared away from the heads of the attackers, there was a moment of bewilderment and then the officer in charge of Norris's party gave them the word to withdraw and push on quietly to the town. It was a narrow escape from a bad business.

The drenching at Wemmer dam brought serious results to Norris. That night he returned to his hotel with a temperature, and the next morning he awoke delirious with an acute attack of the South African fever. For nearly a week he hovered between life and death. It was then that the lonesomeness of his situation came home to him; he might have died if Mrs. Hammond, in the midst of her own troubles, had not found time to aid in pulling him through. He later remarked to Charles Norris that he was so weak when the fever left him that he could not remove the cap from his fountain pen. But his troubles were not yet over. The crisis in the city had sent food up to exorbitant prices; bread was a dollar a loaf, and potatoes thirteen dollars a bag, and in a short time his letter of credit was nearly exhausted. On top of this he learned that his failure to cable home from Cape Town and the delay of his mail during the insurrection had caused consternation in San Francisco. There the press was featuring stories of his disappearance, while his mother, sick with fear, was sending daily messages to the banks of Cape Town and Johannesburg, trying to locate him. After repeated efforts he managed to persuade the Boer authorities to allow him to send through a message telling of his safety and asking for money to come home on.

During the ninth and tenth of January, Johannesburg surrendered its arms to Kruger, and the members of the Reform Committee were arrested to face trial for their lives. Norris summoned up enough strength on the tenth to act upon a demand of the Landdrost to appear before the Boer police. The Landdrost was monosyllabic and impolite, handling his passport as though he wished it had been a death warrant, and from his manner it was evident that Norris was not to be included in the general amnesty which had been proclaimed to all those who would surrender their arms. The Boer officer asked no questions, offered no explanations, but called Norris's name, handed him his passport, inflated himself, and then bellowed: "The Government gives you twenty-four hours in which to leave the Transvaal!" And as a final touch, he mulcted Norris of twenty-five dollars to pay for his passport out of the country.

As he took the train for Cape Town the next day, Norris was a sick boy. Gone were the plans for pushing through to Bulawayo and trekking north to the Zambesi—to Cairo. He was glad to be going home, and on the fifteenth of January, when the *Moor* sailed for England, he entered in his diary,

> "I'm out to sea!   I'm out to sea!
> 'Twasn't half as fine as I thought it would be."

Another disappointed passenger joined the ship as it was anchored out in the stream; it was Cecil Rhodes, the tremendous power who, in manipulating the strings for the Johannesburg drama, had pulled the house down about his ears. Mr. Rhodes left the boat at Plymouth for London to help clear away the débris of the "great fiasco," and Norris went on to New York and California. He arrived home late in February, anxious to rest and recover his strength.

The South African adventure was over. Its direct bearing on his writing was not extensive, for, with the exception of his travel articles, he used it in only two of his short stories, *A Salvation Boom in Matabeleland* and *The Strangest Thing*. Seven articles appeared in the San Francisco *Chronicle*, one in *Harper's Weekly*, and two in the *Wave*. But more important to Norris was the experience it brought to him; experience purchased at a heavy price, for the fever contracted in South Africa was to reappear during a later adventure in Cuba and, in the end, again return to add to the complications which brought on his death. This fever, however, was but a strand in the deterministic pattern of his life; for the present he benefited by becoming more cosmopolitan and world-minded than ever.

★   ★   ★

Chapter 6: Studio Sketches of a Novelist

During the two years following his return from South Africa, Frank Norris exploited the resources of journalism. As its most important objects were constant observation and effective expression, it appeared to be the field particularly suited to his needs. Those who desired only cheap success might "sail paper boats in the creek behind the schoolhouse, or fish with bent pins in the pools and shallows of popular favor"; but it was the duty of the conscientious writer to prepare himself as assiduously as does the artist, with his years of sketching, and the musician, with his repetition of finger exercises. The novelist must obtain his schooling as best he may, for he has no set regime, no formula, no master to point his way. "For the novelist where is the cut-and-dried science which he can learn that will help him? . . . Of all the arts, the art of fiction has no handbook. . . . Of all the arts, it is the most virile; of all the arts, it will not, will not flourish indoors. Dependent solely upon fidelity to life for existence, it must be practised in the very heart's heart of life, on the street corner and in the market place." For the training which he desired, Norris hit upon an ideal

126

position; with almost as much liberty as a free-lance writer, under an editor sympathetic towards his ambitions, and in a city well fitted to his purposes, Norris profited greatly by the two years of observation and writing which were attendant to his work on the San Francisco *Wave*.

Early in April, 1896, Norris took up his new position, after he had passed six weeks in recuperating from the attack of fever contracted in Johannesburg. Much of this time he spent with Waterhouse and two other college chums at the Big Dipper Mine in the cold, invigorating climate of the High Sierras above Colfax. It was a pleasant vacation, devoted to chatting about college days, larking in the snow, taking it easy. With his renewed color and brown eyes contrasting with his rapidly graying hair, his lean and supple five-foot-eleven figure needed only the Uitlander outfit which he had brought home from Africa to make him a completely romantic person. When his usual playfulness had returned, he came down from the mountains to join the staff of the *Wave* on the suggestion of its editor, John O'Hara Cosgrave.

The San Francisco *Wave* had been started at Del Monte by Ben Truman of the publicity staff of the Southern Pacific Railroad with the chief purpose of popularizing the newly opened Del Monte Hotel. In 1890 it was transferred to San Francisco, where it appeared in a new form with the subtitle, "A Weekly for Those in the Swim." During the following five years it advanced from its modest beginning to a position of considerable importance, and, by the time Norris became connected with it, its political and literary departments had relegated the society news to the back pages, and the subtitle had been dropped. In the storm which arose about the notorious funding bill, it was the chief journal backing C. P. Huntington and the railroad interests, carrying on a bitter war with Hearst and Bierce on the *Examiner*, Arthur McEwen on the *Chronicle*, and Frank Pixley on the *Argonaut*. It was a time of corruption and muckraking in San Francisco politics when journalists questioned no methods in gaining their ends. Like the rest of the San Francisco journals, the *Wave* "rode to popularity on the violence of its antagonisms." In its office Norris learned much about politics, particularly about the feud between the farmers and the railroad—already referred to as "the octopus" —a struggle which he was to use later in his fiction.

Of more lasting import than its political axe-grinding, however, was the literary output of this short-lived journal. During the ten years of its existence, contesting for the literary market with two worthy rivals, the *Argonaut* and the *Overland Monthly*, it printed representative work by Ambrose Bierce, Bailey Millard, J. P. Pollard, Arthur McEwen, Yone Noguchi, W. C. Morrow, Gelett Burgess, Ernest Peixotto, John O'Hara Cosgrave, Juliet Wilbur Tompkins, Emma Frances Dawson, Geraldine Bonner, Frank Norris, Will Irwin, Jack London, and James Hopper. Of these, Burgess, Norris, Cosgrave, Hopper, and Irwin served upon its staff at one time or another. No better tribute could be paid to the skill of Cosgrave as an editor than that he mustered this talent in a city which today boasts no successful literary journal; he started with two literary supplements a year and built up the number and quality of his contributions to the point at which he could present a good short story each week.

Frank Norris's nominal position on the *Wave* was that of editorial assistant; in this capacity at times he almost wrote the journal by himself, while at other times, for weeks at a stretch, he would contribute practically nothing to it. Cosgrave, only four years Norris's senior and himself barely started on his career, realized that freedom would give scope to his assistant's talent. What he could not give him in salary—Norris never received more than $100 a month—he gave him in opportunities. The "editorial assistant" wrote short stories, dialogues, descriptive articles, interviews, theatrical and art criticisms, editorials, book reviews, parodies, translations, and football write-ups. Most of his contributions appeared signed, initialed, or under the pseudonym of Justin Sturgis, a name frequently used by both Cosgrave and Norris when limited finances forced them to write the paper alone. The occasional editorials appeared unsigned, as did a number of his feature articles; fortunately, his style is clearly recognizable, so that most of his writing can be identified. At times there was much hack work, ranging from the mechanical write-ups based on the exchange editor's clippings to solemn articles, such as the one mentioned by Condy Rivers, *The Industrial Renaissance in Japan* "compiled after an hour's reading in Lafcadio Hearn and the Encyclopedia." His irregular position gave full rein to enthusiasms—and also to indolence when such had the upper hand. The spirit which pervaded the working force was that frequently found in pioneer journals; Gelett Burgess writes of it in glowing terms. "We all liked Jack Cosgrave, and his only fault was that he could pay us but little. Frank did splendid work, didn't need money, would do what he pleased. . . . We were like brothers; we all regarded it as a lark; we had such freedom. We were learning to write." It was under these circumstances that Norris wrote the stories and articles which Burgess has so fitly called "the studio sketches of a novelist."

*   *   *

A SURVEY of Norris's contributions to the *Wave* reveals three periods of varied activity. The first, during which he wrote chiefly sketches and stories reflecting the plans for his novels, lasted for three months, after which there was a silence for an equal length of time. When he returned to his work in October, it was to devote himself almost exclusively to non-fictional writing—articles, reviews, sport write-ups, and general hack work in profusion—which he continued throughout the winter of 1896–7. This dwindled down into a very small stream which ceased entirely in the early spring. Late in May, the third and most productive period began with a burst of energy probably created by circumstances which will be discussed in the next chapter; it brought with it a cessation of article-writing and a series of short stories which continued without interruption through the summer, fall, and winter, culminating in *Moran of the Lady Letty*, the first chapter of which appeared in January, 1898. The irregularity with which he worked and the changes in the nature and quality of his writing give a good basis for judging the enthusiasms and falterings which were taking place in his life.

In the first period Norris drew upon his experiences and the *milieu* of his two unfinished novels for his subject matter. He used his adventure in South Africa in one story and two articles; he began to develop a sort of Zolaistic journalism in an energetic method of writing articles descriptive of California scenes and customs; but his purpose of setting himself to school was best carried out in the two series of sketches which he called *Western Types* and *Man Proposes*. In the former he made detailed "objective" descriptions of the college man, the plumber's apprentice, the fast girl, and the art student. He utilized aspects of his own education for the sketches of the college man and the art student, and for the fast girl he printed the section of *Vandover* which describes Ida Wade. His plumber's apprentice was a study of life on Polk Street; his name is Jonesie, he drinks steam beer, crosses the bay for picnics on Sunday, and occasionally closes the day's enjoyment by becoming drunk and disorderly. "In front of the corner grocery he will while the time away, talking loud, swearing, spitting, scuffling, and joshing the girls that pass in twos and threes." He is of McTeague's world, the world of slow-thinking and ponderous working men. In addition to this sketch Norris wrote a short story about him, *The Heroism of Jonesie*, in which he surprises himself by kicking a prize fighter in the face in his efforts to save a girl whose honor is in peril; his heroism is the result of "a desperate sort of courage that comes of fear." In another story of this period, Sandy Callaghan, a car conductor, has a girl who runs the soda-water fountain in a candy store on Polk Street. She "wore very blonde hair and imitation alligator-skin belts. She exhaled alternate odors of sachet and chocolate caramels. . . ."

In the series *Man Proposes* Norris played five variations on a single theme. The proposals range from a false avowal made by a society-bred hero in the face of what appeared to be certain death—a situation which Norris liked so well that he used it again as a pivotal incident in his novel, *A Man's Woman*—to an uncouth declaration made by a coal heaver, with small eyes, flat nose, and a lower jaw protruding like the jaws of a carnivore, to a woman, not young, and rather fat, perspiring over a washtub. "Suddenly he took her in his enormous arms, crushing down her struggle with his immense brute strength. Then she gave up all at once, glad to yield to him and to his superior force, willing to be conquered. She turned her head to him, and they kissed each other full on the mouth, brutally, grossly."

Norris was recording what seemed to him to be "the heart's heart of life." He noticed every detail of the lower middle-class dwellers on Polk Street; externally he knew them well, could in quick strokes of his pen summon up the slow-moving workmen and their showy girls. He could not get inside of their heads—see their inmost thoughts—but, as an objective artist, he could use the method of the behaviorist; assuming their internal struggles were mirrored in their external acts, he watched for characteristic habits and mannerisms. Noting them with curious detached eyes, he discovered that they were animals, the creatures of habit, the playthings of forces. He became convinced of the presence of the brute beneath the veneer of civilization. He found ready support for his ideas, for had not the thought of the nineteenth century become obsessed with that slag of evolution, the assumption that the primitive, the primordial, controlled man stripped of conventions? Heredity, circumstances, and the brute nature. "His father had been a coal heaver before him, and had worked at that trade until he had been killed in a strike. His mother had drunk herself into an asylum and had died long ago." Tell the Truth, tell about life, spurn the gingerbread falsehoods of sentimental historical romance, the vapidity of Marie Corelli and the Duchess.

As Norris observed Polk Street, Stephen Crane, similarly interested, was writing about the slums of New York. *Maggie* and *George's Mother* were reviewed in the *Wave* on July 4, 1896, by a hand which appears to be Norris's. It is the comment of one pioneer on the work of another. "In *Maggie*, Stephen Crane has written a story something on the plan of the episode of Nana in *L'Assommoir*. . . . I think that the charm of his style lies chiefly in his habit and aptitude for making phrases—sparks that cast a momentary gleam of light on whole phases of life. . . . The author is writing . . . from the outside. Mr. Crane does not seem to *know* his people. He does not seem to have gotten down *into* their life and to have written from what he saw around him. His people are types, not characters, his scenes and incidents are not particularized. . . . With him it is the broader, vaguer, *human* interest that is the main thing, not the smaller details of a particular phase of life. . . ."

★   ★   ★

ONE afternoon at dusk during this same spring, an
artist riding down Sacramento Street on the "dummy
seat" of a cable car had a momentary vision of an
unknown young man, a slouched figure in an Inver-
ness cape, passing beneath a blown gaslight in a
downpour of rain. Some poignancy of drama in the
scene fixed it in his mind, and the next day he painted
the impression into a somber little canvas which he
called "Spring Floods." The artist was Bruce Porter,
a man whose sensitive nature, reflected in the creation
of murals and stained-glass windows, made it possible
for him to establish an unusually intimate friendship
with the subject of his picture, Frank Norris.

Porter met Norris for the first time a few days later
at Martinelli's Café, when, on May 1, 1896, Les
Jeunes gathered to celebrate a successful year of
publication of the *Lark*. Their host was Frank Gelett
Burgess, editor of the *Lark*, and chief spirit among
Les Jeunes, who had decorated the dinner menu with
a border of "goups," "boneless homunculi," with
interlaced legs and arms. (The press reported that
"a *pâté de volaille* opened and the larks flew out.")
Les Jeunes were of two sorts: the small inner circle
which had given to the *Lark* nationwide fame, and
the "un-larked Jeunes" or friendly supporters,
among whom were Cosgrave and Frank Norris from
the *Wave*. All of the members of the inner circle at
the dinner were to become Norris's close friends.
Burgess, mathematician turned humorist, he had
known as an instructor at Berkeley. Ernest Peixotto,
with whom he had sketched horses at the Presidio,
had been his chum in Paris. Bruce Porter's studios in
San Francisco and New York were to become his

favorite spots of retreat and confession. Porter Garnett, whose interest lay in artistic printing, introduced him to the *Bocce* courts of the Italian quarter;
frequently their companion player was Willis Polk,
in time to be one of San Francisco's leading architects.
These five men, each destined to attain fame in
creative fields, were leading an artistic revolt against
the commonplaces of the literature of the day.

The essence of their rebellion was found in the
Lark, a thin small creature printed on bamboo paper
with uncut pages; the magazine was incredibly *fin-de-
siècle*, posing as an exponent of free and wide-
swinging bohemianism and declaring that "delicate
and interesting is the difference betwixt those who
would rather be, and those who would rather see, a
Purple Cow." Garnett parodied the *Rubaiyat*, Porter
wrote prose idylls, Yone Noguchi composed oriental poems, Polk discussed " *L'Arkitecture Moderne*,"
Peixotto designed covers and posters, and Burgess
followed up the extraordinary success of *The Purple
Cow* with other nonsense verses, accompanied by
capering Goops, such as

> "*I'd rather have Fingers than Toes,*
> *I'd rather have Ears than a Nose,*
> *And as for my Hair, I'm glad it's all there,*
> *I'll be awfully sad when it goes.*"

The *Lark* was the most original and brilliant of
the short-lived brochures, called Dinkey Magazines,
which followed the appearance of the *Yellow Book* in
England. With the *Chap Book* of Chicago and Elbert
Hubbard's *The Philistine*, it represented the best of

136   Frank Norris: A Biography

a movement which had numerous followers throughout America. Whimsical as their contents were, their purpose as stated by Burgess was significant. "The movement . . . aimed to overthrow the staid respectability of the larger magazines and to open to younger writers opportunities to be heard before they obtained recognition from the autocratic editors. Their outbreak was a symptom of the discontent of the times, a wide-felt protest of emancipation from the dictates of old literary tribunals."

This piquant rash was, in fact, but one symptom of the fever attendant upon the break with tradition which marked the literature of the nineties. By the middle of the decade the younger writers were repudiating the New England school with anathemas. They were impatient with its offspring, the local-colorists who wrote carefully and timidly—Miss Wilkins and Sarah Orne Jewett in New England. Edward Eggleston in Indiana, George Cable and Thomas Nelson Page in the South, the writers of the Bret Harte school in the West. They were equally impatient with what seemed to them evasion by the older writers; Henry James had deserted the field for English urbanity; Mark Twain, who intended to voice his inward torments in a posthumous autobiography, was seeking idealism in the musty past by writing a biography of Joan of Arc; William Dean Howells, who had laid the foundation for a hardy American realism in *The Rise of Silas Lapham* and *A Modern Instance*, was content to encourage the young revolters rather than break the bonds of convention in his own novels. No one seemed to dare dig below the surface into the rot and violence of life.

The reaction of the younger writers was thus described by Norris at the turn of the century: "It has been a decade of fads, and 'the people have imagined a vain thing.' . . . For half a century certain great names, from Irving down to Holmes, were veritable Abracadabras—impeccable, sanctified. Then all at once the *fin-de-siècle* irreverence seemed to invade all sorts and conditions simultaneously, and the somber, sober idols were shouldered off into the dark niches, and not a man of us that did not trundle forth his own little tin-god-on-wheels, kowtowing and making obeisance, and going before with cymbals and a great noise, proclaiming a new Great One."

Norris did not do obeisance to the tin-god-on-wheels kowtowed to by the writers of the *Lark*. It was too light, too frivolous—he was for more monstrous aims than the Joy of Life. He did not agree with a creed that held that "amusement is the chief function of fiction, and that fidelity to fact is founded on another ideal." He did not want whimsicality, but angry protest and cries for the "Truth." He enjoyed his dinner with Les Jeunes, he read the *Lark* and laughed, he made its creators close friends, but he did not contribute to its pages. His god was of an entirely different sort; he preferred to attack smug complacency with a bludgeon rather than a rapier, dealing in drama which works itself out in blood in *McTeague* and in slaughter in *The Octopus*. Big ideas, primitive nature, Life with a capital L, adjectives and apostrophes. . . . "Les Jeunes. Yes, there are Les Jeunes, and the *Lark* was delightful—delightful fooling—but there's a graver note and a more virile to be sounded. Les Jeunes can do better than the *Lark*.

Give us stories now, give us men, strong, brutal men, with red-hot blood in 'em, with unleashed passions rampant in 'em, blood and bones and viscera in 'em. and women, too, that move and have their being, people that love and hate something better than Vivettes and Perilles and Goops."

Among Les Jeunes, Norris found that he was doing obeisance to a strange and to them a horrible god. Bruce Porter's quickest memory of him remains that first glimpse which he painted into "Spring Floods." The artist found him "a very dear, a very charming, and a very solitary human being."

★   ★   ★

WHEN Norris returned to the *Wave* in October, 1896, after an absence of nearly three months, the nature of his contributions changed to a marked degree. Instead of continuing his fiction—he produced only two negligible stories during that winter—he put his effort into a series of descriptive articles, which, together with a large amount of routine work, seems to have taken all of his time. For the subjects of these, of which the purpose was to rediscover the region for its inhabitants, he sometimes chose an interesting event, custom, or locality in San Francisco and at other times went outside of the city for his material, to Napa County, to Monterey, or even to the San Joaquin valley. While he was acquainting himself with central California, he discovered novel subjects, about which he wrote in a manner that departed far from ordinary journalism. His method was to work his observations into a creative conception, aiming by means of a few strokes to hit the heart of

reality, and energizing his descriptions with the ideas
he had absorbed from Zola—the endowment of
material objects with life and personality, the recognition of underlying social and economic forces in all
he described, the emphasizing of common elements
welding organic and inorganic life into one.

More than ever he realized it was the *way* he saw
things that gave vitality to his writing. His manner of
observation was paradoxically unlike the idea of it
prevalent among those who have noted his detailed
descriptions. It was not his custom to go out as a
reporter or research worker with a notebook in hand,
collecting facts; rather, he always appeared to be
careless in his observation. As Cosgrave puts it:
"Frank never saw things with his eyes. He had no
faculty of physical attention, but after having been
to a place, exposed to its stimuli, he could describe
it—*on paper*—with complete verisimilitude. I used
to say that his pores served him as visual organs."
Furthermore, Norris looked upon accuracy for its
own sake as an unworthy aim, stating emphatically
that his method of description was never photo-
graphic but selective, like that of the artist in painting. "Accuracy is the attainment of small minds,
the achievement of the commonplace, a mere
machine-made thing that comes with niggardly research and ciphering and mensuration and the multiplication table, good in its place, so only the place is
very small. . . . It is not a thing to be striven for. . . .
To be true is the all-important business. . . . Paint
the horse pea-green if it suits your purpose; fill the
mouth of Rebecca with gasconades and rodomontades
interminable: these things do not matter. It is truth

that matters, and the point is whether the daubs of pea-green will look like horseflesh and the mouth-filling words create the impression of actual battle."

A few examples will show how he turned the writing of feature articles to his own purposes. At Santa Cruz he visited a carnival: "The main street seen in perspective was a weaver's loom, the warp white and yellow, the woof all manner of slow-moving colors— a maze, intricate, changeful, very delicate. . . . There was another voice, that of the sea, mysterious, insistent, and there through the night, under the low, red moon, the two voices of the sea and the city talked to each other in that unknown language of their own; and the two voices mingling together filled all the night with an immense and prolonged wave of sound, the bourdon of an unseen organ, the vast and minor note of Life." At Asti he found Italians making claret. "The odor is overpowering, penetrating; it is the reek of the earth's blood squeezed from the harvest, as it is massacred and tortured here in the tremendous hydraulic presses. . . . Outside there, over those miles of low-rolling hills, stretch the vines themselves, sweltering under the sun, teeming with warm liquor, loaded with heavy fat bunches, a vast, rich life, renewed with every season, inexhaustible, sucking up the red life-blood of the earth and pouring it out in rivers of wine." He watched a fifty-ton gun being pulled into place and mounted on Lime Point. "The sulky leviathan that dragged sullenly back on those groaning wire cables that set the eight-horse-power engine hiccoughing and sweating with exertion, that taxed the ingenuity and energy of a little army of toilers—behold, it comes to hand with sudden and marvelous docility; it has been bridled and bitted; it is obedient, gentle, even. . . . Now a woman's wrist may deflect its muzzle, raise and lower it at will, may guide it about subject to her flimsiest caprice." At Stockton he saw the largest harvester in the world, an "enormous engine at its work, rolling through the grain knee-deep, like a feeding mammoth, its teeth clicking and clashing before it, its locomotive rumbling behind." At the prize fight, men stood upon their chairs, "their faces scarlet and their throats distended with the inarticulate cry of the mob that knows no restraint, *autre temps, autre mœurs*, with a vengeance." . . . "Did you ever visit an oyster bed? You should eat an oyster sitting on the stringpiece of the wharf at Belmont camp, prying open the wet shell with your penknife, the wind in your face and the smell of salt in your nostrils."

Energy! Vitality! Life! Big people fascinated him. "He had been working all day in a squalid neighborhood by the gas works and coal yards, surrounded by lifting cranes, pile drivers, dredging machines, engines of colossal, brutal strength, where all around him were immense blocks of granite, tons of pig iron; everything had been enormous, crude, had been huge in weight, tremendous in power, gigantic in size. By long association with such things he had become like them, huge, hard, brutal, strong with a crude, blind strength, stupid, unreasoning. . . . At a street crossing he picked up a white violet, very fresh, not yet trampled into the mud. . . . In some strange way it appealed to him, and blindly he tried to acknowledge his appreciation. He looked at it stupidly, perplexed, not knowing what to do; then instinctively his hand carried it to his mouth; he ground it between his teeth and slowly ate it. It was the only way he knew." Similarly, he admired physical strength in women. Of Maud Odell: "She strikes one as possessed of tremendous vitality, she grips your hand almost like a man." He preferred the Gibson girl, tall enough to look down on most men, to the smaller demure maiden of Wenzel. "The Gibson girl is more serious perhaps, and you must keep keyed pretty high to enjoy her society. But somehow you feel she's a 'man's woman' and could stand by a fellow and back him up if things should happen."

But more persistent than any other idea which he put in these articles was his conviction that San Francisco was the city among cities suited to the story-teller. "Things can happen in San Francisco. Kearney Street, Montgomery Street, Nob Hill, Telegraph Hill, Chinatown, Lone Mountain, the Poodle Dog, the Palace Hotel and the What Cheer House, the Barbary Coast, the Crow's Nest, the Mission, the Bay, the Bohemian Club, the Presidio, Spanish town, Fisherman's Wharf. There is an air about all of these places that is suggestive of stories." A dozen native populations throng with types for characters, among them Chinese and Japanese in outlandish oriental streets and Spaniards and Italians clinging to the sides of Telegraph Hill, in peril of being blown off by a strong wind. On the streets of the city are forty-niners newly aroused by the gold rush to Alaska, and at its wharf lies the *Percy Edwards*, a two-stick trading brig preparing to leave with a handful of men to found a new colony down below the Marquesas. Within the narrow limits of

Chinatown the See Yups and Sam Yups carry on a tong war, "a war between the House of Have and the House of Want" which, in striking down its most notable citizen, Little Pete, carries its influence to the heart of China itself. The iron hulk of a whaleback steamer is being gorged with wheat from the San Joaquin valley to relieve a famine in India. In the hills near by men pursue bandits with bloodhounds, just as they pursued Evans and Sontag a few years before. To the citizens of San Francisco: "Your dinner is laid for you on the table at home, it is a crime to go armed; you are blasé; you are effete even. . . . The same state of affairs can be found today throughout the Coast Range as existed in the wild days before the fifties, the same romantic, melodramatic, absurd, overwrought situations that sound so impossible in the dime novel and the penny awful."

It was a fruitful schooling. In the issues of the *Wave* Frank Norris placed the germ of almost every idea which he was to use later in his fiction.

Chapter 7: Blix

Norris's implication in the autobiographical *Blix* that his early work on the *Wave* was the product of aimless enthusiasms prepares one for the collapse of his spirit in the spring of '97. Throughout the previous winter he had neglected fiction almost entirely, and by February even the special articles which had at first fired him with enthusiasm took on a sameness and lack of vitality which were signs of a failing interest. Finally in March they ceased, and Gelett Burgess, who had killed the *Lark* in mid-flight, took over practically all of Norris's duties on the *Wave*. Norris had arrived at a *cul-de-sac*. A listless indifference alternated with the fits of depression which took him to Bruce Porter's studio late at night to confess that he was "written out." He seemed to be exhausted, physically and spiritually.

In the light of his customary optimism, it appears strange that he should admit failure at this moment; there were professional and personal reasons enough, however, to account for his dejection. Of the former the most obvious was that, after a year of irregular journalism, he was tired of it. Valuable though his assignments had been in developing versatility, in

adding skill to his descriptive powers, in giving him
contacts with all conditions of life, their worth for
him was now exhausted. He had no desire to become
a reporter or editor; he felt that he was dangerously
near to becoming a hack writer and remaining one.
He was a story-teller, not a newspaper man.

There was little to spur him on to a renewed interest in his fiction. As he thumbed over the manuscripts
of his two unfinished novels, he could not bring himself to complete either one; it seemed to him that
the chances of publishing *Vandover and the Brute*
or *McTeague* as he had originally planned them were
very slight, for their naturalistic themes were decidedly at variance with the type of novel in favor
with the American publisher. How often he had been
told, how often he had observed for himself that a
first novel must be safe and decorous and must assure
the reader that this is a very good world! Had he not
seen this very process of emasculating and sentimen-
talizing going on in the selection of short stories by
the editors of the standard magazines? He vented his
feelings and at the same time revealed his discourage-
ment as he attacked these magazines in an editorial:
"Why is it that the best magazines should fail to
publish the best class of stories? Why are not the
names of Kipling and of Arthur Morrison and
Stephen Crane seen in *Harper's* and in the *Century*
and in *Scribner's* as often as these old familiar stand-
bys, the veterans, the 'steadies,' Brander Matthews,
Octave Thanet, Charles Dudley Warner, Thomas
Janvier, Ruth McEnery Stuart and so many other
'magazinists'? . . . These good people—to all ends
and purposes—died long ago. . . . There is in them

no freshness, no originality, no vitality, no close, keen grip on life or nature. . . . The great merit of the stories of these 'magazinists'—the one quality that endears them to the editors—is that they are, what in editorial slang is called 'safe.' They are safe, it is true, safe as a graveyard, decorous as a church, as devoid of immorality as an epitaph. They have not the vigor or decisiveness to offend the most invertebrate taste. They adorn the center table. They do not 'call a blush to the cheek of the young.' They can be placed—Oh, crowning virtue, Oh, supreme encomium!—they can be 'safely' placed in the hands of any young girl the country over. . . . It is the 'young girl' and the family center table that determines the standard of the American short story."

These practical difficulties might have proved less formidable in the face of a firm determination. There is every reason to believe, however, that Norris had not yet completely outgrown his dilettantism. In light of the strong autobiographical strains in his early novels, one cannot go far wrong in drawing conclusions from them as to the personal issues Norris faced at the time they were written. Thus in *Vandover* he presents a youth of artistic, sensitive nature allowing himself to drift, failing to exert the purposeful aim which would create a masterpiece, softening under continual surrenders. Even after granting much to the use of the naturalistic formula and to Norris's habit of exaggerating his impulses for dramatic effect, one is still faced with a residue of ethical judgment which evades the objectivity of the book. And in *Blix*, a novel largely autobiographical dealing with this period of his life, the issues may be read in

the light of a confession. Just as Vandover came to
tragedy through drifting, Condy Rivers is saved
from a life of aimless enthusiasms only by the ripening
of love, which saves him and gives him a definite
aim in life. There are considerable grounds to assume
that in so far as lack of determination and set purpose
is at the root of the troubles of both Vandover and
Condy Rivers, it was a weakness which Norris
recognized as a dangerous element in his own character.

Norris took refuge in being a playboy, and in San
Francisco, just as at Berkeley, he found an abundance
of friends to play with. He made frequent visits to
his fraternity house, seeing much of his old "Fiji"
friends who were living in the bay region; their
annual reunions at the Poodle Dog after the "big
game" were supplemented by dinners held by the
members of the Thirteen Club, a convivial organization of fraternity alumni. Also, he spent much time
with Les Jeunes and other writers and newspaper
men. At the Bohemian Club the younger men would
sit in the "Owl's Nest" (a bay window overlooking
Post Street and Grant Avenue), commenting on the
passing girls, or gather in the back room to play
poker all night. Occasionally two or three went down
"the cocktail route" on Kearney Street or drifted
over to the Barbary Coast to see the sights. There was
a certain Mexican *bodega* in the Latin quarter where
red wine was served in tin pint measures and visitors
could indulge in endless conversation, as in a European café. There was *bocce* to be played on dimly
lighted stretches of packed earth hidden in the in-
terior of ramshackle wooden houses, there were foot-

ball games across the bay to attend, and a race course where an admirer of good horses could see the pick of the country. There was much to do, and good fellowship everywhere; his friends were nearly all men of real ability, but too much of a good time was conducive to drifting, to enjoying life with a modicum of effort.

Norris reveals in *Vandover* and *Blix* that he divided the women of San Francisco into two groups, the virtuous and the fallen. He had plenty of opportunities to observe members of the latter class, for the city was famed for its demi-monde ranging from the "fast girl" of the type of Ida Wade to the harlots of the Barbary Coast. There is little question that he saw something of the primrose path, but his exceptionally strong respect for women, coupled with his sensitivity, kept him from any very corruptive philandering. His handling of sex indicates that his creed was more Puritan than pagan; it at least allowed for a very lively consciousness of sin which frequently militated against his objectivity as a naturalist. The amoral attitude which he tried to attain in his fiction was acquired rather than inherent. In a review of a contemporary novel in which, after declaring that "the ultimate physical relationship between man and woman is a truly dangerous subject," he excuses sexual irregularity on the ground that it is the heritage of the brute. "The idealists will close their eyes to the fact that men *and women* are after all only human. Even the word *human* is misleading. Is it not even truer that so-called humanity still is, and for countless generations will be, three-fourths animal, living and dying, eating and sleeping, mating and reproducing even as the animals?"

Of virtuous women, the majority of Frank's friends were society girls. He had become very attractive, and women, particularly women of the accepted social order, persisted in falling in love with him. He continually fell in love and fell out again, but, except for two or three close friendships with intellectual women, his attachments seem to have been ephemeral. He was bored and annoyed at the behavior of many of his society friends; his ennui took the form of criticism of their manners. He raised a storm of protest by writing for the *Wave* a series of dialogues between Justin Sturgis and Leander, in which he upbraided them. He considered such important questions as: Should girls smoke cigarettes and drink cocktails on the sly? Should women speak to men who come to functions drunk? Should a young man call on a young lady in the evening dressed in a sack suit, call her by her first name, attempt to kiss her in a darkened parlor? One feels through all of this raillery a spirit at odds with a social code which enforces the letter rather than the spirit of the law.

Norris's rather unwilling precipitation into society life was to a large extent due to his mother. Fond of good breeding and the "upper set," given to frequent entertaining of her church and society friends, she attempted to inculcate in him an orthodox respect for all polite amenities. ("The Doctor's Daughters of Reverend Dr. MacKenzie's church will give a musicale at the home of Mrs. B. F. Norris. Music will be supplied by the mandolin club of Berkeley and the Press Club Quartette.") Norris found open rebellion of little use, but he expressed his objections by frequently shocking her in playful scorn of convention. One night, in spite of her entreaties, he insisted that he would wear a red and white striped shirt to a formal function; on another occasion, when he and Charles Norris appeared in full regalia, he announced to the guests, "The management has spared no expense." Mrs. Norris, distressed at his light-hearted attitude, always resorted to the rebuke, "Go on as you are going on now, young man, and nobody knows where you will end up."

His relations with his mother had more serious and hampering aspects. In continually urging him to stay on in San Francisco to live with her, she was depriving him of a very necessary freedom. He was now twenty-seven years old but was not as yet entirely self-supporting. Moreover, he was subject to the strong personality of his mother, whose fundamentally orthodox tastes were hardly conducive to the free expression of a young naturalist despite the fact that she was keenly eager to further his writing career. (That Norris chose *Blix*, the most idealistic of his novels, to dedicate to his mother was probably not a matter of chance.) Thus, valuable as her influence on him had been, close as was the tie of affection between them, it was necessary for her son, in order to realize his greatest powers, to become financially and spiritually independent.

       ★   ★   ★

AT THIS moment Norris fell seriously in love. This radical change had a threefold result: it renewed his interest in writing, it caused him to avoid an excess of good-fellowship and society, and eventually it gave

him the needed independence. *Blix*, written a year
after the events in it took place, contains Norris's
account of his courtship; in spite of the incidental
fictitious material introduced to round it out, its
central theme of how Condy Rivers was strengthened
by his love for Travis Bessemer ("Blix") is, in its
main essentials, the story of his love for Jeannette
Black.[1] As he states in that novel, it brought to him
a steadying force, a maturing purpose, "a hardening
of aimless enthusiasm into energy and determination."

Norris met Jeannette Black at a sub-débutante
dance late in the fall of 1896. He was at once attracted
to the pretty vivacious girl, nine years his junior,
who was nearly as tall as he, had brown hair and eyes,
and radiated health, youth, and good spirits. "She
impressed one as being a very normal girl. You did
not expect to find her introspective. You felt sure
that her mental life was not at all the result of
thoughts and reflections germinating from within,
but rather of impressions and sensations that came
to her from without. . . . She was just a good, sweet,
natural, healthy-minded, healthy-bodied girl, honest,
strong, self-reliant, and good-tempered." She lived
with her father and mother at the corner of Octavia
and Geary streets. Her father, Robert Black, born
in northern Ireland, had come to California in '49,

[1]Several of Norris's friends have stated to me that *Blix* is not
entirely an account of Norris's courtship of Jeannette Black.
Thus, he did not use "Blix" as a nickname for Miss Black,
but may have used it at an earlier date. However, the major
incidents of the novel, when not purely fictitious, apply to this
period of his life.

had made and lost a fortune in the Virginia City mines, but had put aside enough to enable him to marry Carolina Virginia Williamson, an orphan from the South, and to retire to the life of a semi-invalid in San Francisco. They had three children, a son, Jeannette, and a younger sister, whom Norris amused with unusual games.

Throughout the following winter and spring Jeannette Black and Frank Norris carried on a mild flirtation. It did not occur to him that he could fall seriously in love with a seventeen-year-old girl who had not as yet "come out" in society, and their relations were largely confined to "sub-deb" parties and an occasional call or theater party. One day in April Jeannette made two notable decisions: She decided not to "come out," and she decided that she and Norris were no longer to flirt. She shared with Norris a dislike of the insincerity and conventionality of society life, and she pointed out to him that their own relationship, the product of its standards, was not sufficiently frank.

"'Do you love me?'

"'No, I don't!' he exclaimed blankly, as though he had just discovered that fact.

"'There!' she declared—'and I don't love you.' They both began to laugh."

From that time, the attitude of comradeship they assumed allowed them a freedom which their friends and particularly Norris's mother felt was decidedly unconventional; they asserted their independence, confident that they were right in "hating shams and affectations, happy in the things that were simple and natural and honest." As pictured in *Blix*, their life that summer was idyllic in its spontaneity. They roamed the streets of San Francisco, haunting the spots which (to a pair of young romancers) were most attractive. They climbed aboard the whaleback *City of Everett*, where the first mate told them a story of how as a diver he fell in love with a drowned girl entombed in the cabin of a sunken ship. They ate tea and crackers, watermelon rind, and "China nuts" in a Chinese restaurant three stories above the Stevenson memorial in Portsmouth Square. When, as Norris crooned a Carolina coon song to the accompaniment of his banjo, Miss Black threatened to join in, he "laid the instrument across his knees with exaggerated solicitude, and said deliberately:

"'You are a good, sweet girl, and what you lack in beauty you make up in amiability, and I've no doubt you are kind to your aged father; but you—can—not—sing.'"

Then Norris read Kipling to her until she shared his enthusiasm for "his most venerated author."

They contrived a plot to write to two people advertising for mates in the personal columns of a newspaper, and so arranged it that they should meet each other at Luna's Restaurant. The scheme succeeded, and, although they never saw the couple again, Norris arranged their marriage in *Blix* and introduced the red-haired man for further excitement. They frequently ate supper at Miss Black's house, where Norris sat on the drainboard of the sink, talking about his stories. They played poker for fun, pretending that it was necessary to wean Norris from a soul-gripping vice. They went fishing on Lake Andreas, Miss Black wearing her dog-collar belt, Norris carry-

ing a lunch of "devilish ham sandwiches," a mouth
organ, and a copy of *Plain Tales from the Hills*. Of
all their excursions and adventures, however, the
one that pleased them the most was an all-day walk
which started at Fort Mason, led through the Presidio to the old red-brick fort which overlooked the
Golden Gate, and followed along a deserted stretch
of seacoast "where the bowlders lay tumbled and the
surf grumbled incessantly" to a semicircle of black-
berry bushes halfway up a hill. After eating their
lunch, they would sit for hours upon an old log, "both
of them young and strong and vigorous, the Pacific
under their eyes, the great clean Trades blowing in
their faces, the smell of the salt sea coming in long
aromatic whiffs to their nostrils. Young and strong
and fresh, their imaginations thronged with pictures
of vigorous action and adventure, buccaneering,
filibustering, and all the swing, the leap, the rush and
the gallop, the exuberant strong life of the great,
uncharted world of Romance."

Somewhat carried away by his playfulness when
writing *Blix*, Norris amused himself by caricaturing
his own foibles in the creation of Condy Rivers,
whose childishness, irresponsibility, and absent-
mindedness caused one reviewer to state that "he
has the manners and apparent mental development
of a schoolboy of sixteen, irrelevant, uncertain, and
shallow—positively silly at times." In spite of this,
Condy Rivers was in most ways truly Frank Norris,
and his enthusiasm in finding a companionship which
brought him relief from the flirtations of the social
world is a faithful presentation of Norris's discovery
after his compact with Jeannette Black. The good

spirits which attended their unconventional behavior
suited him more than the doubtful pleasures of leading "germans," acting in society plays, and commenting on girls from the windows of the Bohemian
Club. The vividness with which he portrays the
delights of roaming through the city, fishing and
hiking, eating picnic lunches, and watching the sunset
from Washington Hill shows how truly welcome the
change was to his ingenuous nature. When, in August,
Miss Black announced that she would leave in a few
weeks for Monticello Seminary in St. Louis, he
realized that he felt for his brown-haired, dark-eyed
companion a love more permanent than his previous
infatuations. The crisis came when Miss Black
crossed the bay for a week's visit in Mill Valley; after
four days' absence, Norris followed her to have a very
serious talk. That night after his return, he found his
closest friend, Bert Houston, at a restaurant and
made him walk the ten miles to the Cliff House with
him. His enthusiasm was overpowering, he loved
Jeannette Black and she loved him, he was going
to throw all his energy into writing, gain recognition,
and marry. As they looked out on the moonlit
Pacific, Norris's thoughts echoed Browning: "Life
is better than literature. To live is better than to
read; one live human being is better than a thousand
Shakespeares; an act is better than a thought."

*   *   *

DURING the summer in which the events described in
Blix took place Norris's writing for the *Wave* entered
a third and final period marked by continuous pro-
ductivity. After printing an editorial on May 22, 1897,

appealing to younger writers to turn to San Francisco for subjects for short stories, he illustrated his thesis by writing nearly one story a week for the following seven months. It was from this series of tales that Will Irwin made the collection bearing the title of its leading story, *The Third Circle*, which was to be published by John Lane in 1909. They were short short-stories in which his method was to strike off an incident, decisive and brief, suggesting everything that precedes and everything that follows, a method which put a premium on ingenuity. Many of them were negligible, but a few represented him at his best in a kind of writing to which he was not eminently fitted. He almost invariably used San Francisco as their setting, drawing largely upon his own experience and in some cases on incidents from his novels. In *The End of the Act* and *At Home from Eight to Twelve* he printed two sections from the manuscript of *Vandover*, while *The End of the Beginning* later became the first chapter of *A Man's Woman*. Two of the stories, *Judy's Service of Plate* and *Fantaisie Printannière*, dealt with the characters and milieu of *McTeague;* and *Little Dramas of the Curbstone* and *Reversion to Type* were of the same school, illustrating the favorite theme of naturalism—"implacable fate working itself into tragic climax, and degeneration of the larger sort." Several times he apparently attempted to adapt Maupassant's studies of abnormal psychological types to his portrayal of degeneration, notably in *A Case for Lombroso* and *His Single Blessedness*. Admiration of Maupassant may also have led him to his use of mystery and horror in such stories as *The Strangest Thing, The*

House with the Blinds, and *The Third Circle*, which
helped to convince the readers of the *Wave* that he
intended to make a specialty of the terrible. It may
have been in response to an appeal "to cultivate a
broader field with some space in it for the pleasant
side of life" that he resorted to coltish humor in *This
Animal of a Buldy Jones*, to overstrained satire in
Boom, and to the idyll in *Le Miracle Joyeaux*, in
which he pictured a Jesus without a beard smiling
to please a disappointed urchin. It was undoubtedly
to the composition of his short stories for the *Wave*
that he refers in *Blix:* "Condy had developed a taste
and talent in the matter of writing. Short stories
were his mania. He had begun by an inoculation of
the Kipling virus, had suffered an almost fatal attack
of Harding Davis, and had even been affected by
Maupassant. He went in for accuracy of detail;
held that if one wrote a story involving firemen one
should have, or seem to have, every detail of the
department at his fingers' ends, and should 'bring
in' to the tale all manner of technical names and
cant phrases." As a whole, the stories are best classi-
fied as suggestions for plots, notebook memoranda,
rather than finished tales; their most notable qualities
lie in quick portrayal of atmosphere and setting,
in an occasional impressive situation, and in their
value as exercises for writing longer fiction.

Norris was not satisfied, however, with writing a
short story or sketch for each issue of the *Wave*. He
had a much more important project in mind, a project which had needed only the stimulus of his awakened ambition to be realized. Shortly after Jeannette
Black departed in October to attend school in St.

Louis, he applied to his editor for permission to devote several weeks to the completion of *McTeague*. Because this would necessitate his leaving San Francisco, as he wished to go to the Sierras where he could work in quiet, he apparently arranged that his weekly contributions should continue to appear, writing some in advance and planning to mail the others in from Iowa Hill. Some time in October he arrived at the Big Dipper Mine, determined to finish his novel.

It is chiefly to Seymour Waterhouse, superintendent of the Big Dipper Mine, that we owe the details of Norris's activities while he was in the Sierras. He spent by no means all of his time in writing, but, clad for mountaineering in high boots, riding trousers, rough-neck sweater, and sombrero, he rode and hiked about the gold diggings, observing the methods of hydraulic mining, examining the stamp mills, and trying his hand at washing gravel for gold. He made the acquaintance of the people of the region, planning to use them in stories[1]; there were Charlie Murray, ("Bunt McBride"), loquacious teamster, cowboy, and miner, "who knew his West as the cockney knows his Piccadilly"; "Shorty Stack," bedrock cleaner and amateur pugilist; "Chino Zavalla," Mexican shift boss, who occasionally carried the gold brick over to Iowa Hill; "Félice," his black-haired, green-eyed wife, whom he imagined in intrigue with a college-bred man, ignorant of the laws of a mining camp; and a score of others, blacksmiths, itinerant

[1]Norris used Big Dipper material in six short stories, *Reversion to Type*, *Shorty Stack—Pugilist*, *Dying Fires*, *The Wife of Chino*, *A Bargain with Peg-Leg*, and *The Passing of Cock-eye Blacklock*.

peddlers, cow-punchers, stage-drivers, prospectors, miners. . . . He entered into the life of the camp, accompanying Waterhouse on minor explorations and assisting him as rodman when he surveyed. They both carried guns, as Waterhouse had been twice shot at by workers at a neighboring mine with whom he had a dispute. One shot had imbedded itself in his saddle while the other had pierced his hat. The isolation of the camp was complete; it seemed to have its own government, laws, and customs, and to the city-bred novelist it represented Western life at its rawest.

The outdoor life put Norris in the best of health for his writing. At Harvard he had been in a quandary as to what to do with his burly dentist after the murder of Trina. The influence of the environment in which he now worked may have been partly responsible for the use of an ending more romantic than the rest of the book. He would take McTeague back to the Big Dipper Mine, where he had spent his childhood and had learned his profession from a traveling dentist, would have him move on to Inyo County, intuitively conscious of his pursuers, on down to the Panamint Range, where he would take to quartz-mining, and then out into Death Valley to meet Marcus Schouler in a final dramatic struggle. He had his material at hand in his knowledge of mining in Placer County, and Murray, who knew Inyo County and Death Valley well, would supply him with the final scenes. In writing a vivid description of the mining camp he carried his verisimilitude so far as to include himself and Waterhouse in the group which McTeague faced as he entered the office. "The dentist approached the counter and leaned his elbows upon it. Three men were in the room—a tall, lean young man, with a thick head of hair surprisingly gray, who was playing with a half-grown Dane puppy; another fellow about as young, but with a jaw almost as salient as McTeague's, stood at the letter-press taking a copy of a letter."

As far as can be ascertained, *McTeague* was finished at this time, for when Norris left the mountains, he was prepared to send the manuscript in search of a publisher. It was not to appear, however, until the spring of 1899; in the meantime he was to write and publish *Moran*.

★   ★   ★

EVER since his college days Norris had hoped to reach the book-reading public by means of a collection of his best short stories. After receiving some encouragement from William Doxey, the progressive local publisher who had printed the *Lark*, he had applied himself to the project, editing his manuscripts, drawing illustrations for which Charles Norris and Albert Houston served as models, and considering in turn the titles, *Beer and Skittles*, *On and Off the Asphalt*, and *Ways that are Dark*. For some reason, the arrangement with Doxey failed to materialize, and it is likely that he sent the collection to an Eastern publishing house with no better results. In *Blix* a New York firm rejected a group of Condy Rivers stories, suggesting that since "the best-selling book just now is the short novel . . . of action and adventure" he try his hand at writing one; it is probable that a similar suggestion returned with Norris's manuscript.

Norris's short novel of action and adventure was

Moran of the Lady Letty. Moran wrote itself. It was
partly the child of Stevenson, whose *The Wrecker*
(a novel which, judging from Norris's many references
to it, he had almost memorized) had long made him
wish to write a sea yarn centering around the San
Francisco waterfront. It doubtless carried the parental
strain of Kipling, whose *Captains Courageous*, published the year before, pictured the regeneration of a
millionaire's son during his forced cruise on a fishing
schooner operating off the Grand Banks. But the
factor which was most responsible for *Moran* was
Norris's discovery of Captain Joseph Hodgson.

Hodgson, the Captain Jack of *Blix*, was the sort of
man to delight the heart of a story writer. To discover
him was to discover a mine filled with deposits which
only needed refining to yield a fortune. Born in Blyth,
England, of seafaring stock, he had at seventeen
joined a vessel bound for whaling in the Behring
Straits and had led an erratic life ever since. Whatever may have been the truth about those incidents
of his life in which he pictured himself as an ad-
venturer, operating outside of the law, smuggling
rifles to Mexican revolutionists, selling champagne
made of rock candy, effervescent salts, and Riesling
wine to the Koreans, or robbing Russian posts of
sea-otter skins, there is no question of his having been
one of the crew of the *Rodgers*, the relief ship which in
search for the members of the ill-fated *Jeannette* was
burned off the coast of northeastern Siberia, a catastrophe which forced the men to spend a winter among
the primitive Chuckchi. That his previous experience
in the Arctic made him a valuable man here is noted
by the chronicler of the expedition, who refers to him

as "Hodgson, the Pay Yeoman, who went up the ice-pack in a three-hole canoe and killed ten walruses." There was nothing which he liked better than to tell of his experiences, which, with rare ingenuity and dramatic force, he would spin into yarns studded with phrases and dialogue in nautical lingo. Norris and Miss Black had spent many afternoons at the Fort Point Coast Guard station where Hodgson was in charge, Miss Black sitting upon a hassock with Norris standing at her elbow, the two wrapped up in Hodgson's narratives as the latter paced the room in his stocking feet, puffing at a cigar and gesticulating violently. As Hodgson told of how he killed whales off the California coast and fished for sharks in Magdalena Bay in disreputable vessels manned by Chinese pirates and sailors "shanghaied" from the San Francisco waterfront, the plot of *Moran* grew in Norris's mind. In Hodgson's words, they "wrote the book together," and Norris expressed his gratitude by dedicating the completed novel to his "buccaneer" as he pleased to call him.

Moran was written feuilleton fashion, appearing weekly in the *Wave* from January 8 to April 9, 1898. Norris "shut his eyes to the end of his novel—that far-off divine event—and took his task chapter by chapter, even paragraph by paragraph." He did not, however, sweat much blood over the book. In the midst of its composition he wrote to a friend who was reading the instalments: "I've read what you told me about *Moran* and I like to have you say it's a corking good story. I've had more fun writing the yarn than anything I've got hold of yet. . . . You're quite right about Wilbur, he is a mere nit until after we get into a fight with the beach-combers for the ambergris. That makes a man of him. My game was to [have] 'em all nits and bring Moran out in full value. You see the thing is hardly more than a sketch. I'm glad you find it convincing and consistent. Moran is the only excuse for the yarn. Wilbur is just the protagonist (Mr. W. D. Howells he gimme that word). About finding Greenwich by the altitude of a star, a sea captain told me that point and said it was a feat amongst navigators so I guess it must be O. K. . . . You know Moran and Wilbur have a most God-awful fight in the next chap [ter]. In the fight with the beach-combers, she gets to fighting 'Bersark,' crazy in the head y'know, and turns on Wilbur. He fights back like a good fellow and does her up. That breaks her spirit—you see and *then* she begins to love him—savvy."[1]

Thus far the pursuit of bigness and crude strength had taken Norris—to conceive of a story built around a physical encounter between a society youth and a barbaric Norse maiden, wherein the girl learns to love by being conquered and the boy is regenerated by contact with the primitive. It pleased him to present a modern Siegfried-Brünnhilde struggle in which his Valkyrie is a nineteenth-century girl imbued with the old Viking spirit—a heroine whom he liked to compare in stature and physical prowess with Bradamante, Boadicea, and Berenice. Moran was in reality a child of his interest in saga literature, the effect of which runs like a hempen rope through his writings from the poem about the Austrasian Brunhilda, com-

[1]Letter to Harry M. Wright postmarked New York City, March 13, 1898.

posed during his first college year, to the Grettir-saga stories printed just before his death. He adapted her to the environment of his adventure story, allowing her, like the huge Swedish Goodedal, mate of the *Flying Scud* in Stevenson's *The Wrecker*, to go "Bersark," fighting with the savagery of an Amazon, breaking into pieces the fragile heroine of the fastidious American novel of the nineties.

Norris, with youthful temerity, essayed the difficult task of writing a sea story with the experience of a landlubber. He was not as successful as Kipling in *Captains Courageous*, nor could he stand comparison with Conrad, whose *The Nigger of the Narcissus* had just appeared. Norris's skill more nearly matched that of Jack London, for whom he was breaking the way. Despite occasional errors in detail for which he was much twitted by his friends, *Moran* emerged with a salty flavor. In writing it, he relied entirely on his assimilation of Captain Hodgson's nautical advice; he would have Greenwich computed by the altitude of a star, speak of the garboard streak glancing in the sun, even allow Moran to manipulate a quadrant lying flat on her back on the deck. Why quibble about details? Even if his women friends insisted that their hair could not be knotted, no matter how long or heavy, it delighted him to have Moran so treat her "great ropes of sandy hair which fell over her breast almost to the top of her knee-boots." After all, what does the hothouse plant accustomed to the society of the drawing room know about the behavior of a Valkyrie? Norris showed his hand when he wrote to Isaac Marcosson: "When I wrote 'Moran' I was, as one might say, flying kites, trying to see how far I could go without breaking the string."[1]

* * *

NORRIS's next step on the road to success, his removal to New York City at the call of a publishing firm, came as the realization of a long-cherished ambition, an ambition shared by most of his fellow literary aspirants in San Francisco. To Frank Norris as to Condy Rivers it appeared as the climax to the drama of "arrival," the logical conclusion in a rise to a place of significance. "Of all the ambitions of the Great Unpublished, the one that is strongest, the most abiding, is the ambition to get to New York. For these, New York is the *point de départ*, the pedestal, the niche, the indispensable vantage ground; as one of the unpublished put it: 'It is a place that I can stand on and holler.'" As one reads through the files of the *Wave*, one realizes how customary the succession of events had become; a writer or artist embarked on his career in San Francisco, received some degree of acclaim, and then was drawn to New York as a bar of iron is drawn to a magnet. One sees the notices of departure of each in turn: "Chimmie Fadden" Townsend, Ernest Peixotto, Gelett Burgess, Juliet Wilbur Tompkins, Bruce Porter, Geraldine Bonner, and now Frank Norris. To those who remained behind, hoping to join the exodus, the final proof of its effectiveness came in the form of news items telling of the success of those who had "arrived."

[1]Letter to Isaac Marcosson written about December 1, 1898. *Adventures in Interviewing* by Isaac Marcosson, John Lane, 1919, p. 233.

This Eastward movement, which continually drained San Francisco of its best literary talent, was not new, but it had a particular significance during the last decade of the nineteenth century. The most important factor drawing literary men to New York was the presence there of most of the houses publishing magazines and books, and among these houses a radical movement was taking place. The decade saw the rise of yellow journalism, the innovation of the Sunday edition, the rapid growth of advertising, the improvement of processes for elaborate illustration, and the popularizing of cheap magazines with wide circulations. These new methods, which were cutting the ground from beneath the conservative magazines and newspapers, were put into effect by young men, a considerable number of whom were drawn from regions west of the Alleghanies. As it became the practice for enterprising editors to look to the West for "discoveries," a promising writer contributing to such a journal as the *Wave* would almost inevitably come to their notice. Exactly that happened to Norris. As Jeannette Gilder expressed it in *Putnam's Magazine:* "That wise man of the East, S. S. McClure, always had his eye on the West. He read the *Wave*, as he read almost everything else that was published, and he read *Moran of the Lady Letty*. He immediately sat down and wrote to the author, told him to come to New York and he would publish his book, and that he wanted him to write for *McClure's Magazine;* that, in short, he wanted to be his literary godfather, which in reality he became."

S. S. McClure was one of the most enterprising and possibly the most erratic of the group of men who were revolutionizing the publishing business, a group which included Edward Bok, Horace Lorimer, Frank Munsey, Irving Bacheller, William Randolph Hearst, and Joseph Pulitzer. After his arrival as a peasant emigrant from Ireland in 1866, he had sensed the potentialities of his adventuresome imagination, and, after working his way through college and learning the rudiments of publishing and editing on the staffs of the *Wheelman* and the *Century Magazine*, he had set out with no capital except ideas and the habit of good luck. The two most noteworthy results were the starting of the first newspaper syndicate in 1884 and the inauguration of *McClure's Magazine* in 1893. The magazine, which sold for the unprecedented price of fifteen cents, threatened the supremacy of the older monthlies as it became more and more successful. Mr. McClure has said that his sole qualifications for being an editor were that he was "open-minded, naturally enthusiastic, and not afraid to experiment with a new man." Among his "experiments" were Robert Louis Stevenson, Rudyard Kipling, Conan Doyle, Booth Tarkington, Anthony Hope, and Joseph Conrad. A considerable share of the credit for the success of the venture was due to his friend and associate, John S. Phillips, who served as a balance wheel to check the excesses of his gifted but frequently impractical chief. According to Charles Norris, it was Phillips who first brought Frank Norris to McClure's attention, and later sent for him to come to New York and took charge of him on his arrival.

It was, however, before Norris had received final notice from *McClure's* of his good fortune, that he left San Francisco early in February, ostensibly to collect material for a *Wave* article on the Mardi Gras in New Orleans. One suspects that a more imperious reason for the trip was to see Jeannette Black, for he broke his journey at St. Louis, where he found a wire from Phillips awaiting him at the Planter's Hotel. As it contained an offer for him to join McClure's staff at once, he did not return home, but, after arranging with the *Wave* to complete the instalments of *Moran* by mail, he went on directly to New York.

Norris entered upon his duties realizing that, although he would be pressed for money, he would have independence and considerable freedom. In addition to future royalties from *Moran*, which was to be syndicated and then published in book form, he received a salary of twelve and a half dollars a week in return for his mornings spent at routine. The rest of his day was to be free for writing novels. The routine work was of a varied and apparently irregular nature; soon after his arrival he stated: "You have no idea of the difficulty of keeping up even with the hammer-and-tongs work of a New York publishing house such as the McClure magazine and syndicate. I am writing for *both* and, being naturally anxious to make a formidable impression at the outset, have asked for all assignments and details they can give me. . . . I have started up another Leander-Justin Sturgis dialogue on 'The Little Miseries of Life.' This is for the syndicate, however, and does not appear in the magazine."[1] (The results of his activity have not been traced; no signed contributions appeared

[1] Letter to Mrs. Davenport dated March 12, (1898).

in the magazine, and any syndicated material lies buried in the files of the daily press, uncatalogued, for the McClure records have not been preserved.)

Norris, determined to make his own way, limited his expenses to fit his meager salary. He wrote to Jeannette Black that he was ensconced in a small back bedroom at 10 West Thirty-third Street, was eating his meals out at a restaurant near by, and had just enough money left, after paying for his board, room, and carfare, to buy seven stamps a week. As lack of money and the absence of congenial friends furthered his ambition to work hard, he applied himself during his afternoons and evenings to the continuation of the episodes of *Moran* and the composition of *Blix*, which he may have started before leaving the West. His social life was confined to an occasional dinner with friends from San Francisco, chief of whom were Edward Selfridge and Frederic Juilliard, two of his ubiquitous fraternity brothers, who insisted that he allow them to "set him up to a square meal." He enjoyed the rôle of poverty-stricken author and willingly denied himself most of his accustomed luxuries, confident that he was about to arrive.

Of the incident which served to make his success complete, he wrote thus casually to a friend: "By the way, Mr. Burgess took me to call on the Howells last Monday evening. We had a most charming visit. I find him one of the most delightful men imaginable and, as you told me, especially fond of good talk."[1] Three weeks after his arrival in New York, Norris had called on the dean of American letters, who, after

[1] Letter to Mrs. Davenport dated March 12 (1898).

receiving him kindly, offered to read the manuscript of *McTeague*. One can hardly refrain from quoting Gelett Burgess's account of their visit, an aspect of which illustrated to him Norris's "ironic humor, a kind of Mephistophelean touch tempered with kindness." "Frank called for me that evening at my apartment on Washington Square and found me dressing—we were to call in evening dress. He watched me dress with that ironic, devilish smile of his on his lips all the while. It was not until we had been in Mr. Howells' drawing room for almost an hour that I discovered to my horror that instead of having put on my tail coat, I had by inadvertence put on my cutaway coat with my evening vest and trousers. Frank had known it all the time, and had said nothing to me, letting me make a fool of myself, and enjoying my embarrassment and mortification to the full." If, as one suspects, Trevor in *A Lost Story* is Norris's portrait of their host, it is not likely that the error in dress made any difference to him. "He was a short, rotund man, rubicund as to face, bourgeois as to clothes and surroundings, jovial in manner, indulging even in slang. One might easily set him down as a retired groceryman—wholesale, perhaps, but none the less a groceryman. Yet touch him upon the subject of his profession, and the *bonhomie* lapsed away from him at once. . . . Then he became serious. . . . This elderly man of letters, who had seen the rise and fall of a dozen schools, was above the influence of fads, and he whose books were among the classics even before his death was infallible in his judgments of the work of the younger writers. All the stages of their evolution were known to him—all their mistakes, all their successes. He understood; and a story by one of them, a poem, a novel, that bore the stamp of his approval, was 'sterling.'" When Norris returned a few evenings later, Howells received him in his jacket and lounging slippers, and the two sat for a long time before the fireplace discussing *McTeague*. Howells had been much impressed by the novel and encouraged Norris to make further efforts to have it published.

Is it strange that Norris looked upon life as an adventure? Just a year before, he had been mourning that he was "written out"; then he had fallen in love, successfully courted the girl, finished *McTeague*, written *The Third Circle* and *Moran of the Lady Letty*, achieved recognition in the East, obtained a position with a New York publishing firm, and received the approval of *McTeague* from the leading critic in America. That the succession of events seemed to him like the plot of a novel, he testified in writing *Blix*. His letters sum up his enthusiasm. "New York is *all right*. I've got a nifty little room in a mighty nifty little place just opposite the Waldorf Hotel—hot potatoes—and Eddie Selfridge and I absorb nourishment together at a fairish joint on Madison Avenue. I think I am going to 'get on' now. My stuff seems to take pretty damn well, much better than I expected and lots of people—big people in a way—have patted me on the head and chucked me under the chin. . . . I've passed an evening with Howells as I told you, and have met Chimmie Fadden Townsend. Burgess is here coining money, and Ernest Peixotto is already almost famous. Juliet Wilbur Tompkins draws down $135.00 a

172   Frank Norris: A Biography

month from *Munsey's*, and I hope to be right up
with the procession by next summer. . . . Not much
news here, plenty big grind, no catchum much time
to have-um fun. By the way if you love me you will
write me a criticism of Moran each week.

"Your flen'
"Norris."[1]

[1]Letter to Harry Wright postmarked March 13, 1898.

Chapter 8: Cuban Adventure

On the fifteenth of February, 1898, the *Maine* was blown up in Havana Harbor. In a letter written three weeks later, Norris revealed his reaction to the resulting excitement: "How do you like Moran? I am in two minds about her and do not know whether she should be killed or go to Cuba with Wilbur. I myself have a half promise in the matter of war correspondent for the syndicate in case of 'unpleasantness.'"[1] His better judgment decided the fictional issue by having Moran killed just as Wilbur was preparing to sail with her around the Horn to join the filibusters off the Florida coast. The personal issue was decided by a recurrence of "the attack of Harding Davis," which precipitated him into the midst of the "unpleasantness" which followed, giving him a vivid first-hand contact with the more violent aspects of naturalism.

The story of the development of that "unpleasantness" provides a pertinent study for the determinist, just as it calls forth a smile from the cynic and an apology from the defender of human nature. The well-oiled machinery of propaganda steadily gathered momentum throughout the early spring of '98; with

[1]Letter to Mrs. Davenport dated March 12, 1898.

inexorable force it set going the dynamo of nationalism, galvanizing Norris as he went about his routine work and writing of novels. Rumors of war pursued him. The yellow press worked the public up to the sticking point, Hearst revealed that the Spanish ambassador wrote of McKinley as a "caterer to the rabble and . . . a cheap politician," investigating committees reported that the *Maine* had been dynamited by external hands, and an ultimatum was sent to Spain. On April 23rd the guns of the *Nashville* cracked across the bows of the Spanish merchantman, *Buenaventura*, and war had begun. By May the first, when Dewey destroyed a Spanish fleet in Manila bay, Norris had become a cog in the machine, welcoming the advance of the skirmish line across the Pacific "still pushing the frontier before it," confident that the Anglo-Saxon was now "to fulfil his destiny and complete the cycle of the world."

Norris shortly after the declaration of war went out to Hempstead, Long Island, where his friend Edward Selfridge, first lieutenant in the volunteer 71st New York Infantry, was preparing to leave for Tampa with his regiment. To say good-by to Ned was not his only mission. "I expect to see some fighting as a correspondent. McClure's are building up a big staff of writers for the war and they are going to send me. I'll see you in Havana." In spite of the promising work which Norris had before him in New York, with *Moran* ready to appear in book form, with *McTeague* waiting for a publisher, with *Vandover* lying fallow, with a volume of short stories in the air, the war-correspondent virus and the thirst for adventure were having their way with him. Any hesitation he may have had was swept aside as the rush to report the Spanish-American War became almost a panic. While the army gathered at Tampa, writers seduced from their regular work came down in hordes. Although it is estimated that between 450 and 500 received their passes and sat through the days of May and June on the hotel porches in Key West and Tampa, there were many other applicants turned away. Among the favored were, novelists, Richard Harding Davis, Stephen Crane, Julian Hawthorne, John Fox, Jr.; illustrators, Frederic Remington, R. F. Zogbaum, G. R. Peters, Howard Chandler Christy; veteran correspondents, Stephen Bonsal, James Creelman, Caspar Whitney, Sylvester Scovel, Edward Marshall, *ad infinitum*—even William Randolph Hearst arrived in his steam yacht in time to pull Creelman out of the blockhouse at El Caney. The majority, who were new to the game, made up a nondescript lot; there was a "special" for an agricultural paper, correspondents for religious journals were common, the "Kinetoscope man" was there; hardly a half-score of the entire lot knew a space wheel from a cavalry brigade, and yet they were, in many cases, the best writers from their respective journals. McClure, who covered the war so completely that he doubled the circulation of his magazine, announced that he had "representatives, contributors, artists, and photographers with every branch of the army and navy and at every scene of probable action." Norris was one of the "contributors."

Some few days after the bombardment of Matanzas, Norris arrived in Key West ready for action. His

state of mind as well as his disappointment at what
he found was registered in a manuscript which he
never published. "For him who smelleth the battle
not very far off, Key West in war time is a great disappointment. . . . You ask more for your money than
you actually get. You want to see excitement, turmoil, activity, the marching and countermarching
of troops, the excited going and coming of couriers
a-horseback, the glint of epaulets and brass at street
corners. . . . You want to see the correspondent in all
his glory, leaping from a dispatch boat before she is
even made fast to the docks, dashing ashore in all the
panoply of pith helmet, Norfolk jacket, and field
glasses, a bundle of dispatches in one hand, racing his
fellows to the telegraph office, 'getting in his stuff,'
beating his rivals, making a scoop. . . . Instead you
can easily imagine yourself in a seaport summer
resort at a time when a visiting cruiser or monitor
is lying off the hotel. . . . I shall carry away from the
Key West Hotel only a picture of a row of men in
white ducks and yachting caps sitting on the ver-
andah. . . . They are doing nothing, these war correspondents, waiting merely; waiting for something to
turn up. I have seen a group of officers and correspondents in a devoted circle around one of the three
or four smartly dressed women—officers' wives who
are at the hotel—as if famine and fighting were not
within six hours' easy steaming, as if the *Maine* still
rode the ocean under the eye of heaven, and as if the
Spanish-American War of 1898 had never been
declared."[1]

[1]Manuscript in the hands of Charles G. Norris. Quoted at
length to the end of this section.

It was the rocking-chair period of the war. The American fleet was blockading Havana in the vain hope that it could be starved into surrender, while Cervera's Spanish fleet was "lost" somewhere in mid-Atlantic, causing anxious citizens to fear that the Eastern seaboard would be bombarded at any moment. The army of regulars and volunteers which was slowly gathering at Tampa was impatient at restraint but unprepared to go into action. During the two months between the declaration of war and the end of June, nothing resembling a real fight took place in or near Cuba. Norris could do no more than wait at Key West "where Sampson's fleet pivoted on the mangy little city filled with journalists, harlots, and mosquitoes," or make trips to Tampa where another white-clad army of staff officers and correspondents sat on the porch of a baroque hotel.

Only one incident broke the monotony of waiting. At half-past four of a May morning Norris, awakened by a pounding on his door, heard the voice of a fellow correspondent:

"We're going right out! It's the *Three Friends*. You'll find her at the dock by the Consul's office. You've got twenty minutes."

Pleased at the opportunity to visit the blockading fleet, in fifteen minutes Norris was dressed and on board, and by five o'clock the *Three Friends* had cleared her docks and was drifting out over the torpedo beds and submarine mines of the port of Key West. At breakfast he met his two companions: one, a seasoned newspaper man who had been present at the bombardment of Matanzas; and the other, a young man whose slight build and drooping mustache

made him look like Robert Louis Stevenson. Though
Norris referred to him only as "a young, a very young
personage, celebrated the world round by reason of
his novel of battle and sudden death," he was undoubtedly Stephen Crane, who was already famous
through the publication of *The Red Badge of Courage*
three years before, and whose *Maggie*, still-born in
the year that Norris began *McTeague*, was the American novel most nearly paralleling his own excursions
into naturalism. Possibly it was Crane's iconoclastic
attitude towards the war (he symbolized it by refer-
ring to the "bunch of bananas" which hung in the
cabin of the *Three Friends*), or perhaps it was his
lackadaisical manner, which as Thomas Beer testifies made him "wonderfully disliked" by some of
the Cuban correspondents, that caused Norris to
write of him with a coolness not untouched with envy.
At any rate, as Norris was reticent about "talking
shop" with a stranger, their conversation included
no discussion of naturalism in American letters but
was confined to the subject of war-reporting, at
which Crane appeared a veteran, for he "had been
in peril of his life on a filibustering expedition, was
tanned to the color of a well-worn saddle, and had on
the bridge of his nose the little calloused spot that
comes from the long use of field glasses."

During the two days' cruise Norris strove in vain
to find spectacular news for an article; as they
steamed along the Cuban coast, the only thing that
relieved the monotony of the rolling foothills covered
with grass and clumps of palms was an occasional
glimpse of smoke rising from plantations being

burned by the insurgents; the blockaders, who invariably haled them to ask for news rather than to
furnish it, created excitement but once, when the
Dolphin fired a warning across their bows; and the
only information of hostilities which they were able
to pick up was that the Havana forts had fired at
the *Vicksburg* and that the Cardeñas batteries had
exchanged a few shots with the *Dupont*. As the
stubby-nosed tugboat floundered her way back to
Key West, Norris chaffed at writing his report while
with speculative eyes he watched Crane build up his
"story" out of the meager material. "It will be
long before I forget the picture which the Young
Personage made while at work upon his 'stuff.'
Table there was none, and the plunging of the boat
made it out of the question to write while sitting
in a chair. The correspondents took themselves off
to the cabin and wrote while sitting in their bunks.
The Young Personage was wearing a pair of duck
trousers grimed and fouled with all manner of pitch
and grease and oil. His shirt was guiltless of collar
or scarf and was unbuttoned at the throat. His hair
hung in ragged fringes over his eyes. . . . His dress-
suit case was across his lap and answered him for a
desk. Between his heels he held a bottle of beer
against the rolling of the boat, and when he drank
was royally independent of a glass. While he was
composing his descriptive dispatches which some
ten thousand people would read in the morning from
the bulletins in New York, I wondered what the
fifty thousand who had read his war novel and have
held him, no doubt rightly, to be a great genius

would have said and thought could they have seen him at the moment."

*   *   *

EARLY in June, after Admiral Sampson had bottled up Cervera's fleet in the harbor of Santiago de Cuba, the land forces prepared to move from Tampa to the scene of action. Norris, who had been but loosely attached to the Fifth Army Corps, set about obtaining an assignment to a particular division, a move made necessary by the fact that, once arrived in Cuba, he would be dependent upon the army for rations and for permission to get near the fighting. The division which he chose was the First Infantry, partly because it was made up of regulars from the San Francisco Presidio, and partly because he could thus join forces with an old friend, James F. J. Archibald, whom he had known as a writer for the *Overland Monthly* and who was now field representative of the San Francisco *Post*. Archibald, who in holding the rank of aid-de-camp was assured of seeing action in his double capacity of military attache and newspaper correspondent, had, as a member of the *Gussie* expedition, received the distinction of being the first man wounded in the war. He greeted Norris enthusiastically, assuring him that if he stayed by his side he would see plenty of fighting. Norris accepted the offer and served through the campaign as the comrade of the genial egoist, certain characteristics of whom he later used in portraying Osterman in *The Octopus*.

While the troops were embarking on the eighth of June, Norris and Archibald went aboard the flag-

ship *Securança*, which carried General Shafter and his
staff as well as the more important correspondents.
For a week everyone grumbled as the squadron lay
sweltering in the Florida heat, waiting for the order
to sail, but at last the transports moved out of Tampa
Bay, pushed on to Key West where they were joined
by a convoy, and then struck out for Santiago.

Now that they were actually on their way, Norris
felt sure that he was going to see something of real
war; he was pleased that he had passed the first
eliminative test, for the number of correspondents
had been cut from 500 to 165, the most noted of
whom were aboard the flagship. As the ships steamed
at eight knots along the coast of Cuba towards Cape
Maisi, he made the acquaintance of two men whom
he had long admired from a distance—Richard Harding Davis and Frederic Remington. He was somewhat disappointed in Davis, for the latter's apparent
arrogance, which made him unpopular with many,
kept Norris at a distance; on the other hand, he found
Remington very approachable and glad to chat with
him about art and horses. (In the *Wave*, Norris had
haled him as "Frederic the Great," declaring that his
drawings created a "panorama of the brutal, unleashed splendid life that goes thundering along from
Idaho to Texas. . . .") In spite of the good company,
time passed slowly until, on the 20th of June, they
stopped off Aserraderos, where Norris was one of the
party which accompanied General Shafter on his
interview with the insurgent General Garcia. As the
next moves after the conference were to disembark
the troops at Daiquiri, surround Santiago, and attack
it from the rear, the following two days were given

over to landing on the open coast, where heavy fire from the battleships met with no resistance from the enemy.

On the 22nd of June, Norris rode through the pounding surf, dragged himself up on the high iron pier, and stayed in Daiquiri only long enough to adjust his pack. Ten miles up the coast at Siboney he caught up with the First Regiment, "rolling on the grass and kicking its heels under a grove of cocoanut palms, after the long days of cramped quarters on shipboard." A week of waiting, enlivened by marching and pitching and breaking camp, ended when Young's brigade drove the Spaniards off the trail at Guasimas, and Norris moved forward with the regiment to a point on the Santiago road about three miles south of El Pozo. During these days Norris and Archibald were adjusting themselves to the hardships of life in the jungle growth of south Cuba; they slept in a patent hammock, invented by the latter, which was equipped with flaps so that it could be made into a tent to keep them dry in the drizzling rain; as they hung out of reach, they escaped the huge land crabs which scuttled over the faces of the sleeping soldiers, but occasionally tarantulas dropped in to make them uncomfortable—they shook two off their blanket in one night; they supplemented their meager rations with mangoes fried in bacon grease. As the food and water for the army ran short, the two correspondents found it increasingly difficult to get supplies. One night they dropped in on Lieutenant Selfridge. "They were a sorry-looking couple. I know Frank Norris never knew how to rough it, and if Jim Archibald did, his appearance was decidedly against him—

neither had any kind of equipment and apparently
they had not been near soap and water or a razor for
some time. They had no rations and were ravenously
hungry, so I not only invited them to share my next
meal with me, but gave them hardtack, bacon, and
coffee to take with them."

Before hostilities began, however, they were able to
add to their equipment in a very material way; their
party grew to four in number. Mounts were very
scarce, and, although Archibald was frequently detailed a horse or a mule, Norris feared that he was
going to see the campaign on foot. Luckily, one day
he found a native who was willing to part with his
miserable little white pony for a large sum in American dollars; Norris immediately closed the bargain,
and from that time on there was a company horse,
a "bronco" to share their rations. The final addition
was a Cuban guide, who, after attaching himself
to the two correspondents, became so faithful that
they could not have rid themselves of him if they
had wanted to. As he was very homely, Norris, after
consulting his Spanish dictionary, named him "Bonito." "Bonito" was very proud of and very busy
with his equipment, which consisted of a rifle which
he refused to fire for fear of impairing its immaculate
condition.

Near dusk on the afternoon of June 30th they were
informed that the American forces were to attack
El Caney the following morning. The plan was that
the army, in order to encircle Santiago, should attempt to push back the first line of Spanish defenses,
located in the foothills about eighteen miles from the
city, the line of defenses which ran up from Aguadores

in the south along the ridges, through San Juan blockhouse, and on to El Caney, the largest village in the vicinity. El Caney was to receive the brunt of the attack, as its garrison could be shelled from a hill which overlooked it; if, as was expected, this attack should succeed early in the day, the right flank would push on to cut off the Spanish reserves from the north, forcing the Spaniards to retire from their well-nigh impregnable position on the summit of San Juan Hill. Norris, together with most of the correspondents who had come to El Pozo—now reduced to forty in number—planned to see the issue decided from the heights overlooking El Caney. He little realized that the order of affairs was to be almost entirely reversed, that the stubborn little group below them in El Caney were to be able to hold out till late in the afternoon, while the really important action was to take place on their left, where the American soldiers, trapped under a withering fire in the valley before San Juan Hill, were to make a bloody dash up that hill contrary to all plans and contrary to all supposed possibilities.

*   *   *

DURING the night before the battle Norris rode with Lawton's division to the heights where Capron's small battery of four guns took up its position to bombard the fort and village. "The column went forward through the night by fits and starts, now doubling when word was passed by to close up, now halting in mud up to the legging tops for no assignable reason, now moving forward at a snail's pace, and now breaking up completely, when the tired men

eased belt and blanket-roll and dropped into the
drenched grass by the roadside for a moment's rest.
. . . There was no talking in the ranks, but on ahead
we could hear the battery trundling along. Then
there was the monotonous squash of many boots
churning up the mud of the road, the click of swinging
cups against bayonet scabbards, the indefinable murmur of a moving army that recalls the noise of the sea
or of forests. . . . To our left, far down the valley, was
a cluster of pin points in a faint white glow as of a
nebula. Santiago was there, and from mountain top
to mountain top the Spanish signal fires were flash-
ing."[1]

They stopped within earshot of the Spanish sentinels, and when dawn came Norris could see El Caney
below them and about a mile away "red roofs, a white
wall or two, the twin towers of the church, a blockhouse of unusual size on a sugar-loaf just outside the
town, and, yes, on its salient tower a flame-colored
tongue of bunting, the flag of Spain." From below
to the left he could hear the shots of Ludlow's regiment, fighting its way towards the blockhouse. "The
rifles sputter, as hot grease sputters, the shots leaping
after one another in straggling sequence, sometimes
in one-two-three order, like the ticking of a clock,
sometimes rushing confusedly together." Soon the
artillery on the hill started operations as Capron
shelled a column of cavalry going out of El Caney.
Norris's first reaction was surprise at the absence of
order and precision among the artillery men, who

[1]Throughout this section I have quoted freely from *With
Lawton at El Caney*, the *Century Magazine*, June, 1899.
Quoted by permission of the publishers.

went at the affair very casually, while correspondents
and an attaché or two were dodging in and out, note-
books and kodaks in hand.

"'What's the matter?' cried the captain angrily.
'Why don't you begin?'

"'All ready here, sir. Number four, ready!'

"'Well, fire it, then! Go ahead!'

"'Number four, ready!' began the lieutenant.
'Fire!'

"After the report came a piercing, ear-shattering
sound as the shell took the air and tore across the
valley. All of us went tumbling to the left of the
battery's position, to get out of the way of the smoke
and to see the explosion when the shell burst. There
was a silence for about ten seconds, while a hundred
eyes watched the moving column and the mass of
green bush and hill and pale-blue sky above it. Then
suddenly a little ball of white cotton popped out
against the blue of the distant landscape; the crowd
relaxed its breath.

"'Too high!'"

As the battery was out of range of enemy fire, the
group of correspondents, attachés, and artillery men
were able to watch in safety the drama going on
beneath them. On the left, Ludlow climbed the hill
before the blockhouse, his men falling rapidly under
the heavy fire from the Spanish trenches. Chaffee
came in from the right and moved towards the Santiago road to cut off the rear. The battery, with un-
pitying skill in gunnery, shelled the blockhouse and
the trenches before it. To the men on the hill it
seemed an outright slaughter; they marveled that
the Spanish soldiers could hold on so long with

practically every shell falling in their midst. And yet they did hold on for hours, this handful of men cut off from retreat. . . . The flag was shot down and they saw a man crawl out upon the ledge of the block-house to replace it. Number four of the battery fired. "The shell was still screaming when we caught sight of the man scrambling upon the ledge near the broken staff. Then, right over the fort, right over the staff, and over the Spanish soldier's head, the little ball of white cotton leaped into view. 'Got him!' shouted the entire battery, as the bursting shrapnel wiped the man from the wall of the blockhouse as a sponge would wipe a slate. . . . We shall remember these Spanish soldiers of El Caney, for not until late afternoon, after ten hours of intermittent shelling, did they finally consent to leave—what was left of them."

Then, as they saw Ludlow making the final charge up the hill, the group of men on the hill around the battery went mad with excitement. For the moment Norris found it more interesting than the battle. "It surged forward to the crest of the hill, swarming over cannon and caisson, taking possession of every elevation, eager to see the last move in the game, and it shouted and talked aloud regardless of the answer. A German count, an attaché of legation, wrangled over a question of distance; a brigade commander asked meek questions of a private standing on an upturned cracker box; colonels, majors, correspon-dents, soldiers, Cubans, photographers crowded to-gether, rubbing elbows, gesticulating, advancing opinions, contradicting one another, àll beside them-selves in the tension of the moment."

The cheering of Ludlow's men as they reached the fort was too much for Norris. Down the hill he rode his little white horse as fast as he could go, left him in a grove of cocoanut palms to be retrieved by "Bonito," and, climbing the sugar-loaf hill, reached the line of rifle pits below the blockhouse. What he found there shocked him; for the first time war became an actuality. "The first Spaniard I saw was lying at the bottom of a trench. He was a young fellow—they were all young fellows—his face the color of wax; one poor, dirty hand looked like a buzzard's claw; his arm was doubled up under him and—but the rest is not for words. A bullet wound is one thing, but shrapnel smashes its man, flings him down, and drives and dints him into the dirt. The dead were everywhere; they were in the trenches, in the fields of pineapple, in corners of the blockhouse, and in grisly postures halfway down the slope of the hill. The air was full of smells—the smell of stale powder, of smoke, or a horse's carcass two days unburied, of shattered lime and plaster in the blockhouse, and the strange, acrid, salty smell of blood."

A few minutes later Norris stood with Archibald, a corporal, and five soldiers on the side of a gully which lay between the blockhouse and the village of El Caney. Behind him the troops were occupied with burying the dead and guarding the few prisoners; to his left in the direction of San Juan Hill he could hear fighting still going on. The little town before him gave no signs of life until he and his companions shouted "*Amigos!*" with all their force; then suddenly it swarmed with civilians who came out of their hiding places and advanced towards the gully. "They came hesitatingly, stopping and calling every five steps, then, gaining confidence, came boldly out of the town. . . . In five minutes the town was alive with people, men, women, and little naked pot-bellied children. . . . Most of them were women trembling on the verge of hysteria. . . . One, who was choking with sobs, was at the same time eating sardines from a tin as fast as she could handle the fork, and with no consciousness of what she was doing. For the children . . . it was a new sort of a picnic. . . . A beautiful woman, whose husband, a Cuban, had been killed by one of our shells, was filling the air with her cries . . . till it broke one's heart to listen to her."

The two correspondents together with the squad of soldiers were the first to enter the village. In so far as the squad's mission was to clear the town of fugitive Spanish soldiers, it was foolhardy for civilians to accompany them, but, as James Creelman of the New York *Herald* had just demonstrated in leading the rush into the blockhouse, the correspondents were determined to play the part of soldiers. Norris, with his revolver cocked, passed down the narrow streets and into the houses, the jail, the hospital, the church, the mayor's residence. . . . Luckily for him, what few Spanish soldiers had not been killed were quite ready to surrender. After capturing two in a small blockhouse, he walked them in front of him, allowing himself a free breath only when he had delivered his charges. In pushing his way into these unknown houses he came across sights he could not forget. Soldiers had crawled away into corners to die. In a building on the plaza were forty wounded men too weak to care what happened. Lying on the floor of the mayor's house was the body of a young girl, "her hair across her face like a drift of seaweed." She had been stabbed; the knife still stuck in her breast. There was blood and suffering everywhere he turned.

He was glad to leave El Caney behind him when the time came to join his regiment, which had pushed on three miles down the Santiago road. He found that the victorious troops were also weighed down by heavy depression, the aftermath of carnage. As darkness came on, they received the command to countermarch instead of advancing towards Santiago, for while they had been fighting at El Caney, their comrades had taken San Juan Hill and now needed all of Lawton's men to hold the right flank of their precarious line. Throughout the night of the first of July they tramped wearily, Norris and Archibald taking turns upon the pony which "Bonito" had brought through the confusion. Archibald remembers that sometime during the march "Willie" Hearst joined them and walked for a while so that they could use his horse. While they talked of the campaign, of newspapers, of freeing the Cuban people, Norris could not forget the broken bodies at El Caney. The troops arrived to take their positions in the trenches early the next morning.

*   *   *

THE thin line of American soldiers holding the lizard-like crest of San Juan Hill, busy digging itself in with bayonets and tomato cans, was disheartened by the withering fire from the well-protected Spanish trenches; its situation was so precarious that more than once a retreat to El Pozo seemed inevitable. The base hospitals among the mango trees were filled with wounded men, whose condition was made more wretched by the inadequate supply of food, good water, and medical equipment, while the yellow fever was beginning to get its deadening grip on the army. The correspondents were under fire a good deal of the time, whether they were posted on top of the hill noting the fighting or down in the valley helping to care for the wounded men. By now their ranks had been greatly thinned; only a handful remained at the front, while the rest retired to Siboney and El Pozo to write their stories for the home press. Norris insisted on endangering his life along with Bonsal, Davis, Crane, McIntosh, Remington, Christy, Whitney, Archibald, and a few others. (Creelman and Marshall were now on the casualty list.) Norris later related that Remington with his shirt tail out came running to warn him of the danger of the enemy fire; they met the situation by taking liberal draughts from a bottle of whiskey which Remington carried as his most valued equipment. That these green war correspondents were without caution in exposing themselves to the enemy bullets, was the testimony of Davis and Leonard Wood, who had been busy the day before keeping Stephen Crane from roaming about in a conspicuous English waterproof which seemed to draw the enemy fire. Luck must have been with them. It seemed also to be with the American army, for on July 3rd, at a time when their situation appeared most precarious, Cervera's fleet committed suicide by trying to get out of Santiago bay, and General Toral asked for a truce so that noncombatants could leave the city before Shafter began the bombardment.

As soon as the truce went into effect, the refugees began to pour into El Caney in such numbers that before the end of the first day their situation had become very grave; into a village built for five hundred inhabitants had come ten thousand helpless people, the majority of whom had walked the two leagues from Santiago. The heat, which made shelter unnecessary at night, increased their distress at going without food or sufficient water. When Norris and Archibald rode into El Caney on the second morning of the exodus, they found the central square a seething mass of white-clad Cubans, thousands of men, women, and children, from whom came an insistent plaint for food: "*Comida, comida!*" When the correspondents offered their rations, it took but a moment for ravenous mouths to bolt the hardtack, swallow the raw bacon, and chew up the dry coffee.

Across the plaza, on a terrace in front of the church, the Red Cross in the form of Dr. Bangs of the hospital ship *State of Texas* had established itself. When the two newcomers, after pushing their way across the plaza with considerable difficulty, offered him their services, he accepted promptly, for before their arrival he had faced the problem of feeding the multitude with the sole aid of a couple of inefficient Cubans. Dr. Bangs appeared to Norris a mass of energy; he was stout, had a very red face and a voice like the exhaust of a locomotive, wore a pith helmet battered out of shape, and had a beard a fortnight old. He bellowed as he worked over the kettles full of cornmeal mush. "Now fellows," he shouted, "we want to get at the women and children first. Tell 'em to send up the children first!" Norris went back to the edge of the terrace and shouted as loudly as possible. "*Niños primero. Niños primero.*" "*Comida!*" shouted the crowd in answer, "*Comida! Comida!*"

In spite of the industry with which they collected wood for the fires, it was seven that evening before they had three kettlefuls of steaming cornmeal mush ready for the children; in the meantime the cry for food had become shrill and piping. "Tell 'em," roared the doctor, wiping the sweat from his forehead with the back of his hand—"tell 'em it's 'most done—tell 'em pretty soon now." Norris returned once more to the edge of the terrace and leaned over. "It was yet light enough to see—to see about three thousand children, half of them naked, the other half ragged beyond words. What a mess! Close to the gate the jam was terrific; they were packed as sand is packed, so that they moved, not as individuals, but as groups, and masses, swaying forward and back, and from side to side, without knowing why. I could see but a pavement of faces, crushed together cheek to cheek, upturned, pinched and agonized, shrill-voiced with the little rat that nipped and gnawed at their poor starved stomachs. Farther on, where the press was not so great, the children reached toward me empty cans, pots, pails, tin cups, vessels of all sizes and descriptions, and they put their hands (not their fingers) to their mouths with always the same cry of unutterable distress, '*Comida! Comida!*'[1]

[1]Throughout this section I have quoted freely from *Comida*, the *Atlantic Monthly*, March, 1899, by permission of the publishers.

"'*Poco tiempo!*' I called to them. '*Poquito tiempo.*'"

At last, when Dr. Bangs opened the gate, intending to let in twenty children, hundreds of starving little wretches pushed their way in. Norris helped drive them back into the corner by main strength. "But even as I pushed and thrust, a little hand—ever so little hand—took hold of my wrist. It was that of a tiny girl, almost too weak to stand, but she held a pitiful empty sardine can toward me, and whispered confidentially, with a great attempt at cheerfulness, '*Comida, eh? Comida por me?*' and put her hand, not to her lips, but to her stomach.—We came to know that gesture afterward. So long as they pointed to their mouths we could allow the applicants to wait their turn, but when they pointed to their stomachs we knew that it was almost time for the restoratives."

They fed as many as they could, but there were still twenty left when the cornmeal gave out, twenty who had to wait till the next morning for a bite of food. A sick girl of sixteen almost collapsed on their hands. The days of fighting, the sleepless nights, the suffering around him, a slight touch of fever—all had contributed to shattering Norris's nerves. The night after feeding the children was one of grotesque horrors. It started when, as he led his horse into the church, which had been turned to the uses of a fort and stable by the Spaniards, the pony became frightened by a torn altar cloth and for a moment had the whole place by the ears. "It was a strange, incongruous scene—the shattered chapel, the bayonet scabbards, the Mauser cartridges clinking underfoot, the prim stiff calicoes and ginghams from Waltham, and the cow-puncher's pony shying from an altar cloth woven by fingers that were dust two hundred years ago." Then, as they were turning in, the doctor in his thunderous voice exclaimed, "Well, fellows, here's something I do every night that you can't do at all," and took out his left eye to polish it on the leg of his trousers. Norris, growing faint, decided to sleep outdoors. As he groped about for a smooth place to lie he discovered that the log-like object which he had chosen for a pillow was an amputated arm which had been but half-buried. When he finally fell asleep, it was with this grisly object on one side, two yellow-fever patients on another, a thousand starving refugees on a third, and the desecrated chapel on the fourth. . . . In the morning he found that the boards with which he had built himself a crude shelter from the rain were coated thick with human blood. . . .

They stayed at El Caney during most of the following day, feeding the crowds, who gashed themselves with the sharp edges of tins as they fought for food, caring for the sick, taking pictures of the plaza and the refugees. By that time other support had come to the aid of Dr. Bangs and they were free to depart. "We stayed and worked as long as we could, and a little after noon we rode away in a drenching rain. But for nearly half a mile down the road, as our steaming horses toiled through the mud, fetlock deep, the vague murmur of the crowd in the plaza came back to us, prolonged, lamentable, pitiful beyond expression—the cry of people dying for lack of food.

"*Comida! Comida!*"

*   *   *

THERE followed ten days of waiting while the repeated extensions of the truce made the men grumble, for they preferred fighting to lying idle in their unhealthy bivouac. None knew whether they were to attack Santiago or starve it into surrender, and rumors were the order of the day. In the meantime it rained incessantly, men died of wounds, the yellow fever ravaged hotly. Norris and Archibald found a comparatively dry spot to hang their patent hammock and busied themselves with fighting off the crabs, tarantulas, and yellow fever. The most exciting incident of their enforced rest was the finding of a huge potato in the corner of a deserted Cuban hut. This was highly valued, as food was scarce, and they looked forward to a feast such as they had not had since landing at Daiquiri. They decided to celebrate with a dinner that night, and Norris carefully hid the potato in the saddlebag on his pony. When dinner time arrived, however, Norris suggested that they wait until Sunday, which, he maintained, was a day more appropriate for such a celebration.

Sunday came, and Archibald clamored for the potato. They had succeeded in wrangling a can of tomatoes out of the commissary department, and with bacon and "bald-headed" coffee the feast was in sight. Norris was reluctant. "Let's wait until tomorrow. They say that Toral is going to surrender and we want to do it right."

"Tomorrow rot!" barked Archibald, and started for the saddlebags. Before he reached them, however, Norris crumpled up and told the truth. "I fed it to the pony; he was hungry and looked pathetic. He enjoyed it a lot." Archibald remembers that it was

some time before his rage succumbed to Norris's good
nature; at any rate, they waited until the fall of
Santiago to have their celebration.

Two days before the surrender, Norris and Archibald were assigned to General McKibben's staff and
moved into the Hacienda San Pablo, a six-room villa
used as headquarters of the Second Brigade. The new
quarters furnished a welcome relief from the primitive
camping, the food supply improved in both variety
and quantity, and on the evening of July 16th Norris
felt content with the world as he sat upon the veranda
joining with the orderlies in singing *The Spanish
Cavalier*, watching the Cuban fireflies "like little
electric lights gone somehow adrift," and listening to
the plaint of the whippoorwill hidden in the vermilion
Flamboyana. The singing was interrupted by the
arrival of a mud-splattered messenger who drawled
out: "Say, is here where General McKibben is?"
It was not long before they knew he had brought word
that the Spaniards were to surrender on the morrow.
The fighting of the Cuban campaign was over, and
for the moment all were occupied in trying to find
"any kind of a black tie" for the general to use in
the coming ceremony. There was to be a formal surrender in the fields near Santiago, and at noon the
American flag was to be flown over the Governor's
Palace in the city.

Next morning the two correspondents, realizing
that only by rare good fortune would they be able
to see the *grand finale*, for the orders restricting newspaper men were unusually severe, fell in with the aids
and rode with McKibben's staff to the headquarters
on San Juan Hill. On arrival Norris was struck with

the number of generals who had come to make war
on Spain: "Shafter in his inevitable pith helmet;
Wheeler, small, white-bearded, and wiry; Ludlow,
who always contrived to appear better dressed than
anyone else; Randolph, with his bull neck and fine
salient chin; and others and others and others;
Kent, Lawton, Wood, Chaffee, Young, Roosevelt,
McKibben . . ."[1] As the column formed, it seemed to
Norris that a half of the three hundred men were
brigadier generals, major generals, generals command-
ing divisions, staff officers, and the like. Determined
to stay with the march, Archibald on a scraggly mule
and Norris on the lamentable white pony fell in
behind McKibben's staff, but they were continually
forced to drop behind to give precedence to yet another general until they at last found an inconspicuous
position near the rear of the column, which was now
moving towards Santiago with General Shafter's pith
helmet bobbing briskly along ahead and the band
playing a quickstep by Sousa.

The surrender was simple and quiet. The opposing
forces lined up, Generals Shafter and Toral rode
forward and shook hands, the Spanish soldiers gave
up their arms and walked away. As Norris looked on,
he divided himself in two; with one part he observed
the drama, and with the other he reacted to the
emotional situation. "It was war and it was magnificent, seen there under the flash of a tropic sun with
all the welter of green to set it off, and there was a

[1]Throughout this section I have quoted freely from *The Surrender of Santiago* which was originally published, I believe,
in the New York *Evening Sun*.

bigness about it, so that to be there seeing it all and in a way part of it made you feel that for that moment you were living larger and stronger than ever. Tomorrow nearly a hundred million people, the world round, would read of this scene, and as many more, yet unborn, would read of it, but to-day you could sit on the back of your little white bronco and view it as easily as a play."

The simple intensity of the surrender in the fields, an intensity which brought a lump to Norris's throat, was replaced by a savage exultation as he galloped into the captured city. Here was something more akin to the brutal spirit. "There was no thought of humanitarian principles then. The war was not a 'crusade,' we were not fighting for Cubans, it was not for disinterested motives that we were there, sabred and revolvered and carbined. Santiago was ours—was ours, ours, by the sword we had acquired, we, Americans, with no one to help—and the Anglo-Saxon blood of us, the blood of the race that has fought its way out of a swamp in Friesland, conquering and conquering and conquering, on to the westward, the race whose blood instinct is the acquiring of land, went galloping through our veins to the beat of our horses' hoofs. . . . We rode on there at a gallop through the crowded streets of the fallen city . . . triumphant, arrogant, conquerors."

At noon he watched the forces present arms in the plaza, heard the band play the national anthem, and saw the American flag raised on the staff above the Governor's Palace. It was the most intense moment of the campaign; there was no cheering; for perhaps a full minute they stood with bared heads reverently

watching the great flag as it strained in the breeze . . .
and the great names came to Norris's mind again:
Lexington, Trenton, Yorktown, 1812, Chapultepec,
Mexico, Shiloh, Gettysburg, the Wilderness, Appo-
mattox, and now—Guasimas, San Juan, El Caney,
Santiago. . . .

*   *   *

THE rest was anticlimax. For a while they stayed in
the Palace Hotel and crossed the plaza to eat at the
Café de Venus, where they found beefsteak at $7.50
a plate. Then they moved into an abandoned restaurant, where they hung their hammock in the
corner and used the kitchen to cook their meals.
When the owner appeared he invited them to stay
and opened up the wine cellar for their use. To while
away the time they collected souvenirs. Norris obtained part of the very flag which had flown over the
Governor's Palace before the surrender. He and
Archibald bought all sorts of Spanish decorations
from a jewelry store at fifty cents apiece and played
stud poker for them. Thus they spent three weeks
in Santiago, suffering from the "let-down" which
followed the excitement of the campaign. Their reaction was not in spirits alone, for it brought with it
sporadic attacks of the malarial fever which they had
been fighting off for so long; now it hit Norris with
double force, for it found his system still weak from
the previous siege in South Africa.

Early in August they received permission to board
the transport *Iroquois*, which was sailing for Porto
Rico, whither the scene of the war had shifted, but,
much to their relief, news of the signing of the Peace

Protocol reached them in mid-course, and the boat
headed for New York with the two correspondents
as the sole passengers. They were the vanguard of the
reporters to return from the successful campaign, but
Norris, at least, was too ill to enjoy their welcome at
the Battery. He had planned to return to his work in
the McClure office, but, after a few days of desultory
effort, he realized that he had reached the stage of
collapse. In a letter to Peixotto he confessed his
distraught condition:

"I had your very kind little note day before yesterday and would have replied sooner were it not that
I've been down with fever ever since leaving Santiago.
The thing got a twist on me somewhere between
Daiquiri and San Juan and laid me out as soon as we
got inside the city. . . . I am very much tempted to
accept your invitation to Chadd's Ford and very
probably would if I did not think there was a chance
of me to go out to San Francisco for three or four
weeks. I need a rest very badly and a bit of a change
for a while and a good opportunity to forget a good
many things I had to see during the war. Now that
I can stand off and as it were get a perspective of the
last three months, the whole business seems nothing
but a hideous blur of mud and blood.

"There is precious little glory in war, if the Santiago campaign is a sample, and when you try to
recall the campaign, it's only the horrors that come
to you, the horrors and hardships and nothing of the
finer side. I've made a roof for myself to sleep under,
out of boards that were one glaze of dried blood. . . .
I have seen men who were shot in the throat stretched
out in the sun at the Division hospital who had been

for forty-eight hours without water, food, sleep, shelter, or medical attention. I have seen a woman of seventy trying to carry on her back another of ninety-two, and at Caney I was the first to discover, in one of the abandoned houses, the body of a little girl— Ernest, I don't believe she was fifteen—who had been raped and then knifed to death just before the beginning of the battle.

"I want to get these things out of my mind and the fever out of my blood, and so if my luck holds I am going back to the old place for three weeks and for the biggest part of the time I hope to wallow and grovel in the longest grass I can find in the Presidio Reservation on the cliffs overlooking the ocean and absorb ozone and smell smells that *don't* come from rotting and scorched vegetation, dead horses and bad water."[1]

In a couple of days Norris was on his way out to California to attempt to forget the details of his first-hand contact with naturalism. It was to take him more than three weeks to regain his old enthusiasm.

[1]Letter to Ernest Peixotto written in August, 1898.

Chapter 9: Reaction

THIS time the fever did not burn itself out as quickly as it had after the return from South Africa. Instead of wallowing in the grass of the cliffs overlooking the ocean, Norris went to bed on his arrival in San Francisco, and the three weeks for recuperation lengthened out to nearly two months, spent partly in the hospital and partly in the Hotel Pleasanton, where his mother and brother were now living. In spite of the care of his mother, the temperature returned each afternoon, and, long after he was able to get around, the normal elasticity failed to return to his step. As his health improved, he made visits to the Bohemian Club, where he could sit in the "Owl's Nest," sunning himself as he chatted with the few of his old friends who were still in the city; finally he recovered enough strength to play an occasional game of *bocce* or visit the Fiji house in Berkeley. Needless to say, he spent a great deal of his time with Jeannette Black, and together they took the less strenuous of their favorite excursions, visiting the waterfront, Chinatown, and the Presidio.

The most encouraging incident during his illness was the arrival early in September of *Moran of the*

Lady Letty, fresh from the presses of Doubleday, McClure & Company. In spite of what Norris called "the yellowry-greenery aspect of Moran's new clothes," he was very pleased with the issue, for it was his first novel to appear in book form. As soon as it reached San Francisco, Mrs. Norris read it to Frank and Jeannette Black, who declared it showed marks of genius. Stimulated by this tangible evidence of his progress, Norris summoned up enough energy to put the final touches on the manuscript of *Blix*, which he had all but completed the previous spring; at the same time, he contributed to the *Wave* a short story, *The Drowned Who Do Not Die*, which was the tale in *Blix* the couple heard from the first mate of a whaleback, and Condy wrote up as *Victory Over Death*.

As if to make up for his desertion of fiction during the Cuban campaign, Norris gave himself no further rest but immediately began to lay the groundwork for another novel. His new venture grew out of an idea which he had been considering for some time, an idea which had come to him as he had listened to Captain Hodgson recount his experiences in the Arctic as a member of the *Rodgers* relief expedition. It seemed to him that here was an excellent subject for a novel of force—man's combat with nature at its cruelest; moreover, the popular interest in polar exploration which would make a novel dealing with this unexploited field particularly timely had been aroused by Nansen's trek to within four degrees of the North Pole in 1896, and by Andrée's fatal attempt the following year to drift across the top of the world in a balloon. In *The End of the Beginning*, which had appeared in the *Wave* in the fall of 1897, Norris

had pictured the hardships faced by a group of
explorers marooned on the ice floe off Wrangel
Island. He planned to use this episode as the opening
chapters of his novel, and to follow it with the return
to civilization of the chief of the expedition, Bennett,
a man of action, endowed with almost primitive
strength, with all of the virility of McTeague but
with none of his stupidity. The main part of the
story would concern the mating of this rugged hero
with a woman of equal strength of character, a civilized and cultured Moran engaged in a profession as
strenuous as Bennett's arctic exploring. When, during
a visit to the San Francisco Children's Hospital,
Norris was struck with the grave responsibilities
faced by the graduate nurses, he decided that his
heroine, Lloyd Seabright, should be an expert in that
field. Bennett would pit his strength against hostile
nature; Lloyd would pit herself against death; they
would both pit themselves against each other in the
struggle, which, according to Norris's formula, invariably prefaced the winning of a woman. It would
be another epic of force and he would title it *A
Man's Woman*.

During the remainder of his stay in San Francisco,
Norris applied himself to "getting up" the technical
details of arctic exploring and nursing. For those of
the former he spent several afternoons with his
"buccaneer," who once more became icebound in
Siberia, and, although Norris eschewed the latter's
story of how he avoided a panic among his huskies
by biting off the nose of his lead-dog, he was not long
in acquiring an easy skill in talking of aleuronate
bread, McClintock sledges, mock moons, and "the

abnormal fatness of starvation, the irony of misery, the huge joke that arctic famine plays upon those whom it afterwards destroys." For medical information he went to his old chum Bert Houston, who was attending the Lane Medical School in San Francisco. Over the luncheon table he learned methods for combatting virulent cases of typhoid fever—"quinine for the regular morning and evening doses, sulphonal and trional for insomnia, ether for injections in case of anæmia after hemorrhage, tincture of valerian for the tympanites," etc. . . . to "crushed ice wrapped in flannel cloths for the cold pack in the event of hyperpyrexia." A visit to the hospital operating room taught him how to describe the excision of a hip joint. . . . Good naturalistic details these—starving wretches and painful operations.

On October 12th Norris wrote to a freind: "On the very day I had planned to call upon you I must find myself enroute for New York again. . . . *McClure's* have sent me passes for all the way—*me voila parti.* I hope to be 'on the square' (Washington Square of course) from now on if I can."[1] The letter expressed more cheer at departing than he actually felt. Despite his three months' vacation he was returning to New York with the fever still in his blood and the horrors of the war still on his mind. It was to be another six months before he was to regain his customary vigor; in the meantime he was to pass a wretched winter during which the reaction from his Cuban campaign was to be felt in his life and in his fiction.

★   ★   ★

[1]Letter to Mrs. Davenport postmarked October 12, 1898.

IT IS not surprising that Norris looked forward to living on Washington Square, for, during this era before the inroad of tourists hunting for bearded and long-haired talent, it offered an ideal location to the indigent writer, combining the triple advantages of interesting surroundings, cheap lodgings, and congenial company. Furthermore it lay in the heart of a section of the city with which fully one half of the best of New York local-color fiction had concerned itself. The settings made famous by the stories of Henry James, Brander Matthews, G. W. Curtis, Julian Ralph, "Chimmie Fadden" Townsend, and H. C. Bunner could all be found within five or six hundred yards of the white Memorial Arch. Tradition had kept the north side of the square in mansions of red brick, but the international shabbiness which had invaded the southern border and broken it up into lodging houses, shops, beer gardens, and saloons made it possible for Norris to rent at a very reasonable figure a small front bedroom in an old house at 61 Washington Square, South.

Norris did not find the traditionally congenial company, the "New Bohemia" of the Square, to his liking. He had no time for convivial parties, and he soon found that he was annoyed by the would-be artists who spent their time in pawing over literature and literary men. He looked upon their ideas as effete—almost decadent. He disliked anyone who made a cult of literature. Doubtless he was willing enough to join in an argument at the Judson Hotel, where he took his meals, frequently winding up with a playful, "Now, don't agree with me or I'll know I'm wrong"; but it is questionable that he felt in

sympathy with the group which Juliet Wilbur
Tompkins pictures as made up of "self-conscious
adventurers who slept under the stars and strewed
pennies to pay for the night's lodging." Rather, he
turned for companionship to a few intimate friends,
to John Harrold, who lived at the Benedict, to Selfridge and Juilliard, who occasionally dropped in to
see him, and particularly to the Peixottos, who lived
in an apartment a few doors below his lodgings.
The following summer he told the latter couple how
completely he had been dependent upon their company to keep him cheered during his season of distress. "I don't dare think of going back to Washington Square with you people away. New York can
never be a *very* lovely place to me but New York
minus Mr. and Mrs. Billy Magee—well, we won't
think much about that just yet. . . . Will I ever forget
how much you both helped to make this hard winter
of '98–99 easy for me? What I should have done
without you I honestly don't know, because there
were times when the whole thing was something of
a grind, and it didn't seem worth while to go on at
all. Well, somehow one does pull through."[1]

Later he was to delight in the green leaves which
transformed Washington Square in the springtime,
but now he was cold, ill, and lonesome; it was his
first winter in the East, and it took his utmost cheerfulness to combat the bleak skies and the snow and
slush. A new element was added to the causes for
depression when he received the news from San
Francisco that Jeannette Black was critically ill with

[1]Letter to Ernest Peixotto dated Hotel Pleasanton, San Francisco, May 7, 1899.

a mastoid infection. He telegraphed that he was coming home at once, and it was only the receipt of a
wire from Jeannette telling him of a successful operation and urging him to remain in New York that kept
him from taking the first train West. . . . Before the
winter was over, his nostalgia had become a habit.
He wrote home: "New York is not California nor
New York City San Francisco and I am afraid that
because of the difference I shall never be reconciled
to the East. . . . There is not much color here and
very little of the picturesque. . . . I have almost forgotten how a mountain looks and I never can quite
persuade myself that the Atlantic is an ocean—in
the same sense as the Pacific. I miss the out-of-
doorness of the West more and more and the sea fogs
and the Trade Wind, and I don't suppose I shall
ever feel at home away from there. Indeed I have
come to look forward to the time when I shall come
back to San Francisco to live for good and all. I was
talking to Mr. Howells about this and he rather
encouraged me to do my work wherever the surroundings were most congenial, and told me that as soon
as I had 'once established my connections' in New
York there was no reason why I could not 'go home'
and that a 'literary' man could do his work any-
where. He has been very good to me this winter."[1]

Howells's goodness was not confined to frequent,
informal hospitality. In December he devoted several
paragraphs of his department in the newly founded
Literature to a review of *Moran of the Lady Letty*.
After giving a genial summary of the story, at the

[1]From letter to Mrs. Davenport dated 61 Washington Square
South, March 22, 1899.

same time implying that it was not the writer's best work, he had ended with direct praise: "Whoever desires a thrill may find it in this fresh and courageous invention which gains a certain effectiveness from being so boldly circumstanced in the light of common day, and in a time and place of our own." Although the critics were inclined to take Howells's encouragement of young writers at a discount—one critic insisted that if he continued patting beginners on the head he would soon have all the young people in the country taking to fiction—his position as dean of letters was sufficient to make his conspicious notice of *Moran* of signal aid to Norris. Critics came to refer to him as a promising discovery brought to light by McClure and hailed by Howells, a double endorsement which made him worth watching. Otherwise, *Moran* created no ripples; it was uniformly ignored by the standard reviewing journals, and the newspapers passed it by with the comment that it was a sea story somewhat overladen with incident. There was one notable exception in Isaac Marcosson, then literary editor of the Louisville *Times*, who read it with enthusiasm, wrote a very commendatory review, and started a correspondence with Norris which later led into a friendship.

Norris's disheartenment at this time was not relieved by the situation which he faced in making a living. *Moran*, despite Howells's encouraging remarks, had not attained a sale which promised much in royalties; nor had his position with the publishing house proved highly remunerative. As the subject of McClure's enthusiasm, he may have found himself at the mercy of a visionary temperament which blew hot

and cold. McClure himself, who states in his autobiography that he usually lost interest in a scheme as
soon as it was started, was in Europe most of the time
that Norris was adjusting himself to living on fifty
dollars a month and meeting the assignments of his
firm. Norris's ambitious plans for writing for the syndicate and magazine seem to have proved abortive. It
is true that *Moran* had been serialized in the New
York *Evening Sun* and two of his *Wave* stories were
reprinted in the magazine, but so far as is known
nothing written specifically for them was published.
Moreover, although he had gone to Cuba as a special
writer for *McClure's Magazine*, to his bitter disappointment that journal found no room in its
pages for his articles; the general features of the
campaign had been adequately covered by Stephen
Bonsal, a veteran correspondent, and what special
articles were needed were ready in abundance from
such first-hand sources as the British Consul at
Santiago and Admiral Alfred T. Mahan. Norris was
forced to place his war observations elsewhere;
The Surrender of Santiago appeared in the *Evening
Sun*, *With Lawton at El Caney* in *Century*, and
Comida in the *Atlantic Monthly*.

After all, Norris's desk work was a diversion; he
was primarily concerned with writing novels. Not
long before he was brought East by McClure, the
latter had joined with Frank Doubleday in founding
a book-publishing firm, Doubleday, McClure & Company, which, although it maintained a couple of
box-stall offices at *McClure's*, was an independent
concern guided by Doubleday and his staff. It was
this firm which had published *Moran*, was preparing

to publish *McTeague* in February, and planned to turn out *Blix* after an appropriate interval. As Norris states in a letter of the time, "I hardly write to anyone nowadays except to authors of rejected manuscripts,"[1] it is probable that an arrangement had been made between John Phillips of *McClure's* (who gave Norris every help he could) and Frank Doubleday to have him spend most of his time reading stories for the book-publishing firm. But whatever the exact arrangements were, his position was too irregular and his pay too meager to reassure him greatly.

★   ★   ★

DURING the winter, as Norris worked on *A Man's Woman*, he went about his writing in the frame of mind described in *Blix*, "grinding out the tale, as it were by main strength, driving his pen from line to line, hating the effort, happy only with the termination of each chapter, and working away, hour after hour, minute by minute, with the dogged, sullen, hammer-and-tongs obstinacy of the galley-slave, scourged to his daily toil." The further he proceeded, the more he realized that the novel was not good, but he kept at it persistently, determined to complete it in some form or other. It seemed as if the book, like the winter, would never end. It was better to be busy than idle, however, better to get the depression out of one's blood by writing than by moping; the result could at least be used as a pulp-magazine thriller, a book to be spoken of with excuses. When once he got it out of his way, and when spring and

[1]Letter to Mrs. Davenport dated March 22, 1899.

his health should return he might again write with
the pleasure and ease which had been his when working on *McTeague* and *Moran*.

In spite of his dogged obstinacy, the story in *A
Man's Woman* failed to move. No matter how ve-
hemently Norris expounded his conflict, it remained
forced and disagreeably unreal; his *motif* he stated
openly and repeated frequently: "Two characters of
extraordinary power clashed violently together."
The characters are the arctic explorer, Ward Bennett,
endowed with an indomitable will and a manner
"like the slow moving of a piston," and the resource-
ful nurse, Lloyd Seabright, "tall and of a vigorous
build—full-throated, deep-chested, with large, strong
hands and solid, round wrists," "a grand, splendid
man's woman." When they clash violently together,
Bennett transfers the tactics of exploring to the sick-
room, forcing Lloyd to sacrifice the life of his best
friend in a scene which is so incredible that the reader
refuses to stomach it. After this major error, they
repent and marry, and the book ends with Lloyd
proving her heroic mettle by sending Bennett to the
arctic once more to discover the North Pole on a
hundred per cent American expedition. Throughout
the latter part of the book runs the refrain spoken
by Adler, Bennett's faithful hanger-on, "Don't let
him chuck, don't let him get soft; make him be a
man and not a professor."

It is difficult to agree with Christopher Morley that
this book, despite its melodramatic nature, contains
many evidences of Norris's ability. One may grant
some credit to the originality of the heroine at her
best in contrast to her paler sisters in contemporary

fiction; she was, as one reviewer pointed out, "as far
from any ideal of the man's woman heretofore presented as the East is from the West." On the other
hand, her partner in crime, Bennett, is much more
of a human gorilla than a second Edward Fairfax
Rochester. Something also may be said for the impressive closing scene, which, in its quiet realism,
surpasses most of the endings of Norris's novels.
But as a whole the book reveals the writer's favorite
methods misused to the point of caricature. Norris
realized that his attempt to civilize Moran and to
give intelligence to McTeague had proved abortive,
that his apotheosis of force had this time resulted in
a thick-boned skeleton without flesh and blood.
Details piled up so thickly that Norris was tempted
to burlesque his method in his account of the death
of a nurse: "dicrotic pulse, diarrhœa, vomiting,
hospital, thrombosis of pulmonary artery, *pouf*,
requiescat." He attempted to make his strong situations real by dithyrambic processes, flooding his
manuscript with adjectives, favorite phrases, eter-
nally appearing catchwords such as "bourdon,"
"diapason," "primitive," "primordial," "simian,"
"prehensile"; he emphasized his forces by writing
Enemy with a capital E, the ever-present Enemy,
which in turn represented the drifting away of
Lloyd's loved one, the menace of the polar ice, and
the clutch of death in the operating room. Most unfortunate fault of all, Norris continually made the
mistake of talking about his action, analyzing the
motives for it, instead of presenting it objectively.
The central chapters of the book move painstakingly
from one crisis to another—the crises existing in the

minds of the characters—and whereas one such crisis might be dealt with adequately in a novel, six can not. Thus, in Lloyd's attempt to regain her self-respect after she had abandoned her patient at the point of death, Norris attempted to do in a few pages of analysis what Conrad did by objective methods in all of *Lord Jim*. Finally, there is a vagueness about portions of *A Man's Woman* which reveals that its subjects have been only partly assimilated by the writer; it fails in verisimilitude; it is a homeless orphan, for it alone among all his novels is laid in a city without a name.

Of special interest to the biographer is the insistence of two notes running through this novel written during a period of reaction: the pervading air of the sick-room tainted with the vitiating warmth of malarial fever; and the emphasis on the gruesome and horrible which reflects memories of a boy who had recently slept under boards glazed with human blood and seen soldiers writhe in the base hospitals outside of Santiago. The atmosphere of ill health and suffering is not confined to the accounts of the three sick-room cases which form much of the latter part of the book, but it is sensed in the high-strung nerves of the principal characters as they face their successive problems, a delirious intensity which does not permit of relaxation. The violent and frequently grotesque ordeals faced by the characters are motivated and heightened by an unrelenting fever; the clinical thermometer does not go down throughout the entire book. The action is incrusted with scenes of brutality. In the arctic, marooned men, bloated with starvation, move about on their hands and knees, their tongues

"distended, round and slate-colored, like the tongues
of parrots, and when they spoke they bit them hopelessly." A corpse lies with the men "frozen so hard
that a touch upon it resounded as if it had been a log
of wood." One of the men loses both hands through
frostbite and gesticulates with a spoon tied to the
right stump. Moreover the brutalities do not stop
with a return to civilization. An Alaskan husky
calmly starts eating the heroine's dog after killing
him in a fight; the hero kills a beautiful horse by
braining him with a geologist's hammer; and when
Bennett, a remarkably ugly man with a simian jaw,
a contracted forehead, a deforming cast in one eye,
and prehensile fingers, is stricken with typhoid fever
"his great body collapsed upon itself; the skin of the
face was like dry, brown parchment, and behind it
the big, massive bones stood out in great knobs and
ridges." A detailed description of the excision of a
girl's hip joint, a description filled with references to
knives, bistouries, integuments, blood, incisions,
and periostal elevators, ended with the heroine dis-
locating the child's hip while the surgeon cut off the
protruding head of the bone with a chain saw. The
writing of it may have relieved some of Norris's
emotion, but it proved too strong for his reading
public and was cut out of the later editions. One feels
that Norris had attempted to rid his mind of the
horrors seen during the Cuban campaign by consign-
ing them to paper with a cruel twist of the pen.

Norris realized that in *A Man's Woman* he had
reached the nadir of his career. When it was ready
for publication he confided to Marcosson: "The next
book of mine to appear is the *Man's Woman*. It's a

kind of theatrical sort with a lot of niggling analysis
to try to justify the violent action of the first few
chapters. It is very slovenly put together and there
are only two real people in all of its 100,000 words.
It's different from my other books, but it is the last
one that will be."[1]

[1] Letter to Isaac Marcosson, written November, 1899. *Adventures in Interviewing*, N. Y.: John Lane, 1919, p. 238.

Chapter 10: The Dentist

T HE hard winter of '98–99 ended in a promising spring. *McTeague* was released by Doubleday, McClure & Company in February, 1899; although it did not meet with a very cordial reception, its publication heartened Norris, for he felt that it represented his best work. Toward the end of February *Blix* was accepted by the publishers, who arranged to serialize it in the *Puritan* during the summer and bring it out in book form for the fall market. Early in March *Moran* appeared in England under the title, *Shanghaied*, published by Grant Richards, who was to bring out all of Norris's novels in English editions. *Shanghaied* received more attention and more favorable comment from British reviewers than it had been accorded in the American press. Finally, on March 22nd, the last word of *A Man's Woman* was written, and the disagreeable and unsatisfactory novel was turned over to the publishers to await their pleasure. Thus it was that, at the time when Norris came into some critical prominence, the tag end of materials, the stories half-digested and hastily formed were cleared from his desk and he was ready for a new project which was to absorb his energies more than anything which he had yet attempted. Before consideration of that project, however, something must be said of the reception of *McTeague* and of the significance of its appearance in contemporary fiction.

Norris looked upon *McTeague*, which he commonly referred to as "the dentist," as his best novel. (It was also his first, for he had started it before any other.) Throughout the six years between the time he began it and the date of its publication he never lost faith in its ultimate appearance, although he was aware that the odds were clearly against it. Enough has been said of its genesis and growth; the reader need only be reminded that Norris began it during his first enthusiasm for Zola, probably in 1893, that he wrote two thirds of it at California and Harvard, and that he completed it during the fall of 1897. That four years passed during its composition does not imply that he slaved over it during all of that time, reforming and revising it; on the other hand, the evidence indicates that when he worked on it, he wrote easily and smoothly, imparting to its pages the freshness of first composition. There are no signs of the deadening process of over-revision. The portions of its manuscript which still exist show a considerable amount of interlinear revision but appear to be a first copy rather than a second or third draft. Thus, in spite of the delay in its completion, it was essentially the product of two comparatively short periods of enthusiasm; it emerged unified in its emotion and conclusive in its imaginative logic.

When *McTeague* was finished there still remained the problem of finding a publisher. Undoubtedly Norris felt that there would be little chance of an

editor accepting it as long as publishers continued
to place "safety" above everything else in evaluating
a first novel by an unknown writer. The immediate
disposal of the manuscript is not known; Charles
Norris remembers that it "at once started its journeys
Eastward, and from there it periodically returned
with never a word of encouragement." Even Norris's
personal touch with the publishing house which was
to bring out his first four novels—it was at this time
that he joined the staff of *McClure's*—failed at first
to bring results, for, although the young and progressive Doubleday, McClure & Company was far more
likely to sponsor "the dentist" than any of the older
and more conservative houses, it did not dare to do
so until it had paved the way with *Moran.*

In 1899 the publishing firm rightly looked upon
McTeague as a strong and dangerous book. The
present-day reader, accustomed to a liberty which
has swept aside many taboos, is hard pressed to find
anything objectionable in it; on the contrary, he is
inclined to accuse Norris of prudishness in carefully
avoiding the extremes of Zola. Such a charge is hardly
just, for Norris handled his subject as frankly as he
was able, attempting to retain all of its virility without warping its effect by injudicious emphasis on
objectionable detail. Thus he met the taboo against
an open treatment of sex by presenting it in general
rather than specific terms, deftly contriving to make
the scene in which McTeague falls in love with Trina
while she is in his dentist chair strongly realistic and
yet acceptable, tracing with a firm hand the sexual
reactions of Trina from her first hesitant yielding to
McTeague's aggressiveness to her later pathological

submission to his sadistic brutalities. Similarly he tempered his treatment of the unsavory by keeping within the bounds of the prevalent code of decency and at the same time presenting his sordid subject in realistic terms. Anyone who feels, however, that Norris leaned over backward in order to write a book that was marketable, underestimates the skittishness of the reading public of his day. No better example of the spirit which supported Comstock could be cited than the outcry which caused the publishers to alter page 106 of *McTeague* after the appearance of the first issue. The reviewers said that the author had mentioned the unmentionable; readers of the novel wrote in to voice their protest against the inclusion of an incident which had no place in print. Their verdict was that Norris, in portraying a minor domestic misfortune, had besmattered his novel with vulgarity.

The questionable episode came at the end of the Orpheum party to which the dentist took his *fiancée*, Trina, her mother, and her young brother, "Owgooste." The expurgated page reads as follows: ["However, while the unfortunate Irish comedian went through his 'act' to the backs of the departing people, Mrs. Sieppe woke Owgooste,] very cross and sleepy, and began getting her 'things together.'

"'Save der brogramme, Trina,' whispered Mrs. Sieppe. 'Take ut home to popper. Where is der hat of Owgooste? Haf you got mein handkerchief, Trina?'

"But at this moment a dreadful accident happened to Owgooste; his distress reached its climax; his fortitude collapsed. What a misery! It was a veritable catastrophe, deplorable, lamentable, a thing beyond words! For a moment he gazed wildly about him, helpless and petrified with astonishment and terror. Then his grief found utterance, and the closing strains of the orchestra were mingled with a prolonged wail of infinite sadness.

"'Owgooste, what is ut?' cried his mother, eyeing him with dawning suspicion; then suddenly, 'What haf you done? You haf ruin your new Vauntleroy gostume!' Her face blazed; without more ado she smacked him soundly. Then it was that Owgooste touched the limit of his misery, his unhappiness, his horrible discomfort; his utter wretchedness was complete. He filled the air with his doleful outcries. The more he was smacked and shaken, the louder he wept.

"'What—what is the matter?' inquired McTeague.

"Trina's face was scarlet. 'Nothing, nothing,' she exclaimed hastily, looking away. 'Come, we must be going. It's about over.' The end of the show and the breaking up of the audience tided over the embarrassment of the moment."

The incident was replaced by a page describing McTeague's difficulty in finding his hat.

*　　　*　　　*

ALTHOUGH the publishers announced *McTeague* as "a great novel, in the truest sense of the word," with its chief figure "a herculean dentist . . . who sloughs off his thin veneer of civilization altogether under the influence of misfortune—a most daring conception"; although many of the critics who reviewed it condemned it as sordid and evil—one even going so far as to declare, "We must stamp out this

breed of Norrises!"; the novel did not become a
succés de scandale. It received more attention than
had been accorded *Moran*, however, and to Norris,
whose hopes were modest, its sale was encouraging.
He wrote to Peixotto a year after its publication:
"McTeague is in his twelfth thousand—ain't it glory-
halleluyah—though a great part of that is a paper
edition."[1] A sale of 12,000[2] meant a good deal to a
beginner, for it brought his name before the public,
but it was insignificant beside the 520,000 copies of
David Harum, also a first novel, consumed by the
public during the same year. Most of the readers of
David Harum were unaware of the existence of
McTeague.

The majority of reviewers acknowledged that the
novel had strength of a kind and showed promising
talent, but they were almost unanimous in advising
Norris to abandon the school of naturalism and embrace American idealism. The verdict of the book
critic on the *Outlook* was typical: "It is a misfortune
that he should have devoted so much skill and virility
to the description of a life so essentially without
spiritual significance, and so repulsive in its habit and
quality. There is a touch of idealism in the relations
of the two elderly lovers who appear in the story;
otherwise the reader is immersed in a world of bald
and brutal realism from beginning to end, and is
brought into association with none whose vulgarity
and brutality is unrelieved by any higher qualities. . . .

[1]Letter to Ernest Peixotto dated February 16, 1900.
[2]The trade sale of *McTeague* was approximately 4000. The
paper edition selling at fifty cents ultimately reached nearly
28,000.

It is to be hoped that Mr. Norris will find subjects better worthy of his power." Other reviewers, like the one on the *Argonaut*, resorted to invective: "seven tenths of the story the normal reader will peruse with a mixture of depression and disgust. We have heard Zola called '*Apôtre de ce qui pue.*' Similarly, Mr. Norris riots in odors and stenches. He might have changed his sub-title and called his book 'McTeague: A Study in Stinks.'"

Some critics, like the one on the *Independent* (who the week before had called Henry James's *Turn of the Screw* "the most hopelessly evil story that we have ever read in any literature, ancient or modern"), declared openly that *McTeague* was dangerous to the commonweal: "There is a certain fascination in a book like this—the fascination of murder and other hideous crimes. . . . Such a story will find its audience, perhaps a large one, but no person will be better for reading it. It has no moral, esthetical or artistic reason for being." This social objection was expressed more calmly by Miss Nancy Huston Banks of the *Bookman*, who had grappled with Zolaism before. With satisfaction she had noted the diminishing of Zola's popularity in America and had assumed that "the celebration of the painful and unclean had passed from fiction forever"—had been permanently swept away by "the sudden on-rush of ideality and romance, which rose like a fresh, sweet wind to clear the literary atmosphere." Now the old enemy had appeared once more in *McTeague*, a native product poisoned by foreign evil. The defenders of virtue must not abate their efforts; "recurrence of the old contention seems to be demanded by the unexpected

revival of realism in its most unendurable form."
Finally there were the critics who considered that
silence was the best way of showing their opposition;
the *Nation*, the *Atlantic Monthly*, and the "big
three," *Harper's*, *Scribner's* and the *Century*, ignored
McTeague.

On the other hand, there were a few to greet Norris
as a coming writer and welcome *McTeague* as a good
influence on American letters. The New York *Tribune*
gave a column to the novel, stating that it had
"merits of an uncommon sort" and commending
Norris for having "a fresh vigor which is captivating
in these days of mediocrity." On the Louisville *Times*,
Marcosson hailed *McTeague* as a masterpiece, at the
same time commending the author for "disdaining
all pretensions to style." Among the critical journals,
the *Critic* and *Literature* lined themselves behind
Norris. Jeannette Gilder, editor of the *Critic*, was
enthusiastic: "Everybody is talking about this
strange and impressive story. . . . Mr. Norris, who,
I believe, is only twenty-eight, has a future before
him. As we are so fond of names of comparison in this
country, I should say that he might be called the
American Balzac."

The most influential as well as the most intelligent
review of *McTeague* was the lengthy paper which
William Dean Howells published in *Literature*,
March 24, 1899. The review was titled "A Case in
Point," for Howells found *McTeague* an illustration
of his statement made two weeks before that expansion in the field of the American novel was impending
and would come through foreign influence. Because
the review is a pertinent and thorough comment on

McTeague, because it reflects so typically Howells's encouragement of the young revolters, and because it has escaped the extensive reprinting of Howells's criticism, it demands quotation at length. "The question of expansion in American fiction . . . seems to me again palpitant in the case of a new book by a young writer, which I feel obliged to recognize as altogether a remarkable book. Whether we shall abandon the old-fashioned American ideal of a novel as something which may be read by all ages and sexes, for the European notion of it as something fit only for age and experience, and for men rather than women; whether we shall keep to the bonds of the provincial proprieties, or shall include within the imperial territory of our fiction the passions and the motives of the savage world which underlies as well as environs civilization, are points which this book sums up and puts concretely; and it is for the reader, not for the author, to make answer. There is no denying the force with which he makes the demand, and there is no denying the hypocrisies which the old-fashioned ideal of the novel involved. . . .

"It ought not to be strange that the impulse in this direction [the use of European methods] should come from California, where, as I am always affirming rather than proving, a continental American fiction began. I felt, or fancied I felt, the impulse in Mr. Frank Norris' *Moran*, and now in his *McTeague* I am so sure of it that I am tempted to claim the prophetic instinct of it. In the earlier book there were, at least, indications that forecast to any weather-wise eye a change from the romantic to the realistic temperament, and in the latter we have it suddenly, and with the overwhelming effect of a blizzard. It is saying both too much and too little to say that Mr. Norris has built his book on Zolaesque lines, yet Zola is the master of whom he reminds you in a certain epical conception of life. He reminds you of Zola also in his lingering love of the romantic, which indulges itself in the end in an anticlimax worthy of Dickens. He ignores as simply and sublimely as Zola any sort of nature or character beyond or above those of Polk Street in San Francisco, but within the ascertained limits he convinces you, two-thirds of the time, of his absolute truth to them. He does not, of course, go to Zola's lengths, breadths, and depths; but he goes far enough to difference his work from the old-fashioned American novel. . . ."

After a detailed summary of the story, Howells proceeds: "This is rendering in coarse outline the shape of a story realized with a fulness which the outline imparts no sense of. It abounds in touches of character at once fine and free, in little miracles of observation, in vivid insight, in simple and subtle expression. Its strong movement carries with it a multiplicity of detail which never clogs it; the subordinate persons are never shammed or faked; in the equality of their treatment their dramatic inferiority is lost; their number is great enough to give the feeling of a world revolving round the central figures without distracting the interest in these. Among the minor persons, Maria Macapa, the Mexican charwoman, whose fable of a treasure of gold turns the head of the Polish Jew Zerkow, is done with rare imaginative force. But all these lesser people are well done; and there are passages throughout the book that live strongly in the memory, as only masterly work can live. The one folly is the insistence on the love-making of those silly elders, which is [apparently introduced as an offset to the misery of the other love-making; the anticlimax is McTeague's abandonment in the alkali desert, handcuffed to the dead body of his enemy.

"Mr. Norris has, in fact, learned his lesson well, but he has not learned it all. His true picture of life is not true, because it leaves beauty out. Life is squalid and cruel and vile and hateful, but it is noble and tender and pure and lovely, too. By and by he will put these traits in, and then his powerful scene will be a reflection of reality; by and by he will achieve something of the impartial fidelity of the photograph. In the meantime he has done a picture of life which has form, which has texture, which has color, which has what great original power and ardent study of Zola give, but which lacks the spiritual light and air, the consecration which the larger art of Tolstoy gives. It is a little inhuman, and it is distinctly not for the walls of living-rooms, where the ladies of the family sit and the children go in and out. This may not be a penalty, but it is the inevitable consequence of expansion in fiction."[1]

*   *   *

NORRIS was, as a whole, well satisfied with the reception given *McTeague*. A month after its appearance he wrote to Marcosson: "I was very much afraid you would not approve of the dentist, and am rather un-

[1] Miss Mildred Howells has kindly permitted me to quote at length from this review.

certain as to his reception by the G. P. [General Public]. But so far the critics have been unusually good to me. . . . You saw every point I tried to make in *McTeague* and didn't misunderstand where many critics have been thick-witted enough."[1] He was particularly grateful to Howells for following up the praise he had accorded *McTeague* when he had read it in manuscript, by devoting his entire department in one issue of *Literature* to his review of the novel. In thanking him, Norris stated his attitude toward his comments: "Need I say how pleased and delighted I am over your review? . . . It has encouraged me more than anything that has ever been said of my work. . . . I agree in every one of your criticisms, always excepting the anticlimax, the 'death in the desert' business. I am sure that has its place. . . ."[2]

The adherence to the "'death in the desert' business" (odd echoing of a Browning phrase— Browning, whose melodrama had entered Norris's blood as naturally as his mother's milk) indicates how thoroughly Norris's method was conditioned by his story-teller's sense. He defended the anticlimax in spite of its departure from the realistic tone of the rest of the novel, because he favored it as a strong ending, a dramatic conclusion, a conception Zola-esque, Hugoesque, which gripped his youthful imagination just as it later appealed to Hollywood and the

[1] Letter to Isaac Marcosson dated March 14, 1899. In *Adventures in Interviewing*, N. Y.: John Lane, 1919, p. 234.
[2] Letter to William Dean Howells written late in March, 1899. In *The Life in Letters of William Dean Howells*, N. Y.: Doubleday, Doran, 1928, v. 2, p. 102. Quoted by permission of Miss Mildred Howells.

moving-picture public in Von Stroheim's *Greed*. One may object that this story-teller's sense which frequently leads to the excesses of melodrama is at odds with the demands of consummate realism, but there is no escaping the fact that it is this very imaginative spirit which makes *McTeague* more vital and hence more effective than the majority of naturalistic novels. It is the source of the fire which burns the story into the mind of the reader; it is the creative power which has kept *McTeague* alive while the multitude of its companion novels have died.

It is only when *McTeague* is viewed in the light of Norris's operating formula that one can analyze both its strength and its weakness. As he made clear in theory and in practice, his novels resulted from his "sense of fiction" operating upon reality as he saw it; both his perception and his expression he attributes to the retention of a youthful outlook on life; he absorbed reality from his immediate environment through eyes which still held the fresh directness of boyhood, and then manipulated it into stories by allowing his imagination free play. His handling of *milieu*, of character, and of plot are all explicable on such a basis. To Norris's eyes the commonplaces of Polk Street were uncommon, and through his touch the realistic background of his novel ceases to be drab; he catches the drama in monotony. So it was with his characters. He once remarked to a friend that his concern was with the "raw man," that he was not interested in the secondary emotions of human orchids, the orderly, well-conditioned, conventionally clad gentlemen, but he wanted "man with his shirt off, stripped to the buff and fighting for his life." Such a figure his imagination created by converting a college friend of exceptional physical prowess into an ignorant dentist, giving him the dress and habits of the people he had seen on Polk Street, magnifying his strength so that he might put up a better fight in his struggle against adversity, even equipping him with an atavistic instinct or "sixth sense" to aid him in the unequal struggle. The result is convincing because, as Norris points out, the author *feels* rather than *knows*. The force of his imagination working on reality likewise created his minor characters, some of which were more successful than others. He was fortunate in catching the dramatic value of a Maria Macapa, using his mother's memory of a servant girl who, when cornered, always resorted to the formula, "Had a flying squirrel and let him go." He was less fortunate in presenting the elderly lovers, patently to supply contrast for his story, characters whom he had watched in real life at the Cambridge boarding house where his mother ate.

The very enthusiasm which gave strength to his novel not only frequently led to the creation of grotesques but it resulted in excesses in other ways. Without being aware of it he accentuated the symbolism in the book until the emphasis on gold—the ten-dollar gold pieces, the huge gold tooth, the gilt paint on the Noah's ark, the golden sunshine on the floor, the metallic gold in the Panamint Hills, etc.—became strained in having McTeague's yellow canary in a gilt cage remain his companion even to his death in the desert. The reader's credulity is pushed to the limit when Norris has the bird still alive and occasionally singing after the dentist has carried it for three days through the heat of Death Valley. No doubt he felt that it added to the drama of the ending: "McTeague remained stupidly looking around him, now at the distant horizon, now at the ground, now at the half-dead canary chittering in its little gilt prison." When Norris was twitted by his friends for creating such a hardy canary, he defended himself with a smile.

"Well, I did say that the canary was *half* dead."

Although the chief virtue of *McTeague* lies in its portrayal of life, it owes no small part of its effectiveness to the skill with which Norris handled the formula of continental naturalism. This formula he had assimilated empirically, by reading novels rather than theory, by analyzing *L'Assommoir* and *Madame Bovary* rather than by studying *Le Roman experimental*. He recognized that the principles which he must follow were frankness, objectivity, the retention of an amoral attitude, and adherence to the implications of determinism. On this basis he made of *McTeague* the study of an individual in relation to his environment; an individual handicapped with a sluggish mentality and inherited tendencies towards viciousness when under the influence of drink; molded, tried, and defeated by circumstances, by forces greater than himself which he cannot even recognize. His life, like the lives around him, is completely comprehended in the total of environment and heredity, and the action which involves him is inexorable in its adherence to the principle of cause and effect and pitiless in the chance turns which it makes. As in the most common pattern of the

naturalistic novel, the conflict between the individual
and external forces leads to internal maladjustment,
misfortune, degeneration, and catastrophe; the whole .
is viewed through the eyes of the detached, realistic
chronicler.

There is no question that the influences of Zola on
McTeague are many and pervasive, but, because
Norris saw his subject at first hand and allowed himself freedom in treating it, the novel is not as imitative
as others of his works. Zola's most characteristic
novels deal with "the sociological study of background, with a multitude of characters dwarfed by
the *milieu*," rather than the psychological study of an
individual. In none of Zola's novels is found a sim-
plified, concentrated study of degeneration such as
Norris used in "the dentist"; the closest approaches
to it are in *L'Assommoir*, *Nana*, and *La Bête humaine*.
Probably these three novels guided Norris at this
time more than any others by Zola; one need hardly
point out that the detailed portrayal of the weakening
of Gervaise Macquart had much to do with the
treatment of McTeague and Trina. In addition, the
Zolaesque multiplication of details, emphasis on
strong sensory descriptions, particularly of smell,
and use of contrast and symbolism are apparent.

The influence of continental naturalism was not
confined to Zola, however; there are strong grounds
for assuming that Flaubert's *Madame Bovary* contributed to *McTeague*. That such should be true is
apparently paradoxical, for *Madame Bovary* is most
noted for its consummate style, while Norris evinced
throughout his writing an insensitivity to and lack
of care for stylistic artistry that would have made

Flaubert writhe. Excessive attention paid to Flaubert's style, however, has tended to overshadow appreciation of his story-telling; it was this latter quality which captured Norris, who read and reread *Madame Bovary* as one of his favorite books. So it is that in *McTeague* occasional incidents and methods show similarity; for instance, the mentalities and professions of McTeague and Charles Bovary, the argumentative natures of Marcus Schuler and Homais, and the descriptions of bourgeois festivals, such as the marriage of the principal characters, the theater performances, and the selling of the family furniture. Moreover, Norris is like Flaubert in his ability to focus on his major characters—dull people miraculously made interesting—to limit the *milieu* to its direct bearing on their action, and to build the plot organically about them. It is to the vital conception of Trina and McTeague, the convincing description of their surroundings, and the imaginative logic of the story as a whole that *McTeague's* claims to distinction must rest.

*   *   *

THE extrinsic importance of *McTeague* grew with history. Its appearance coincided with the crest of the most prolific revival of historical romances that the country has seen; *Janice Meredith, When Knighthood Was In Flower, Hugh Wynne, To Have and to Hold,* and *Richard Carvel* represented the best sellers of its day; the flood of tawdry and hastily written romantic novels had become so great that in England the *Academy*, deploring this artificiality and unoriginality, stated that the art of fiction had stood

still in America for fifty years. From such literary
conditions one would hardly have forecast that the
main trend of American fiction for the following
three decades would be naturalistic; on the other
hand, the majority of critics in 1899 looked upon
Norris's novel as a belated imitation of a school which
was already passing away in Europe and would never
gain a foothold in the United States. But the majority
of the critics were wrong; far from being in its death
throes, the school to which *McTeague* belonged was
here to stay. Once it was planted in American soil, it
took root, and despite its sickly and stunted growth
during the pre-war era when its gardeners were nearly
all drawn away by muckraking and reforming, it lived
to become the gnarled and hard-wooded tree which
completely overshadowed its neighbors after the war.
Much of the credit for planting it was due to Frank
Norris; he had written a pioneer novel.

Nor was the importance of *McTeague* confined to
its aid in introducing a specific school of writing. As
Howells pointed out in his review of *McTeague*, it
was a step forward in the expansion of American
fiction; it dealt with life in more serious and realistic
terms than did its companion novels; it defied the
attitude long prevalent in the country that fiction
must be both safe and optimistic enough to suit all
of the members of the American family. Moreover, it
appeared at a time when its influence was most
needed. Norris was not far from the truth when he
said that the young girl and the American center
table determined the standard of the nation's fiction.
It was inevitable that with the growth of literary
consciousness, this barrier should be broken down

and a larger field opened to the serious novelists. For some time the attackers had been forcing it at various points. One opening had been made in the preceding decade when the novels of Zola had achieved limited and frequently surreptitious circulation. As time went on, more and more foreign novels seeped into the United States, and, despite the objections of the righteous, the works of Flaubert, Tolstoy, Strindberg, Shaw, Hardy, Ibsen, and others made their way to the general public, which even while it stifled its native realists tolerated the frankness of these outside writers. The defense of imported novels by such liberal critics as William Dean Howells, Harry Thurston Peck, Jeannette Gilder, Percival Pollard, James Huneker, and Frederic Taber Cooper made the reading of them seem respectable. Native writers became adventuresome; by 1899 Howells was able to cite eight contemporary novelists who had dealt with "the greater problems of existence"[1] before he was forced to resort to naming *Uncle Tom's Cabin*, *The Scarlet Letter*, and *The Blithesdale Romance*.

Cautiously, sometimes almost timorously, the younger generation had advanced. As early as 1887 Harold Frederic looked sternly on rural life in *Seth's Brother's Wife*. In *Main-Travelled Roads* (1891) and

[1]Howells mentioned Fuller's *The Cliff Dwellers* and *With the Procession*, William Payne's *Money Captain*, Robert Herrick's *Gospel of Freedom*, the works of Stephen Crane and Harold Frederic, particularly *The Damnation of Theron Ware*, Mary Wilkins's *Jane Field*, George W. Cable's *Grandissimus*, and Henry James's *What Maysie Knew* and *The Awkward Age*. *Literature*, March 10, 1899.

Rose of Dutcher's Coolly (1895), Hamlin Garland, continuing in the footsteps of Kirkland and Howe, began to apply continental methods to the school of local color, coining for them the name "veritism" and defending them in *Crumbling Idols* (1894). The pioneer work of these men did much to kill the superficiality and widen the scope of treatment of rural life. Others turned their attentions to the cities. H. H. Boyeson introduced Tolstoyan realism into the drab pages of *The Mammon of Unrighteousness* (1891), *The Golden Calf* (1892) and *The Social Strugglers* (1893). More forceful were the ironic studies of Henry Blake Fuller, *The Cliff Dwellers* (1893) and *With the Procession* (1894), in which he cut deep into the rosy picture of mushroom Chicago. In 1897 Harold Frederic published *The Damnation of Theron Ware*, achieving realism and strength in a study of religion. In the immediate field of naturalism, Stephen Crane had published but not circulated the slight though effective *Maggie* in 1893 and had gained great popularity with his impressionistic study of the Civil War, *The Red Badge of Courage*, in which he showed a debt to Tolstoy rather than to Zola. His talent and his popularity make his contribution commensurate with that of Frank Norris.

Thus the movement towards expansion in native fiction had gained some headway by the time of *McTeague's* appearance. At that moment, however, it had met with a check in the revival of historical romance, an opposition which became almost completely victorious with the deaths and defections of the leading members of the new school. Fatalities seemed to pursue the movement. Boyeson died in

1895, Harold Frederic in 1898, and Stephen Crane in 1900—all of them comparatively young men. Hamlin Garland had turned his attention to Western adventure, and H. B. Fuller had forsworn realism, drawing within his shell to protect his sensitivity. Norris stood practically alone when he published *McTeague*, a book too formidable to be neglected and too strong to be forgotten. The novel was kept before the public by his rapid rise in popularity; he continued his experiments in naturalism in *The Epic of the Wheat*. In 1900 he engineered the publication of Theodore Dreiser's *Sister Carrie*, a novel which was started shortly after *McTeague* appeared, and with the publishing of Robert Herrick's *Web of Life* in the same year, it was clear that the movement would continue to live. Two years later Norris relinquished his leadership, but by that time there were others to carry it on, among them Theodore Dreiser, Robert Herrick, Stephen Graham Phillips, Upton Sinclair, and Jack London. William Dean Howells at that time stated his contribution: "Frank Norris' two mature novels [*McTeague* and *The Octopus*], one personal and one social, imparted the assurance of an American fiction so largely commensurate with American circumstance as to liberate it from the casual and occasional, in which it seemed lastingly trammelled."

Chapter 11: An Idea as Big as All Outdoors

I HAVE the idea of a series of novels buzzing in my head these days. I think there is a chance for somebody to do some great work with the West and California as a background . . . which will be at the same time thoroughly American. My idea is to write three novels around the one subject of *Wheat*. First, a story of California (the producer), second, a story of Chicago (the distributor), third, a story of Europe (the consumer), and in each to keep to the idea of this huge Niagara of wheat rolling from West to East. I think a big epic trilogy *could* be made out of such a subject, that at the same time would be modern and distinctly American. The idea is so big that it frightens me at times. but I have about made up my mind to have a try at it."[1] Thus, in the same letter in which Norris thanked William Dean Howells for his praise of *McTeague*, he revealed his plans for writing *The Epic of the Wheat*. The letter is but one of several in which he announced his scheme to his

[1] Letter to W. D. Howells written in the latter part of March, 1899. In *The Life in Letters of William Dean Howells*, N. Y.: Doubleday, Doran, 1928, v. 2, pp. 102-3. Quoted by permission of Miss Mildred Howells.

friends, all similarly contagious—almost incoherent—in their enthusiasm. One sees their youthful writer gripped by an idea which held him as completely as had the lead-soldier epics of his childhood, an idea which was not to relax its control on his imagination for the following two years, an idea which for the first time promised him the breadth of canvas suited to his talents. It was, in Norris's words, "an idea as big as all outdoors."

Before he wrote to Howells, Norris had talked his plans over with Bruce Porter, now living in the Benedict, diagonally across the Square from Norris's rooming house. Porter's arrival early in March did much to relieve the depression and loneliness which Norris had felt during the winter, for once more the writer made the artist his confidant, dropping in for a chat at odd hours when he saw a light in the studio. Porter had sympathized with Norris over the difficulties he faced in writing *A Man's Woman* and had shared his pleasure at the reception of *McTeague*. Now, when he asked what the plans were for the next novel, Norris said he was working on an idea. He was looking for an original subject, one which would measure up to the standard of *McTeague*, deal with the primitive, portray man's struggle with nature—elemental, all-pervasive; one which would utilize the genuine romance of the American frontier, a field which had found expression to date only in dime novels; one which would suit itself to the methods of naturalism, would have sociological significance. . . . Norris was now sure that he was at his best when writing of California, and yet he would write none of the bric-à-brac of the Bret Harte local colorists. . . .

Could his subject be widened enough to include the two most striking American themes, the conquering of the frontier and the growth of business enterprise—phenomena which had transformed the country in forty years? Why not write a series of novels illustrating the economic forces which were changing civilization from an agricultural to an industrial society? It was the greatest of all possible subjects, the most timely—and yet no one had attempted it.

They talked over the possibilities. What could be done to make these ideas concrete? Norris would need specific incidents which he could present as typical of general conflicts; they must be dramatic enough to serve as climaxes in narrative. He must build up a significant background, a panorama of American life. As they pooled their knowledge of California, suggestions came in abundance: the feud between the railroad and the farmers resulting in bloodshed in 1880, wheat ranches in the San Joaquin, gold mines in the Sierras, cattle ranches as big as Eastern states, missions and Spanish traditions, outlaws, grain ships filled with California wheat to relieve famine in India, vigilante committees, gunmen, cowboys, irrigation, barbecues. . . . Plans accepted, rejected. . . . One morning at five o'clock Norris burst into Porter's rooms and flung himself on the foot of the bed, exhausted but satisfied. He had made his leap in the dark an hour before, had cleared his entanglements and had his story and his form, and couldn't contain himself till daylight. From that moment he used Porter as a springboard; he'd sit for hours listening to the compelled memories of the California he had missed. Then, suddenly, he'd pounce! Here was what he wanted! Here was what he could use!

Norris planned to write three novels, an epic trilogy. The central character would be Wheat, typifying the force of nature—a subject as important and elemental as anything he could think of. "Indifferent, gigantic, resistless, it moved in its appointed grooves. Men, Lilliputians, gnats in the sunshine, buzzed impudently in their tiny battles, were born, lived through their little day, died, and were forgotten; while the Wheat . . . grew steadily under the night." Nature would produce the wheat, nature would triumph when the wheat reached its destination on the other side of the world. The epic would be built around three dramatic incidents typifying the production, the distribution, and the consumption of the wheat. The central episode of the novel of production would be the Mussel Slough affair, in which seven men were killed in a fight between the railroad and the farmers, an event symbolizing the conflict between distributors and producers, more widely the issue between the Trusts and the People, still more widely between centralized industry and individual production. It would be laid in the San Joaquin valley in California. The novel of distribution would tell of the effort of one man to corner the wheat market, would capitalize upon the romance and excitement of business, would concern the middleman in his manipulation of the world's produce. It would be laid in Chicago. The novel of consumption would picture the relief of a famine as the wheat reaches its destination, it would illustrate the process of expansion of trade and world distribution, it would show how the resources of one continent could be used to feed another. It would be laid in Europe. Thus Norris worked out his plan so that he could use three situations which contained an abundance of drama and could place his action in three *milieus* with which he was familiar; he had spent twelve years in California, fourteen years in Chicago, and two years in Europe. The reasons for Norris's enthusiasm over the trilogy are apparent when one notices the almost fortuitous manner which his scheme fitted together in its many parts. Moreover, his enthusiasm was justified, for he had hit upon an idea which, in spite of its grandiose proportions, affirmed his time and environment to a degree surpassing anything attempted before in American fiction.

One morning Mr. Phillips was confronted in his office by the young enthusiast, who, almost trembling with excitement, told him of his plans for the trilogy. Mr. Phillips was impressed, and so was Mr. McClure; they offered to continue Norris's salary while he made a trip West to obtain material for the first novel of the series. In a short time he had cleared the manuscript of *A Man's Woman* from his desk and was ready to start. He wrote to a friend at Cambridge:

"I am leaving for California Monday next to be gone, very likely, until fall. It has happened quite unexpectedly but is the result of a talk I had with the firm here. They believe with me that the big American novel is going to come out of the West—California. . . . I've got an idea that's as big as all outdoors and McClure is going to back me up while I put it through. (And me pay goes marching on the whiles.)

It involves a very long, a very serious, and perhaps a very terrible novel. It will be all about the San Joaquin wheat raisers and the Southern Pacific, and I guess we'll call it The Octopus—catch on? I mean to study the whole question as faithfully as I can and then write a hair-lifting story. There's the chance for the big, epic, dramatic thing in this, and I mean to do it thoroughly—get at it from every point of view, the social, agricultural, and political—just say the last word on the R. R. question in California. I am going to study the whole thing *on the ground* and come back here in the winter and make a novel out of it. What do you think of the idea?"[1]

Just before his departure Norris again suffered an attack of the fever which had kept him weak throughout the winter. He left New York too ill to do more than sit gaunt and shaken in the hansom that carried him and Bruce Porter to the station. Established in his section, he revived to a grin:

"Bruce, see that?" as he waved a little swagger stick between his hands. "I'm going to walk down Sutter Street, swinging that!—and they'll say 'That's Frank Norris!'"

*   *   *

IT WAS good to be back in San Francisco. On the seventh of May, Norris wrote of his contentment to Ernest Peixotto and his wife, who were traveling in Europe. (The unusual salutation illustrates Norris's habit of giving pet names to his friends. Thus, Peixotto was Billy Magee—the Billy after Du Maurier's "Little Billee," the Magee intuitive.)

[1]Letter to Harry Wright dated April 5, 1899.

"MY DEAR OLEMAN AND MRS. BILLY MAGEE:

"I wanted to write you aboard your steamer to say *bon voyage* but of course I have forgotten the boat's name. It's a wonder I don't forget my own name these days, I'm having such a bully good time. Feel just as if I was out of doors playing after being in school for years. Jeannette and I spent the whole afternoon on the waterfront yesterday among the ships (*on* and all over *one* of them), came back and had tea and pickled ginger on the balcony of our own particular Chinese restaurant over the Plaza, and wound up by dining at Luna's Mexican restaurant 'over in the Quarter.'

"The Wheat stuff is piling up B I G. Everybody is willing to help and *McTeague* is soon to be perpetrated in England. . . . I may be here longer than I first expected. Mebbe till late in the fall, and I dunno why I should not write my immortal worruk at a wheat ranch anyway. Tell Burgess I'm full of ginger and red pepper and am getting ready to stand up on my hind legs and yell *big*. . . .

"I have seen Hodgson—my buccaneer chap—and I have gone (naturally not alone) out to the Presidio Reservation and sat down and wallowed in the grass on just the spot I told you about and done everything just as I had planned we should and I'm just having the best time that ever was—*voila tout*.

"Goodbye—or *au revoir*, whichever it is to be.
                                      "NORRIS."[1]

(He invariably signed his letters "Norris," no matter how intimate they were. He did so as a gesture in the

[1] Letter to Ernest Peixotto written May 7, 1899.

game, just as he frequently gave his characters last
names only—Vandover, Annixter, McTeague, Presley, Osterman, Vanamee.)

Norris first turned to the material in the Mechanics'
Library and to the files of the San Francisco *Chronicle*
to dig out the facts concerning the Mussel Slough
tragedy, which he planned to use as the central
episode of his production novel. In the early seventies
settlers had moved into the waste lands of the Mussel
Slough district, lying in the east part of what was
then Tulare County; and had in a decade through
hard labor, irrigation, and extensive improvement
transformed the region into productive farms. The
titles to a portion of their property were in dispute,
for the Southern Pacific Railroad, which had built
a line through the district on a questionable franchise,
claimed the odd-numbered sections on either side of
their road under a Congressional act of 1868. From
the first the settlers had recognized the rights of the
railroad, for that corporation in inviting them to open
up the district had indicated that the railroad sections would eventually be sold to them at the rate
on undeveloped property, an average of $2.50 an
acre. After the region had been developed, the railroad
regraded their sections and notified the ranchers that
the lands were for sale to anyone at $25 to $30 an
acre. They offered nothing for the improvements
which had made the land valuable. The ranchers
fought the corporation bitterly; they formed a
Settler's League of six hundred members, they peti-
tioned Congress, they conducted expensive lawsuits.
The railroad, long experienced in political lobbying,
defeated them at every turn. The feeling in the region

grew intense; the ranchers asserted that the corporation planted insolent agents in their midst, tightened its monopolies on banking and the press, and cut down their profits with arbitrary freight rates. A crisis was reached when, on the eleventh of May, 1880, the federal marshal and three deputies rode into a mass meeting of settlers at Hanford and asked for a conference with the ranch leaders. Planning to take advantage of the absence of the men from their homes, they had come to serve papers to depose them. During the conference a shot was fired, by whom no one knows; in the confusion the deputies shot indiscriminately; during the fight six men were killed instantly and a seventh was mortally wounded. Among the dead were two deputies and five ranchers, only two of whom were armed. The people held the railroad entirely to blame, and, as time went on, the event was magnified into a massacre of innocents, victims to the greed of the corporation.

When Chris Evans and John Sontag appeared on the scene ten years later, they were hailed by many as righteous avengers of the men killed at Hanford. Each of them had a grievance against the railroad; Evans had been ruined when his farm was taken from him after the Mussel Slough affair, and Sontag, who had been injured while working as a brakeman, limped as the result of a premature discharge from a company hospital. When the two men were accused of committing four train robberies near Visalia, they fought their way out of Chris Evans's house and hid in the Sierras, where, with the aid of sympathetic ranchers, they evaded the man-hunting posses for nearly a year, twice making trips into the valley to see the Evans family. Finally they were cornered; Sontag was killed and Evans was captured, but after having been convicted for murder, he broke jail and was again free. A year later, tricked into visiting his home in the belief that one of his children was ill, he was recaptured and sent to San Quentin. In the career of Chris Evans, whose exploits had been assimilated into the saga of the conflict with the railroad, Norris saw a wealth of dramatic material, parts of which he planned to use in portraying the misfortunes of Dyke, a discharged locomotive engineer.

Although the Mussel Slough affair was to be used as the central incident of his novel, Norris did not intend to present it with historical accuracy. Just as he planned to turn the "sandlappers" into landowners operating on a large scale, he intended to present his locale as a rich wheat-bearing country. His search for large wheat ranches hardly led him in the direction of Hanford, for, although wheat had been one of the staple products of that district in 1880, it had since been partially supplanted by other crops. Norris watched the wheat grow elsewhere. Although there is a spurious story that he made an extended visit to a Miller and Lux ranch near Visalia, the fact is that he spent little time in the San Joaquin valley in his search for material. He apparently visited the town of Tulare, which he pictures as Bonneville, he possibly attended a rabbit drive, which he used as a feature of the valley life, but he created the country of *The Octopus* by ingeniously transferring a section of San Benito County to the lower San Joaquin, in the process flattening out the hills, enlarging the estates, and moving a Spanish mission over the Coast Range. Thus he concentrated his California.

Not long after Norris arrived in the West to collect data for "The Squid," as he nicknamed *The Octopus*, he was invited to visit Santa Anita Rancho, near Hollister, in the Coast Range some hundred miles south of San Francisco. The invitation came to him through the Peixottos, who were close friends of Mr. and Mrs. Gaston Ashe; Mrs. Ashe, *nee* Dulce Bolado, had inherited a ten-thousand-acre estate, one of the original Spanish land grants, more than one half of which her husband was farming in wheat. On the Santa Anita ranch Norris saw all of the steps of the growth of the wheat except the planting, which, however, was described to him in detail; and when, during the harvest, he helped on the sacking platform of one of the first combined harvesters and threshers, he felt that he had become one of the cogs in the machinery of production. There was wheat in abundance, for as far as he could see from the hills back of Tres Piños, the valley was covered with fields of grain.

Life at Santa Anita Rancho was so pleasant that Norris's stay of a week lengthened out to nearly two months. The ranch house was the rendezvous for young people from San Francisco who devoted most of their time to camping out, horseback riding, and deer-hunting. As Norris was less active than the other visitors and preferred conversation to deer-hunting, he spent much of his time eating green apples, smoking his pipe, and discussing politics and farming with Gaston Ashe, who was very fond of

arguing. When he discovered that his twenty-year-old
hostess, who had studied and traveled abroad, was a
devoted admirer of Walter Pater, George Meredith,
and Austin Dobson, he entered into lively arguments
over naturalism, praised Zola to the skies, and insisted that "only the elect had nerves" and that "if
a book had entrails in it, it did not have to have
style." He was always on the alert for story material,
and not only used both his host and hostess in "The
Squid" but persuaded Dulce Bolado to tell him
stories about her Spanish forebears so that he would
be able to introduce them into his book. It was in
this manner that he picked up the tales of early
California which Presley was to hear from the centen-
arian at Solatari's in Guadalajara, of De La Cuesta,
Governor Alvarado, and the bandit, Jesus Tejada.

As Norris stayed on at the ranch, his book began
to take form. Here was all the raw material which
he could desire. A dance given in the huge Bolado
barn, attended by everyone who lived within a day's
riding distance, suggested an entire chapter. The
Spanish background could be made concrete by introducing a mission into his synthetic picture, so he
made a number of trips to the near-by San Juan
Bautista which he called San Juan. The old Spanish
town of San Juan Bautista, seat of the mission,
became Guadalajara in the novel. The idea of using
a flower-seed ranch as the background for his
Vanamee-Angéle idyll came to him as, from the
mission gardens, he saw Morse's Seed Ranch spread
out between San Juan and Hollister—or, perhaps,
the sight of the blooms suggested the romance to
him. When he returned to San Francisco he had

more ideas than he could effectively use in one novel.

After four months spent in California, Norris was ready to return to New York, his mind filled with impressions for his panorama. He remained in San Francisco as long as he could, thankful for each additional day which kept him in the company of his friends, Jeannette Black, Charles Norris, and his mother. He even submitted to a modicum of lionizing; when his mother introduced him to the members of a literary club of the city, he was amused at the earnestness of the prominent member who, addressing him fervently with clasped hands, gushed, "Oh, Mr. Norris, *when* did you first *know* that you had this *wonderful* power?" He chuckled as he thought of how he would use her as Mrs. Cedarquist in "The Squid." When it came time to say good-bye, it was particularly hard to leave Jeannette Black; they had been engaged for nearly two years, and the prospects for marriage in the near future were still slim. How could one marry on a reader's salary supplemented by a semiannual trickle from book royalties? Miss Black, realizing the difficulty, had started training to become a nurse so that she would have a means of support.

When he reached New York there still remained a little work to be done in completing the documentation, interviewing, corresponding, reading. At this time he talked with Collis P. Huntington, who gave him the other side of the railroad controversy. The progress of his work in November is shown in his letter to Marcosson written early in that month:

"If you have been involved in politics recently, perhaps you can give me a pointer or two. I am in a beautiful 'political muddle' myself in *The Octopus*,

which I have just started. You know this involves, in
California, the fight between the farmers of the San
Joaquin and the Southern Pacific Railroad. I was
out there this summer getting what stuff I needed,
but I did not think that I should need political notes.
Now, I find that I do, and should have got 'em long
ago. I have gone to work on this and have found out
a good deal about politics and political 'deals' but
I want to find out more.

"The situation in my story is this: There is a certain group of farmers who, despairing of ever getting
fair freight rates from the Railroad or of electing a
board of Railroad Commissioners by fair means
themselves, set about gaining their ends by any
means available. What they want to do is to cause
the nomination and election of railroad commissioners
of their own choosing, with the idea that these commissioners will make proper reductions in freight
rates. They are prepared to spend a very large amount
of money to accomplish this. They want to put the
deal through among themselves, because they have
tried to organize the rest of the farmers in the State
and have failed. I think they form a kind of a ring
of six or eight men. They are all fairly rich men,
but are in a pretty desperate situation, the railroad
having pushed them to just about the limit.

"Can you tell me just about how they would go
about to get their men in? Do you think it *could*
be done at all? What I am anxious to get hold of are
the *details* of this kind of game, the lingo, and the
technique, etc., but at the same time, want to understand it very clearly. . . .

". . . I am going back *definitely* now to the style of

McTeague and stay with it right along. I've been sort of feeling my way ever since the *Moran* days and getting a twist of myself. Now I think I know where I am at and what game I play the best. The Wheat series will be straight naturalism with all the guts I can get into it."[1]

★   ★   ★

AFTER his material was in hand, Norris spent a full year in writing *The Octopus*. In working on his earlier novels he had been guided by the evolution of the story, but now he assumed the attitude of a research worker, carefully planning his work beforehand. He wrote plot summaries, he worked out an "index sheet" for each character, he tabulated and arranged his notes, he made a map of the country where his action was to take place. He played the game of organization with zest, pleased with the formidable piles of notes, gleefully enthusiastic about the map. He went about his work methodically and scientifically, for he was writing "a novel with a purpose."

In his essay, *The Novel with a "Purpose,"* Norris discusses the methods and principles which he followed in writing *The Octopus*. He divides novels into three sorts, those that tell something, as *The Three Musketeers*, those that show something, as *Romola*, and those that prove something, as *Les Misérables*. The third, which is to him the highest form, is the sociological novel which "draws conclusions from a whole congeries of forces, social tendencies, race impulses" and "devotes itself not to the study of

[1]In *Adventures in Interviewing*, N. Y.: John Lane, 1919, pp. 237-8.

men but of man." This conception of "proving
things" in fiction had been presented by Zola in his
discussion of the "experimental novel"; the French
naturalist had maintained that the novelist could
enter the field of social science; that, by making
himself aware of the laws, biological, social, and
economic, which control mankind, he could write
enlarged case studies revealing "the Truth"; that
he could conduct an experiment with puppets created
from observation which would tell his readers what
man is and how he behaves. Thus the novel becomes
a study in behaviorism. Stripped of its scientific
assumptions, Zola's definition says again what has
come to be generally accepted, that in good fiction,
plotting as well as background and character moves
towards the inevitable.

To understand what he was about, it is necessary
to note carefully Norris's interpretation of the purpose of fiction. In his eyes the novel with a purpose
did not attempt to manipulate a story to prove a
theory but rather attempted to present the evidence
from which theories could be deduced. On no other
issue was Norris more outspoken than that the
novelist should avoid propaganda; he must tell his
story and let theory take care of itself. Norris wrote
serious novels because he believed that he could
picture life realistically. He wrote the novel with a
purpose because he was convinced of the futility and
falsity of the novel without a purpose—"the amusing
novels, the novels that entertain. The juggler in
spangles, with his balancing pole and gilt ball, does
this—a flippant paper-covered thing of swords and
cloaks, to be carried on a railway journey and to be

thrown out of the window when read, together with the sucked oranges and peanut shells." He felt that he must tell the truth because it was apparent that most of his contemporaries were telling lies.

In writing "the novel of purpose" Norris placed himself in a dangerous position. Would he remain a novelist or would he become a propagandist? Few people can point out the truth about society without succumbing to the temptation to try to improve its conditions; and the naturalist, who concerns himself with misfortune and maladjustment, is particularly likely to end up a reformer. Once he becomes one, he ceases to be objective, thus forsaking the cardinal principle of his school. Such was the nature of the capitulation of Zola, who abandoned the principles which he had formulated to become a reformer, a novelist with a message. Such was the fate of many of his American followers, of Jack London, Stephen Graham Phillips, Upton Sinclair, Robert Herrick. . . . The naturalistic movement carried within it the seeds of its own destruction.

Norris was not only writing a type of novel which easily degenerated into polemics, but he was riding the crest of a wave which was to carry most of the American naturalists of the following fifteen years straight upon the shoals of "muckraking." Moreover, his personal contacts were such as would tend to turn him in that direction. As he wrote *The Octopus*, he was living in a hotbed of incipient muckrakers. Before he had left San Francisco, one of his mother's friends had carried on a campaign designed to persuade him to introduce a "social sense" into his novels, hoping that he would help to solve the problems of

society. Through her influence he had met friends in
New York with similar interests, the most notable
of whom was the Reverend W. S. Rainsford, the
energetic rector of St. George's. Rainsford not only
interested him in his settlement work among the
poor but persuaded him to give talks to his young
people's meetings. He faced a most insidious attack
at the office of *McClure's Magazine,* where he worked
beside Ray Stannard Baker, Ida Tarbell, and Lincoln
Steffens, under whose bombardment the muckraking
movement was about to be inaugurated. At the same
time, "Teddy" Roosevelt was getting a good grip
on his big stick and Congress was busy muzzling the
trusts; in a short time the entire nation would be
doing its best to make reformers out of its novelists.

That Norris was aware of the danger he faced is
clear from his discussion of purpose in the novel. "It
is important as an end and also as an ever-present
guide. For the writer it is important only as a note to
which his work must be attuned. The moment, however, that the writer becomes really and vitally interested in his purpose his novel fails. Here is a strange
anomaly. Let us suppose that Hardy, say, should be
engaged upon a story which had for purpose to show
the injustices under which the miners of Wales are
suffering. It is conceivable that he could write a story
that would make the blood boil with indignation. But
he himself, if he is to remain an artist, if he is to write
his novel successfully, will, as a novelist, care very
little about the iniquitous labor system of the Welsh
coal mines. It will be to him as impersonal a thing as
the key is to the composer of a sonata. As a man Hardy
may or may not be vitally concerned in the Welsh

coal miner. That is quite unessential. But as a novelist, as an artist, his sufferings must be for him a matter of the mildest interest. They are important, for
they constitute his keynote. They are *not* interesting
for the reason that the working out of his *story*, its
people, episodes, scenes, and pictures is for the moment the most interesting thing in all the world to
him, exclusive of everything else."

How far would Norris carry out his theory in practice? As one reviews the evidence, he finds little to
justify an assumption that Norris would turn social
reformer with his fellows. He was interested in stories,
not reforms. He was comparatively untouched by
suffering and misery, and his sense of the dramatic
outweighed his sympathies whether he was concerned
with a murder, a fight between farmers and railroad
employees, or the torturing of a cat. By nature he was
almost as detached from his subjects as was Flaubert.
He was much more a story-teller than a social philoso-
pher, and there is every reason to believe that he
would have remainded so.

The fact remains, however, that *The Octopus*, as
Norris worked it out, did lend itself to a propagandic
interpretation, which was furthered by a misreading
of the novel on the part of a public which asked for an
attack on the railroads. However, *The Octopus* was
not written to reveal the injustice of the railroads or
to attack the control of the trusts. We have seen that
Norris approached it as an integral part of the epic
of the wheat and selected the railroad-farmer issue
because it promised him the most drama. His purpose
in *The Octopus* was to reveal the working of economic
forces, to portray the clash between producer and

distributor, and to picture a segment of American civilization. It is very probable that his personal attitude toward the central conflict agreed more completely with Shelgrim's than with Presley's; he had far more in common with the employer than with the anarchist. His failure in his intention of presenting the conflict objectively, in stating both sides of the issue, was not the result of a social theory but of a love for stupendous action. Once he considered the railroad as an octopus, crushing out the lives of those whom it reached with its tentacles, the dramatic possibilities piled up; as he discovered injustice after injustice in the California records, he added them to the story to strengthen his climax. The railroad must be made as powerful as possible in order to put up a good fight. It is once more the apotheosis of force.

With his general conception in mind, Norris next turned his attention to his characters. The novel with a purpose "must penetrate deep into the motives and characters of typemen, men who are composite pictures of a multitude of men. It must do this because of the nature of its subject, for it deals with elemental forces, motives that stir whole nations. These cannot be handled as abstractions in fiction. . . . The social tendencies must be expressed by means of analysis of the characters of the men and women who compose that society." In writing this epic novel, then, his typemen must represent a cross-section of the society of the period—that is, central California of 1880. They must be numerous enough to give substance to his picture, and yet distinct enough to be individuals. Thus he made a list of the principal characters of the

novel, some thirty in number; ten farmers ranging
from the leader, Magnus Derrick, to the immigrant
tenant, Hooven; five railroad men, including the
president of the road, a renegade politician, an editor,
a cowboy with a grudge, and the local representative;
eight women variously aligned in their interests from
the dairy maid, Hilma Tree, to the city clubwoman,
Mrs. Cedarquist; the older Spanish settlers centering
about the mission, Father Sarria, Angéle Varian,
and by alliance Vanamee; a misused engineer who
turns bandit, a trouble-breeding saloon keeper, and
Presley, a writer from the outside world who ties
the action together. Naturally, he could not hope to
make all of these characters live. Some of them were
to become distinct individuals, most notably Magnus
Derrick, Annixter, Hilma Tree, and Dyke; some
were to remain types without individualities, serving
to further the action or supply contrast; a few were
to be no more than symbols, failing to take on
semblance of flesh and blood *The Octopus* was to
emerge as an imperfect synthesis, a canvas on which
appeared clear-cut figures as well as blotches, a ragout
in which many ingredients formed a powerful dish,
parts of which are nutritious, others indigestible.

For each person in the novel, Norris prepared a
character sketch which included notes on the physical appearance, the personality, whatever symbolic
value there might be, and the labeling phrases which
he intended to repeat, like Homeric refrains, whenever the character appeared in the story. A sheaf of
notes remains to illustrate his method; thus we know
Annixter before the novel was begun. "P.s. 13-14-15.
Annixter. A male cast of countenance. The jaw heavy,

the lower lip thrust out. The chin masculine and deeply cleft. . . . Stiff yellow hair, always in disorder. A little tuft of it always standing out from his crown like a feather on an Indian's scalp.—Continually seeking an argument. 'In a way it is and then again in a way it isn't.' David Copperfield. His stomach— eats *dried prunes*. A ferocious worker. Extremely inconsistent. Obstinate, contrary, dictatorial, wilful, perverse. Great executive ability. Very shrewd, far-sighted, suspicious. Admiration for Presley. The two great friends. Accepts no direct statement with modification—*a woman hater. Contradicts everything. 'Fool feemale girls'* to take up a man's time. Suspicious that all women are 'trying to get hold on him.' Fear of involving himself in a petticoat mess. Clumsy when women are about. Talks about his 'nature' and his stomach. His worst insult is to call a man *a Pip*. Spits with wonderful accuracy. 'Whit.' Hates Derrick's cat. Belligerent, truculent, turbulent, irascible. 'Hooks, nails and fetters,' 'Horse, foot, and dragoon,' 'lock, stock, and barrel'."[1]

As Norris worked on his *dramatis personæ*, he furthered his realistic aim by using his acquaintances as prototypes for characters. In so doing he found that he was most successful when he fixed upon some oddity of manner or some pronounced trait of character of a friend and then proceeded without further reference to his original. This selective method made it possible for him to draw both Vanamee in *The Octopus* and Corthill in *The Pit* supposedly from characteristics of Bruce Porter; on the other hand, in Annixter he formed a composite character, who

[1] Notes in the possession of Charles G. Norris.

possibly inherited his argumentativeness from Gaston
Ashe and his appearance and some mannerisms from
Seymour Waterhouse. He drew upon other acquaintances to varying degrees: James J. F. Archibald
may have suggested both the appearance and personality of Osterman; Dulce Bolado's literary tastes
but not her youth were transferred to Annie Derrick;
Rita Sandé, the pretty Spanish nurse at the Santa
Anito Rancho, became Angéle Varian; traditions of
Norris's own family and a portrait of his maternal
grandfather aided in the creation of Magnus Derrick;
a prominent member of a San Francisco literary
club was caricatured in Mrs. Cedarquist; Norris's
impressions of C. P. Huntington are said to have
furnished the appearance as well as the ideas of
Shelgrim; Chris Evans suggested Dyke in actions
rather than in figure; and a boyhood friend of Bruce
Porter became S. Behrman. Doubtless there were
other "instigations from reality" among the actors
of "The Squid," for Norris always described real
people when he could do so. Presley, whom many
have considered to be a portrait of Norris himself,
emerged almost entirely as a literary device without
marked personality, an organism upon which to
register impressions. Through him Norris put forward
his theories of romance and reality, expanded his
conception of the epic nature of Western life, and
ridiculed the divorcing of literature from reality.
Once more he adapted an actual incident to his uses
when, in describing the composition and sale of the
poem, *The Toilers*, by Presley, he clearly referred to
The Man with the Hoe, published by Edwin Markham
in the San Francisco *Examiner* on January 8, 1899,

and reprinted and discussed in numerous journals of America and Europe.

In one instance at least, Norris thought of his characters first as symbols rather than types or individuals. This confusion of methods explains the presence of Angéle Varian and to some extent Vanamee. His notes on Angéle state that she is to be "a contrast with Hilma. The Embodiment of Night —pallid gold and pale carnation. She is the symbol of the wheat." Under Hilma Tree: "Contrast Hilma and Angéle. Hilma is always seen in the sun. Angéle at night under the moon. One hale, honest, radiant. The other mysterious, troublous, perplexing. Hilma is the embodiment of day." Angéle is to die, leaving a daughter who is to appear to Vanamee on the same night in which the wheat comes up. The effect is to be heightened by the blossoming of the flowers in the seed garden. With the return of Angéle in the form of her daughter, the grave will be vanquished. "Life out of death, eternity rising from out of dissolution. Angéle was not the symbol but the proof of immortality." So with the fecundity of the earth, with the wheat, with all creation. . . . Angéle is to be drawn from the flower bed by Vanamee's will power. Here Norris planned to use a subject which had long fascinated him. He had listened to Bruce Porter discuss mysticism, hypnotism, thought transference. He had been impressed by Du Maurier's use of Svengali's powers in *Trilby*. He had endowed McTeague with a sixth sense, an intuitive awareness of danger. Now, again, he planned to exploit an unnatural sense in a dramatic manner, giving to Vanamee the power of attracting others by thought transference. It would be another power, the force of will, symbolic of the force which brought the wheat to the surface. Finally, the Vanamee-Angéle incidents would furnish an idyllic element to contrast with the stark tragedy. Once more Norris attempted to create one extreme to balance another; it was to be one of the major mistakes of the book, an extraneous and formless blur on the canvas, the most indigestible portion of the ragout.

With purpose and characters in mind, Norris now completed his action. "It is impossible to deny that the *story*, as a mere story, is to the story-writer the one great object of attention." Here he was almost uniformly successful, for only in a few places did he fail to sustain his dramatic action. He started with a slow approach, worked into gradual development, and then drove home a strong climax. Dyke's dash across the valley and his fight from the captured locomotive, the ball in Annixter's barn, and the last stand of the ranchers in the ditch in the wheat fields he developed with his utmost skill. The chief difficulty was that as he built up the complex situation, planning for a "great, smashing climax," his impetus became so great that it was difficult for him to stop. The fight by the ranchers was effective, the downfall of Magnus Derrick was effective; but the movement carried on beyond the melodramatic pathos of Mrs. Hooven starving on the streets of San Francisco while railroad barons ate ortolan patties and discussed art, to end with a final hollow crash in the stifling of the arch-villain, S. Behrman, beneath a deluge of wheat—a melodramatic conclusion rivaled only in the works of Dickens and Hugo.

His action he placed in a background diverse enough to represent the lives and activities of his entire society. He made his canvas swarm with actualities—"plowing, planting, harvesting, sheep-herding, merry-making, rabbit-killing, love, labor, birth, death. . . ." His feasts are Homeric, prodigious, earthy. He portrayed the fecundity of nature with some of the boldness of Zola in *La Terre;* he described the planting as "the long stroking caress, vigorous, male, powerful, for which the Earth seemed panting. There, under the sun and under the speckless sheen of the sky, the wooing of the Titan began, the vast primal passion, the two world-forces, the elemental Male and Female, locked in a colossal embrace, at grapples in the throes of an infinite desire, at once terrible and divine, knowing no law, untamed, savage, natural, sublime." With all outdoors to work in, he succeeded by his enthusiasm and by his keenness of vision in making his action significant, in giving the feeling that his subject was elemental and all-embracing.

Norris wrote with little revision on large foolscap sheets, in a fine handwriting, six to eight hundred words to the page. The minor corrections for clarity and additional emphasis which he made on this first draft were not numerous enough to make typing necessary. He made no attempt at subtlety, and his rhythm was spontaneous; the effect of his diction is cumulative rather than detailed. His attitude towards words is well illustrated by the postscript of a letter to Marcosson. "I re-open this letter to thank you for a new phrase. I want that expression 'majestic din,' and you must give it to me. Have been working

for just the idea the words suggest and now, Eureka!"[1]
His style became direct and crisp as dramatic tension
increased, but when drumming his "bourdon" he
often deadened his effect with dithyrambic pounding
on words. At other times, his piling up of epithet in
a Whitmanesque manner gave the desired effect; such
moments caused Howells to call him "a poet among
the California wheat-fields." His style bears the virtues as well as the vices of an uncontrolled enthusiasm.

In September, 1900, Norris reviewed his labors:
"The Squid is nearing conclusion. Hooray! I can see
the end. It is the hardest work I ever have done in
my life, a solid year of writing and four months'
preparation—bar two months—and I think the best
thing far and away I ever did. You've no idea of the
outside work on it. I've been in correspondence with
all kinds of people during its composition, from the
Traffic Manager of a Western railroad to the sub-
deputy-assistant of the Secretary of Agriculture at
Washington. Also in connection with it all I've helped
run and work a harvester in the San Joaquin—that
is, I've helped on the sacking platform—but of course
you don't know where that is. Well, the thing is
mostly done now and I know when it slumps and
I know when it strikes and I think the strikes are the
most numerous and important. I know that in the
masses I've made no mistake. You will find some
things in it that—for me—are new departures. It is
the most romantic thing I've ever done. One of the
secondary sub-plots is pure romance—oh, even
mysticism, if you like, a sort of allegory—I call it

[1]Letter to Isaac Marcosson, dated November 15, 1899.
Adventures in Interviewing, N. Y.: John Lane, 1919, p. 236.

the allegorical side of the wheat subject—and the fire in it is the Allegory of the Wheat. The movement of the whole business is very slow at first—don't really get under weigh till after the first 15,000 words (it's about 200,000 words long), then, with the first pivotal incident it quickens a bit, and from there on I've tried to accelerate it steadily till at the last you are—I hope—just whirling and galloping and tearing along till you come *bang!* all of a sudden to a great big crushing END, something that will slam you right between your eyes and knock you off your feet—all this *I hope* for. *Sabe?* There will be about twenty characters in the book, ten really important, ten (about) secondary, and five or six mere supers. In the front matter I am going—maybe—to insert a list of *dramatis personæ* and—this *surely*—a map of the locality. . . ."[1]

✳   ★   ★

FORTUNE was kind to Norris during the year in which he worked on "The Squid," for she brought him a new position and a wife. His association with the McClure magazine and syndicate was terminated when, late in 1899, Doubleday and McClure severed their business connections, and Doubleday, with the aid of Walter Hines Page, Henry Lanier, J. L. Thompson, and S. A. Everitt, founded an independent publishing firm, Doubleday, Page & Company, which opened its offices on the third floor at 34 Union Square on the first day of the new century. When Norris was offered a position as special reader for the new house, he accepted gladly. The change

[1] Letter to Isaac Marcosson, dated September 13, 1900. *Adventures in Interviewing*, N. Y.: John Lane, pp. 238–9.

was of advantage to him in several ways: he could abandon journalism permanently, leaving *McClure's Magazine* just as it was starting the muckraking campaign; his new duties promised to keep him in close touch with contemporary fiction and its writers; and the increase in salary assured him of a more settled financial status.

Marriage became a possibility when Frank Doubleday arranged to have Norris's royalties paid in monthly rather than semiannual installments, which with his salary assured him of a regular monthly income of one hundred and twenty-five dollars. He at once sent for Jeannette Black and, on the twelfth of January, 1900, they were quietly married at St. George's. They celebrated their honeymoon by moving into a little suite of rooms at the top of The Anglesea, rooms which had once been occupied by Oliver Herford, later by Gelett Burgess, and, during the previous winter, by Ernest Peixotto. Norris was very happy. He wrote to Peixotto, "It doesn't seem quite real, yet, but there's a good long time to find it out in." In his letters he told of his plans. "As for me, *on fait son petit chemin tout doucement,* though you might have gathered that from the fact that I can afford to be married. The books have done fairly well this year, well enough so that we have quite a bit ahead in case of emergency, which is bully. . . . It sure does seem strange to remember last winter and to think how far away it seemed then!"[1] "You are quite right as to the charm of old Washington Square in the summer time. We are just beginning to get a foretaste of it now, and there are indications of leaves

[1]Letter to Ernest Peixotto dated February 16, 1900.

on almost all the trees. . . . We are coming back [to San Francisco] *sure*, when, it is hard to say. Just as soon as Literychoore will allow us."[1]

Friends who were invited to their apartment found that the couple made a game of housekeeping, and, as their acquaintances grew in number, they dined out frequently and met many literary people. Hamlin Garland's notes tell of a dinner at Juliet Wilbur Tompkins's home, at which the Norrises were present. "Tall, slender, with prematurely graying hair and fine, candid, humorous glance, he looked the poet rather than the realistic novelist. . . . We at once ranked Norris with Edward McDowell as one of the handsomest men of our acquaintance."[2] Norris and Ernest Thompson Seton discussed the Boer War. When Norris questioned the justice of England's rule, Thompson Seton defended the war with fiery eloquence. "His black eyes glowed with a menacing light, but Norris held his own with entire good humor. He knew what he was talking about." Thurston Peck, editor of the *Bookman* was surprised to find "the author of the terrible *McTeague*"[3] to be "a pleasant, cultivated young gentleman, inclined to be obstreperous—and humorless—in arguments on realism, but in every other respect a very pleasant boy," whereas Jesse Lynch Williams felt that "he was not exactly humorless, but he didn't show much humor in conversation. . . . His face suggested an

[1]Letter to Mrs. Davenport dated April 8, 1900.
[2]Hamlin Garland in *Companions on the Trail*, p. 103; Macmillan (1931). Quoted by permission of Mr. Garland.
[3]Thomas Beer's *The Mauve Decade* (1926) p. 190. Alfred Knopf. Quoted by permission of the publishers.

old-time tragedian—Edwin Booth, perhaps. He had Booth's eyes."[1] Norris's gravity was exemplified when he suggested to a group of his friends that they precede him to a fashionable restaurant, nudge each other on his entry, and loudly whisper, "That's him!" He assumed the rôle of young genius gracefully.

In the busy offices of Doubleday, Page & Company, a human, intimate, flavorous place, Norris was very much liked. Arthur Goodrich, who was managing editor of the newly founded *World's Work*, remembers that "whenever he stopped at my desk for a chat, it always gave a new lift to my day. There was a sort of tonic quality about him, quiet and simple though he was, that stirred and warmed you." He became a close friend of Henry Lanier, who invited him up to his home in Greenwich, Connecticut, for a week-end, took him to a little reservoir pond a few miles north, and taught him to cast a frog for July bass. After experiencing all the backslashing, casting away of baits, and other troubles of the novice, he got fast to a three-pounder—and an angler was created there and then. When Norris returned to the office he declared:

"I'm a great success as a fisherman. I'm going to rent a cottage near a lake in a few weeks and fish all summer."

He found the cottage on Greenwood Lake in New Jersey, where he forgot "The Squid" for black bass.

During this summer Norris made his most notable "find" as a manuscript reader for the company, a discovery which proved to have more literary than financial significance. His employers, who realized

[1] *Ibid.*, p. 190.

that he was not a balanced reader for a young firm which must make money or go out of existence—he had no conception of the business side of publishing and no sympathy with the book which provides entertainment merely and makes a profit—asked him to read the novels which bordered on his own field. One afternoon he brought home to his apartment the draft of a book which he declared to be a naturalistic masterpiece, and he and his wife sat up all night in order to finish it. The next day he turned the office by its heels in his enthusiasm for the discovery; a few days later the firm signed a contract with Theodore Dreiser for the publication of *Sister Carrie*. Before the issue was off the press, however, a distressing mix-up had taken place concerning it; opposition had developed to the publication of a novel telling of the success of an immoral woman; it was felt that the public would not accept the story with the same enthusiasm that Norris had displayed. What actually happened has never been fully revealed; all that is known is that, though a number of copies were sent out to reviewers, the issue proved abortive as far as the general public was concerned. Mr. Dreiser maintains that most of the copies of the novel were locked in the cellars of the publishing company in order to dispose of them with the least trouble. It was not until seven years later that Norris's estimate was justified by the second American edition of *Sister Carrie*, issued by the Bev Dodge Company.

In October, Norris and his wife thought up a new game. Partly in order to escape some of the disagreeable aspects of city life during the winter season,

partly in order to be more alone than it was possible
to be in Washington Square, where their acquaintances had increased with alarming rapidity, they
decided to move out of New York City. But where
to go? They agreed to leave the matter to chance;
they would take a suburban train and stop at the
first place which looked attractive from the car windows. Chance selected Roselle, New Jersey, where
they rented a thinly built frame house, little realizing
how difficult it would be to keep it warm during the
winter. They made an event of moving from two
rooms into six, but the six rooms remained cold as
the heating system proved to be inadequate. In the
evening Norris would go down to stoke the furnace
carefully, only to stand over the grate the next morning and declare:

"There is only a *little* cold air coming up."

For five months they led a quiet life in Roselle.
Norris occasionally went into the office to bring out
a suitcase full of manuscripts, a few friends ventured
out to see them, two fraternity brothers and their
wives stopped for week-ends on trips to the East.
In November, when the day for the annual Big Game
in California came around, the "Fijis" who gathered
to celebrate at the Poodle Dog in San Francisco read
An Exile's Toast, which Norris had sent them.

*"Gesundheit! Ach mein lieber vriendts, dot note she
    gome today,
You're dinin' bli der Poodle in der same ol' yolly way,
While me, Ach Gott, du lieber Gott, I've set me down
    undt wept
Dot your kindt invitationing I cannot yet accept. . . ."*

On December 15, 1900, Norris finished *The Octopus* and delivered it to the publishers. When it appeared the following April, it was to mark several milestones in American fiction; it was to be the first of a long stream of novels dealing broadly with economic currents in American life, it was to make the first noteworthy stride towards the fiction of the Western frontier, and, through its vigor and breadth, it was to make still another inroad upon the hold of sentimental and petty fiction, offering a model of substance to the younger writers who were to carry on.

Chapter 12: An Epic Continued

The Octopus brought Norris to the attention of the public. The comprehensive sweep of the first volume of *The Epic of the Wheat* took the popular fancy, the indigenous plot and characters centering around a strife with the Ogre Trust coincided with general sentiment, and the extensive advertising given to the book by its publishers paved the way for a sale of 30,000 copies. From the time of its appearance, a month after Norris's thirty-first birthday, he faced problems which had not existed for him before. As an unknown writer he had been free to experiment, free to try his hand at the adventure yarn in *Moran*, at the naturalistic tragedy in *McTeague*, at the idyllic autobiography in *Blix*, and at the roughpaper plot in *A Man's Woman*. Now he was in danger of losing his independence. He was on safer ground when being condemned for *McTeague* than when being praised for *The Octopus*. A number of pæans sounded a dangerous note, exemplified by B. O. Flower's lengthy review in the socially conscious *Arena*: "It is one of the most powerful and faithful studies to be found in contemporary literature. It will quicken the conscience and awaken the moral sensibilities of the reader, exerting much the same influence over the mind as that exerted by Patrick Henry in the House of Burgesses in Virginia. . . . If it is impossible for you to procure more than one work of fiction this season, my advice—my unhesitating advice—is to buy *The Octopus*, read it aloud to your family, and then lend it to your neighbors." How far would Norris be able to withstand the force of popular opinion asking him to turn propagandist? What would be his attitude as he assumed "the responsibilities of the novelist"? Was he to realize that one of the dangers of having a big idea is that the creator may become a victim of his scheme? The enthusiasm for the wheat epic had carried it beyond his control; just as the existence of *The Octopus* necessitated the writing of *The Pit* and *The Wolf*, it created a public which demanded a second and third novel that would carry out the "bigness" and "moral purpose" of the first.

As *The Pit* was to concern itself with wheat speculation on the Chicago Board of Trade, Norris's first move was to acquaint himself with his subject. In this new field he had to start at the very bottom, for he was now dealing with a world to which he was a stranger. Instead of having the thousands of acres of fertile earth in the San Joaquin valley as his background, he must set his story in the cramped quarters of a city which he had heretofore considered devoid of romance; instead of dealing with healthy farmers fighting in the open, he must concern himself with grain manipulators, their chicanery and wholesale gambling; instead of handling the pioneer life of the Western frontier, he must portray the parvenu

society attendant on business enterprise. In spite of
these disadvantages, Norris had confidence that on
La Salle Street he would find dramatic matter to
suit his methods; his Chicago, unlike the drab and
ugly city pictured by Fuller in *The Cliff Dwellers*,
by Dreiser in *Sister Carrie*, and by Herrick in *The
Web of Life*, was to be the "Great Gray City where
beat the Heart of a Nation," the center of trade, the
embodiment of the spirit and power of America.

In the early spring of 1901, even before *The Octopus*
appeared, the Norrises gave up their house at Roselle
to go to Chicago, intent on mastering the principles
of high finance. But Chicago literary society welcomed them so effusively that they found themselves
giving far more time to social engagements than to
visiting the Board of Trade, interviewing financiers,
and making notes at the library. After a month they
said good-bye to their friends, officially departed for
California, left the train just outside the city, and
returned incognito to one of the modest hotels of the
city. There they remained another month, undis-
turbed. Norris now for the first time found difficulty
in mastering the technical details of a subject.
George Gibbs, "Fiji" from California who was in
on the secret, tells how he spent hours in trying to
explain short selling to Norris, who easily grasped
the drama of the sales on the floor of the pit, but had
difficulty comprehending how a man could sell a
thousand bushels of wheat when he did not own
them. Realizing that he could learn the details of
brokerage as well in New York as Chicago, he concentrated on absorbing the atmosphere and activity
of the wheat pit. He was particularly interested in

stories about Joseph Leiter's spectacular corner on wheat, which he intended to use with modification as the pattern for his central action. In 1897 Leiter had attained the strongest wheat position ever held in the trade. After buying up the nation's supply during a lean year when reserves were low and the United States was the only exporting country with a surplus, he had forced up the price to nearly $1.50 a bushel. But with every advance in price, wheat appeared as if by magic; the Northwest scraped its granaries, Russia ate rye and emptied its mill bins of wheat, Argentina swept the floor. As the price went up, Armour moved six million bushels into Chicago in midwinter by keeping steel-prowed tugs plowing up the ice at the head of the lakes. Leiter continued buying until the opening of the Spanish-American War caused the panic-stricken European countries to suspend their import duties on wheat. Before he could sell, the fifty million bushels of wheat which he had purchased crushed him with their weight, and with the fall in the market he was ruined. His career was exactly suited to the purpose of *The Pit*—to show how the force of the wheat was greater than that of the man who tried to control it. It was to be a fight between fecund nature and a gambler who would battle to the last ditch.

With the Chicago material in hand, the young enthusiasts took a much needed vacation, spending two months in San Francisco and three in the cabin at Greenwood Lake, where they had passed the previous summer. Norris fished a good deal, read some of the books which he had been wanting to read, entertained friends from New York, and had very business-like pictures taken of him "in his working hours." The photographs, which were for the publishing company, were planned to give body to the myths rising about the American Zola. One caught him at work before the pigeonholed desk which his wife had given him for his birthday so that he could systematize his notes; one showed him reading, pipe in mouth, serious expression on face; one found him sitting in a Morris chair, backed by a library and flanked by a copper tea kettle, closed book in hand, eyes turned straight towards the camera, lips firm and chin determined. He wore a comfortable smoking jacket and boldly striped socks. Despite their propagandic nature, which suppressed the usual smile, the portraits gave an accurate impression of his appearance at thirty-one; the face had filled out, accentuating the weight of the chin and the fullness of the lips, the hair was quite gray, framing an olive complexion which photographed dark; the tall figure had become heavier with just the suggestion of an abdominal bulge, of which he was proud. In the picture at his desk he might have been writing to Arthur Goodrich: "I send you herewith the proof of the *World's Work* stuff and, as you see, I have written 'larger type' over against the author's name. . . . God give me humility, but I do like to label the work and stand by it, be the platform ever so lowly. Even the poor showman who expatiates upon the Circassian lady and the sword swallower has that privilege—and, if the lady and the swallower do not justify his pretensions, his is the one responsibility—ain't ut? . . .

So do let me strut a little in the eye of the public. It is a harmless innocuous vanity at the worst."[1]

Early in September the couple rented an apartment overlooking the Hudson, where Norris started to write *The Pit*. He was now able to give all of his time to composition, for after the completion of *The Octopus* he had discontinued reading manuscripts for the publishers. In order to master the details of stock manipulation which had puzzled him in Chicago, he made an arrangement with a young broker, George D. Moulson, to spend evenings explaining away the difficulties which Norris met during the day. The chief problem was solved when Moulson invented a game to illustrate his lessons; a wire was run from the radiator grate in the floor to a hook in the ceiling, and upon this wire was threaded a float which rose and fell with the fluctuations of heat from the furnace. A rising feather indicated a bull market, a falling one activities of the bears. Norris gambled on a rise, and his wife on a fall; they kept their figures in good order and had great fun in speculating in high finance. *The Pit* was taking form. . . .

On the ninth of February, 1902, Jeannette Norris, Junior, was born. Although she was christened Jeannette in deference to the custom of giving feminine names to girl babies, from the first she was called Billy, a nickname her parents gave her because it was great fun to call "Billy" and have a girl appear. As Norris and his wife were inclined to look upon her as a playmate, she soon fitted satisfactorily into the

[1]Undated letter to Arthur Goodrich, managing editor of *World's Work*.

game which was going on in the apartment overlooking the Hudson. With a thump on his chest, Norris
announced to his friends:

"*Maintenant je suis bon bourgeois, moi—père de
famille!*"

★   ★   ★

SOMETIME during the years which Norris spent in
New York, probably during his first wretched winter
on "the Square," he wrote a story which he called
Dying Fires. In it he told of the disappointing career
of a young writer, Overbeck, who lived in Colfax,
California, where he worked on his father's newspaper.
Overbeck wrote a novel which was a good book because it was written as a true observation of life,
unspoiled by self-conscious literary aims. "The novel
was good. It was not great—far from it, but it was not
merely clever. Somehow . . . young Overbeck had got
started right at the very beginning. He had not been
influenced by a fetich of his choice till his work was a
mere replica of some other writer's work. He was not
literary. He had not much time for books. He lived
in the midst of a strenuous, eager life, a little primal
even yet; a life of passions that were often elemental
in their simplicity and directness. His schooling and
his newspaper work . . . had taught him observation
without—here is the miracle—dulling the edge of his
sensitiveness. He saw, as few, few people see who live
close to life at the beginning of an epoch."

Overbeck was called to New York to work for the
publishing house which found merit in his novel.
There he made the mistake of associating with the
members of the "New Bohemia" who he honestly

believed made up the true literary force of New York. These third-raters praised his novel. They told him there was more harmony of phrase in it than in everything that Bret Harte ever wrote. They said that he had succeeded where Kipling had failed, and called him a second Stevenson—with more refinement. He was misled by their literary discussions, picked up their phrases. "He could talk about 'tendencies' and the 'influence of reactions.' . . . He knew all about 'tones' and 'notes' and 'philistinisms.' . . . An anti-climax was the one unforgivable sin under heaven. A mixed metaphor made him wince, and a split infinitive hurt him like a blow." . . . Then the women of the set began to flutter and buzz around him. They objected to the healthy animalism of his novel, objected that his characters were coarse in fiber. "'Not so much *faroucherie*, you dear young Lochinvar!' they said. 'Art must uplift. . . . The spiritual is the great thing. We are here to make the world brighter and better for having lived in it. . . . Every book should leave a clean taste in the mouth, should tend to make one happier, should elevate, not debase.'"

Under their influence, Overbeck began to be ashamed of his first book and decided to try "something literary." As the result he wrote a book which the publishers called foolishness. When he realized his mistake and returned to Colfax, it was too late. The fire was dead—extinguished by the pernicious influence of New York smallsters. "The fire that the gods had allowed him to snatch . . . had been stamped out beneath the feet of minor and dilettante poets."

Dying Fires does more than accomplish Norris's immediate purpose of ridiculing the Washington

Square dilettantes who had so annoyed him when he first reached New York. It reveals his attitude towards a problem which was constantly in his mind. He felt that his gift, like Overbeck's, was the ability to record life with freshness and enthusiasm, and he did not intend to have these qualities impaired. He proposed to keep his own creative fires active by taking three precautions: by avoiding self-conscious literary company, by reading few novels, and by getting out of New York as soon as possible.

Thus Norris attempted to carry out his conviction that "the important thing in writing is *not* to be literary." He preferred to be looked upon as anything but a writer. He would rather talk to business men than to poets, declaring that the man of action was more interesting than the man of letters. He avoided "talking shop." On no subject was he more outspoken than on the obnoxious nature of the members of "New Bohemia," who, as he put it, drank beer out of teacups; into this group he lumped all pretenders to talent, all academic critics, and all adherents to literary clubs. "Of all the influences which tend to stultify ambition, warp original talent, and definably and irretrievably stamp out the last spark of productive ability, one knows of none more effective than the literary club."

Because of this attitude the friends which Norris made in New York were few in number and close in companionship. He always welcomed fraternity brothers from the University of California. When they were in the city, he saw much of Bruce Porter, Ernest Peixotto, and Gelett Burgess. He made close friends of the members of the Doubleday, Page staff: Henry

Lanier, Arthur Goodrich, J. O'Hara Cosgrave, who had left the *Wave* to edit *Everybody's*, Ruth Frederic, Frank Doubleday, Russell Doubleday, and Walter Hines Page. Although he knew many of the leading writers of the day, he seems to have become well acquainted with only Howells and Garland. Soon after his arrival in New York, he had met Mrs. Isobel Osbourne Strong, Mrs. Stevenson, Austin Strong, and Lloyd Osbourne, whom he had long respected as the co-author of *The Wrecker*. They became close friends, as did Mrs. Katherine Herne, the widow of James A. Herne, and her two daughters, Julia and Chrystal. Hamlin Garland describes Norris as his New York friends saw him: "He was the best company in the world. His eyes glowed with humor. His face shone with roguery and good cheer. His antic manner was never coarse, and his jocular phrases were framed in unexpected ways. . . . I saw a good deal of Norris during the time when this story [*The Pit*] was forming in his brain, and I confess I was more uneasy than he. He smoked his pipe and made merry and discussed everything else under the sun—and appeared quite at ease."[1] Norris was never a writing man when he was away from his desk.

The wonder of life in the frontier town of Colfax so overpowered Overbeck that he had no thought or care for other people's books. Norris approved of this. In order to carry out his creed that "life is better than literature," he tried to adhere to the principle that the novelist should read as little as possible and experience as much as he could. With Norris the

[1]Quoted from Hamlin Garland's *Companions of the Trail*, Macmillan (1931), pp. 170, 171, by permission of the author.

principle had its advantages, for it resulted in a fresh portrayal of life which gave strength to his fiction; on the other hand, it had its disadvantages, for his limited reading tended to influence him too greatly. As Howells pointed out, "By what Frank Norris wrote we might easily know what he read." Of this reading, the French influenced him the most: apparently he read most of Zola's novels—always in the original—often rereading his favorites, *L'Assommoir*, *La Terre*, *Germinal*, *L'Argent*, and *La Bête humaine;* he admired Flaubert's *Salammbô* and especially *Madame Bovary;* his fondness for Hugo influenced both his style and his handling of plot; in his essays he presents Dumas as his example of the born story-teller of the highest order; he was interested likewise in Guy de Maupassant, the Goncourt brothers, and Daudet. The extent of his reading in Balzac is uncertain, but one frequently thinks of M. Grandet as he notes Trina's miserly habits.

The English influence was not so great, though his short stories show Kipling's influence, and many echoes of Stevenson's *The Wrecker* are to be found in his novels. Scott was a boyhood favorite, while Conrad, discovered when he read the manuscript of *Lord Jim* for Doubleday, Page & Company, became a new passion with him. Dickens he always admired, but George Eliot, he declared, lacked the story-teller's gift. He would not read Meredith and made fun of his friends who did; no doubt he classed him as an "over-literary stylist" along with Pater and Arnold. Among the older American writers, he admired Howells, Mark Twain, and Henry James, the last chiefly for *The Turn of the Screw.* Among the younger group he saw promise in Harold Frederic, Stephen Crane, Hamlin Garland, Theodore Dreiser, Robert Herrick, and Owen Wister. Of the Russians he spoke only of Tolstoy, whom he accredited with "magnificent genius." This reading, together with memories from his mother's reading of Browning, Shakespeare, and the Bible, formed most of Norris's literary background.

For the rest, he preferred to walk the streets of New York, looking for "dramas of the curbstone"; to join in the current craze of ping-pong; to fish at Greenwood lake; or to go to unending trouble to bind his paper-backed French novels. Frequently when asked what he was reading, he would reply, as he displayed *Moran* or *McTeague*, "I'm reading a darn good book by Frank Norris."

*   *   *

"TO MAKE money is not the province of the novelist." Such was the firm conviction which caused Norris to attack in no uncertain terms the writers who prostituted their art. "We know them . . . and know their work is false. . . . These gentlemen who are 'in literature for their own pocket every time' have discovered that for the moment the People have confounded the Wrong with the Right, and prefer that which is a lie to that which is true. 'Very well, then,' say these gentlemen. 'If they want a lie they shall have it'; and they give the people a lie in return for loyalties. . . . The man who can address an audience of one hundred and fifty thousand people who—unenlightened—*believe what he says*, has a heavy duty to perform, and tremendous responsibilities to shoul-

der; and he should address himself to his task not
with the flippancy of a catch-penny juggler at the
county fair, but with earnestness, with soberness, with
a sense of his limitations, and with all the abiding
sincerity that by the favor and mercy of the gods may
be his."

Norris could say truthfully that he had never
altered his ideas or methods to increase the sale of
his books. That his novels achieved a limited popularity was not due to any softening of their realism
but to the force with which he recorded life as he saw
it. They were dramatic because life itself was dramatic, exciting because existence was a game. He
tried to write so that he would be able to say, "'I
never truckled; I never took off the hat to Fashion
and held it out for pennies. By God, I told them the
truth!'"

In fact Norris did not look upon financial returns
as an important factor in the game he was playing.
If he had enough money to satisfy his comparatively
modest demands he was happy. During his first two
years in New York, when he had lived on barely fifty
dollars a month, he had overlooked his privations in
his enthusiasm for writing; and when he had married
with a potential income of one hundred and twenty-
five dollars a month, he declared it was "bully" to
have "a bit ahead in case of emergency." He expected
little from royalties, which he called "those micro-
scopic sums that too, too often are less royal than
beggarly." In the light of his estimate that the
moderately successful novel selling 2500 copies would
net the author $250 one may assume that the indi-
vidual returns on his first four novels had been not

much greater than that amount.[1] The sale of *The Octopus* assured him for the first time of substantial royalties, but even the returns on his fifth novel, which were just beginning to come in, were not large when divided by the twenty months he had devoted to its composition. Now, having given hostages to fortune in the forms of a wife and a child, he found it necessary to write short stories and articles, which he preferred to compromising with the public in his novels.

His wife remembers that in the fall of 1901 Norris decided to write a short story, the proceeds from which were to be used in buying her a Christmas present. When the story was finished, he feared that he might not be able to sell it, so he wrote two more; eventually all three of them appeared. As other demands for petty cash arose from time to time, he ransacked his desk for rejected manuscripts and re-

[1]The Doubleday, Doran records show that Norris's early novels had comparatively small sales. The trade sales were as follows: *Moran*, 1,804; *McTeague*, 3,974; *Blix*, 4,076; *A Man's Woman*, 5,334. His first royalties were supplemented by minor returns from the fifty-cent paper editions of the last three, from the syndicating of *Moran* and *A Man's Woman*, from the serial rights on *Blix*, and from the sale of the English editions of all four. However, only during the last year of his life, with the 33,420 sale of *The Octopus*, is it likely that his royalties became fairly large. He did not live to benefit by the 94,914 sale of *The Pit;* although, as Kathleen Norris testifies, he was able to write a $500 check after selling the serial rights of *The Pit* to the *Saturday Evening Post*. The San Francisco *Chronicle* of November 7, 1902, stated that Norris's estate was estimated at $1,000 in cash and royalties. American sales to date on his novels are *The Pit*, 189,751; *McTeague*, 67,272; *The Octopus*, 59,985; *A Man's Woman*, 54,032; *Blix*, 19,029; *Vandover*, 9,107; *Moran*, 2,559.

vised and completed a number of stories which he had put aside. To these he added a few more new ones, so that eighteen of his short stories appeared in various magazines between the publication of *The Octopus* and the appearance of his collected works in the fall of 1903. As they were, almost without exception, inferior to the quality of his novels, it is doubtful that he would have favored their reprinting in book form in the posthumous *A Deal in Wheat*. He looked upon these tales as hack work; his creative energy he threw into the writing of *The Pit*.

Five of the stories thus produced, Cosgrave used in *Everybody's*. In *The Riding of Felipe* Norris erred in turning *Yvernelle* into a prose tale, but he was more successful in *Buldy Jones, Chef de Claque*, in which he again drew on his Paris experiences. These, together with the two adaptations from Morris's translation of the Grettir Saga, *Grettir at Drangey* and *Grettir at Thorwall-Stead*, had probably been written at earlier periods. *A Deal in Wheat*, however, was obviously a five-finger exercise written in connection with *The Pit*. The *Saturday Evening Post* printed a football story, *Kirkland at Quarter*, while the *Ladies' Home Journal* brought out *A Statue in an Old Garden*, harmonics in the manner of the Grannis-Miss Baker idyll. The three stories written for his wife's Christmas present were *A Memorandum of Sudden Death. A Bargain with Peg-Leg*, and *The Passing of Cockeye Blacklock*. Of these the best is the first, in which a reporter tells how he felt as he and his companions were killed one by one during an attack by Arizona Indians. The story was suggested by Remington's picture, "Caught in the Circle." The other two, trick stories with surprise endings, are dialect yarns concerning Bunt McBride, teamster at the Big Dipper Mine; *The Wife of Chino* uses the same setting for an ineffective melodrama. In a Kipling vein are *Two Hearts That Beat as One*, *The Dual Personality of Slick Dick Nickerson*, *The Ship That Saw a Ghost*, and *The Ghost in the Crosstrees*, which are all concerned with the adventures of the Three Black Crows in their unlawful practices on the Pacific. They no doubt find their sources in Norris's conversations with Hodgson at the Life-saving Station in San Francisco. Finally there are *The Guest of Honor*, in which Norris once more speculates on the nature of death, *The Lost Story*, concerning the temptation which comes to an authoress who reads manuscripts, and *Dying Fires*, an attack on the members of "New Bohemia." With a few exceptions these stories, written "to eke out the alarming brevity of royalties," make up the tag ends and remnants of his fiction.

But the articles Norris wrote under the same spur offer a compensatory store of information about his ideas. That he should be asked to write of his ideas after the publication of *The Octopus* was inevitable. Thus, while he was collecting material for *The Pit* in Chicago, the newly established Chicago *American* requested his opinions on literary life in New York. During the following winter the Boston *Transcript* published twelve of his essays, varying in subject from *Truth versus Accuracy* to *The National Spirit—As Related to the "Great American Novel." World's Work*, published by Doubleday, Page & Company, printed in October, 1901, *The True Reward of the Novelist*, the first of the series of articles that appeared in that magazine which were to form the backbone of the posthumous *The Responsibilities of the Novelist*. Of the *Salt and Sincerity* papers which appeared monthly in the *Critic* beginning April, 1902, Jeannette Gilder, editor of that journal, wrote: "After [Norris] came to New York, even after the publication of several of his novels, he was not making a great deal of money, nothing like what he ought to have made with his reputation, and he was obliged to do other writing than that of fiction. We engaged him to do a monthly turn for the *Critic*. . . . It was a sort of go-as-you-please, having the general title of *Salt and Sincerity*. The title was a good one, for everything that Norris wrote was sincere, and the salt brought out the flavor."

These essays contained Norris's declaration of faith. Hastily written, filled with contradictions and excesses, they served their purpose in encouraging the younger writers of his time. To the present-day reader they mirror Norris's virtues and failings; emotional rather than intellectual, exhortative rather than critical, immature in reflective power, they bear witness in every line of the enthusiastic spirit which captured the imaginations of the young rebels for whom they were written. Through them one can understand why Cosgrave, when he asked Norris for an editorial, demanded, "Now, don't think—write. If you think you will be wrong." The irregularity of their composition is illustrated by an exaggerated anecdote which Norris told of the writing of one of them; he started it with enthusiasm, was interrupted, and returned to finish it with a fresh burst of energy, only to find on re-reading that he had completely

reversed his opinion during the intermission. Since
the haste and irregularity with which they were
written made them uneven in quality, it was no
wonder that reviewers pointed out inconsistencies
in them when, un-edited by their writer, they were
published in book form after his death. As a whole,
however, the merits expressed in *The Responsibilities
of the Novelist* outweighed the faults apparent to
captious critics. At a time when his voice was most
needed, Norris boldly and courageously announced
his principles; he pleaded for more substance in fiction; he demanded a conscience of its writers; he
insisted that American life of the moment should be
used as the subject for novels; he cried out against
the neglect of the frontier for tawdry historical
themes; he defended the right of the novelist to deal
frankly with all of the emotions; and he appealed
to the writers of America to be sincere in their search
for the truth of life, no matter how elusive it might
be. He was terribly in earnest when he wrote: "It is
not right that the public be exploited and deceived
with false views of life, false characters, false sentiment, false heroism, false notions of self-sacrifice,
false views of religion, of duty, of conduct, and of
manners. . . . Fiction may keep pace with the Great
March, but it will not be by dint of amusing the
people. The Muse is a teacher, not a trickster. Her
rightful place is with the leaders, but in the last
analysis that place is to be attained and maintained
not by cap-and-bells, but because of a serious and
sincere interest . . . a well-defined, well-seen, courageously sought-for purpose."

*   *   *

IT WAS unfortunate that Norris's last novel was *The Pit*, for *The Pit* was neither as great nor as individual as *The Octopus*. That its comparative failure was not due to capitulation to public taste or to a dying out of his individuality is clear to anyone who makes a close study of Norris's life and writing. As he worked on the second novel in his trilogy of the wheat, he realized that his scheme for an epic in three parts was forcing him to write a novel for which his talents were not well suited. His widow states that never before did he approach his work with such trepidations, tear up so many false starts, become so despondent about his writing. He did not enjoy the composition of *The Pit*, but worked at it steadily, remembering that it was but a link in his chain, putting faith in the possibility that *The Wolf* would carry him once more into the open and back to a subject more promising than speculation and domestic intrigue. He rightly assumed that with a better subject he would write a better book.

Norris wove three strands into *The Pit*. Of these the first and most fundamental was to tie the book to the other members of the trilogy. It was to be shown that the wheat was greater than its manipulators. The characters in the story were to be "dominated by the great forces at the back of them; by the teeming earth, the monstrous machinery of production and distribution, and by the colossal organization of the great game of speculation." The Wheat was to remain the chief actor, defeating the efforts of those who attempt to control it, causing Jadwin's failure in the end. "He had laid his human grasp upon Creation, and the very earth herself, the great mother,

feeling the touch of the cobweb that the human in-
sect had spun, had stirred at last in her sleep and sent
her omnipotence moving through the grooves of the
world, to find and crush the disturber of her appointed courses." Norris's difficulty in handling his
dominant theme in this novel lay in the fact that the
Wheat was never able to appear. It remained in the
background, out in the farms of the West and Middle
West, sacked in the granaries of Odessa and Singa-
pore, feeding the peoples of Russia and Italy. It did
not even come into Chicago; the manipulation of it
upon the board of exchange was the manipulation of
paper representing paper. Norris's perplexity at learning of the methods of dealers who did not even own
the wheat they sold must have turned to despair as
he realized that his force must remain an abstraction,
a thundering off-stage, a "diapason" whose im-
materiality would make its presentation labored and
unreal. The Wheat in *The Pit* was to be found in the
few pitiful sacks of samples, fingered by the dealers
and fed to the pigeons—the only wild life near the
exchange. Here could be no pictures of the fruitful
teeming earth or panoramas of the wheat growing on
the ranches; the very source of Norris's effectiveness,
the concrete presentation of his primal force, was
closed to him. It is a tribute to his genius that in
spite of these difficulties, he did succeed in creating a
sense of the strength of production and the demand
for distribution leading up to and controlling the
action of *The Pit*.

The second strand in the book, a strand which,
pleasing Norris, became the strongest in its texture,
concerned the portrayal of the American business man

as a romantic figure. It had always been one of Norris's tenets that the business baron was motivated by the excitement of making a fortune rather than by the desire for money, which served only as counters in the game. The business man was to him the man of action of the nineteenth century. "Had Mr. Carnegie been alive at the time of the preachings of Peter the Hermit he would have raised a company of *gens d'armes* sooner than all of his brothers-in-arms, would have equipped his men better and more effectively, would have been first on the ground before Jerusalem, would have built the most ingenious siege engine and have hurled the first cask of Greek fire over the walls." He contended that the ablest men of his generation had devoted their energy to the creation of great enterprises, and that their struggles were as well suited to the purposes of the story-teller as were the wars of the barons. In his attitude Norris differed from most of the naturalists, who have shown the financier activated by greed. However, after the passing of three generations of novelists, "muck-rakers," and "debunkers" who have busied themselves with attacks on the capitalists, we are now ready to accept Norris's conception of the spirit back of the business enterprise of his era as the more nearly accurate.

It was the theme of his trilogy which doubled back on Norris, forcing to involve his leading figure, Jadwin, not in the building of a transcontinental railroad, nor in the opening up of the resources of an undeveloped country, nor in the creation of a steel monopoly, but in the comparatively unworthy act of cornering the wheat market. Thus Jadwin became a gambler rather than an empire builder; for the creative gambling spirit of the frontiersman, Magnus Derrick, Norris was forced to substitute a passion which became an obsession as the game escaped the control of the player. The conflict in Jadwin's soul reflected a division in Norris's sympathy. He prized grain manipulation as a source of drama, but, at heart, he condemned the practice as antisocial; his story-telling sense was at war with his moral sense. However, he retained the amoral attitude. *The Pit* was an arraignment of speculation only in so far as it showed that it was impossible for a man to corner the world's wheat; this lesson rested on fact rather than theory. On the other hand Norris's faith in the dramatic value of his subject was borne out in his novel. From the start of Jadwin's buying to the time when the excess of wheat crushes him, the action moves smoothly and logically, gaining momentum for the effective climax on the floor of the pit. In plot structure *The Pit* was a technical improvement over his earlier books.

In a search for a secondary conflict to give his novel substance—for the speculation theme alone was too thin—Norris fixed upon a struggle between love and business. This was the third and weakest strand in *The Pit*. Theoretically, the move was sound; as the typical American marriage is based upon a love match, it is probable that the chief conflict in the life of a man like Jadwin would be one between the rival demands of home and career. Such a domestic crisis was as much in keeping with the spirit of the American novel as was the philandering of Saccard in *L'Argent* of Zola. The difficulty lay not with the subject itself but with Norris's ability to handle it, for his temperament, his interests, and his methods made his treatment of the relations between Jadwin, Laura Dearborn, and Corthill weak. In portraying Laura he was forced to "analyze a woman's soul," and his analyses were never as good as his action. In portraying Corthill his desire for contrast once more caused him to overreach himself; he caricatured the man of letters in order to exalt the man of action. His artist never became more than a shadow, just as the intrigue never took on life.

In using the eternal triangle Norris entered a field long exploited in contemporary fiction, and likewise, in giving his novel a happy ending he duplicated the performance of almost every novelist of his day. An analysis of his procedure in writing *The Pit* shows that just as he introduced the former because it was most logical to his purposes, he used the latter because it was the only honest thing to do. After the crisis—the collapse of Jadwin's corner on wheat— any ending would have been an anticlimax. The formula of the naturalist demanded tragedy, but tragedy here would but have accentuated the melodrama of the story. To kill Jadwin would be foolish and illogical in the light of his character; to have Laura run away with Corthill would only reduce an already foolish situation to the absurd. Jadwin's and Laura's reconciliation and resolution to keep on living was the natural, the obvious, the real thing for them to do. It is probable that Norris realized that the naturalist could become as much a victim of his pattern as the sentimentalist, and that the inevitably tragic ending is as untrue to life as the assump-

tion that the characters "live happily ever after."
His sense of artistry was at any rate sounder than
that of one noted critic, who stated in the *Bookman*,
"We wish we had been called upon to forgive her
[Laura]; that Norris had found it within his conception to let her go out with Corthill into the night,
and brought Curtis Jadwin, broken in body, mind
and purse, to his vast desolate home. 'Old girl—
Honey!' How that feeble cry in the gloom would have
told, with only the echo of the empty dark to answer."

The Pit was finished on the fourth of June, 1902,
and appeared serially in the *Saturday Evening Post*,
starting in September of that year. The book, which
was released in January, 1903, had a wide sale; critics
were as a whole lenient, pointing out that it showed
a definite improvement in structure over Norris's
earlier novels, although some regretted that it lacked
the strength of *The Octopus*. The popular imagination
was captured, the dramatic version was very successful, and a new card game, *Pit*, was invented. The
second novel of the wheat trilogy was a worthy
contribution to the fiction of American business.

★   ★   ★

AFTER finishing *The Pit* Norris's first move was to
leave New York. Every completed page of his manuscript had fortified the conclusion which he had come
to when he first reached the East, that he could not
do his best work there. Almost in anger he announced
that New York was *not* a literary center. It contained
no indigenous writers, its atmosphere was not stimu-
lative to endeavor, and its living conditions were not
attractive. "Not only this, but one believes that

actual residence in New York is hostile and inimical
to work. The place teems with literary clubs. . . . The
best thought is not in New York; and even if it were,
the best thought of other men is not so good for you
as your own thought, dug out of your own vitals by
your own unaided efforts, be it ever so inadequate.
You do not have to go to New York for that. Your
own ideas, your own work will flourish best if left
untrammeled and uninfluenced." Those who believe
that Norris created a straw man to knock down
have but to examine the careers of other frontier
writers and reflect on the surrender to culture of
Bret Harte, Joaquin Miller, Mark Twain. . . . Norris
saw that the traveler from Red Gulch frequently lost
his vitality in the atmosphere of Parnassus and determined that he for one would return to the source
of his strength.

Chapter 13: The Last Adventure

NORRIS and his wife planned for their next adventure to make a trip around the world in a tramp steamer collecting material to be used in writing *The Wolf*. Accordingly, on their arrival in San Francisco in the middle of July, 1902, they set about making definite arrangements for the voyage, upon which they hoped to embark as soon as they had said "hello" to their friends and relatives, straightened out their finances, and disposed of Billy, who, not as yet a hardy member of the vagabond firm, was to remain with her grandmother and a nurse during her parents' absence. The details of the trip were to work themselves out according to the chances which turned up. Had he been able to afford it, Norris would have carried out his dream of chartering a yacht as Jack London did a few years later, but under the circumstances he was forced to be satisfied with interviewing shipping clerks and captains of cargo vessels in his search for a likely ship going in the right direction. The couple wished to be the sole passengers on a tramp steamer bound for the South Seas and Australia, then on to China, to India, to Port Said, to Italy.... They wanted to bunk in a cabin on the forward deck, get acquainted with the officers and the crew, join in the fun of running a ship, build up a store of energy by leading a healthy seafaring life. Before they returned to San Francisco after sailing the seven seas, they hoped to visit many ports where they would learn what happened when the world's supply of wheat was held up by speculators in the Chicago grain pit. They would investigate foreign living conditions, seek out dramatic incidents in wheat distribution. Somewhere en route they would find the best *locale* to be used in *The Wolf,* a spot where famine would be relieved by "the timely appearance from across the sea of three huge American schooners—wheat ships—loaded to their capacity with the great crop that, in spite of the quarrels of the farmers and the railroads, and in spite of the manipulation of the bulls and the bears on the stock market, was to fulfill its destiny as 'the nourisher of nations.'"

As there was no hurry about starting on the voyage, the Norrises lingered in San Francisco enjoying themselves. They had "arrived"; it was great fun to be well known, to be pointed out, to be recognized as leading actors in the drama. Old residents of the city turned to look at the couple as they walked down Market Street—a distinguished young man with a spring in his step accompanied by a pretty, healthy-looking girl, both keen, eager, stimulating as the ocean breezes. Captain Jack called them "nifty" and spoke expansively of "putting on the dog" when Norris (in knickerbockers) and his wife called with Billy and her beribboned French maid. They went over to Berkeley, where Norris, who had become a myth, read a story to an assembly of students, after stating that his impulse on being introduced was to answer as he had always done in college days— "Unprepared." Attentions of the spectators at the first football game of the season were divided between the action on the field and the enthusiastic alumnus who strode up and down the sidelines, cheering once more for "Anglo-Saxon fighting spirit."

With Charles Norris, who was now attending the university and had developed literary aspirations of his own, Frank had many talks about writing. It did not seem long since they had played together with lead soldiers in Paris. As they discussed the old times, the dedication of *The Pit* took form in Frank's mind: "To my brother, Charles Gilman Norris, in memory of certain lamentable tales of the round (dining-room) table heroes; of the epic of the pewter platoons, and the romance-cycle of '*Gaston le Fox*,' which we invented, maintained, and found marvelous at a time when we both were boys." To Charles he told his plans for *The Wolf*, stating that he had decided to change the title of the novel. He also spoke of a trilogy which he hoped to write after completing *The Epic of the Wheat*, a trilogy in which each novel would tell of one day of the fighting at Gettysburg, mirroring through the portrayal of a crucial moment in national history the epic strength and growth of America. As the brothers spent a great deal of time together, they developed an intimacy they had never reached before.

Frank Norris was also getting acquainted with his daughter at this time. Condy and Blix now took the Presidio walk in an abbreviated form, for Billy could

not be carried all over the rocks north of Fort Point.
It was on one of these trips that Norris for the first
time realized that the baby was a human rather than
a toy; the enlightenment came when Billy, whom her
father was carrying, was frightened by the whistle
of a steam engine and nuzzled into his shoulder.
"By Jove! The child has brains!" He began to speculate upon children; discipline was interesting. You
must never say "no" unless you mean it, or there will
be no such thing as a big "no." Interesting story
situation of a man who was raised by the wrong
method. . . .

★   ★   ★

NORRIS's modesty and sincerity were not affected
by his popularity. He played his rôle, enjoying his
success in an ingenuous, youthful spirit, but never for
a moment did he forget the seriousness of his purpose
as a writer. If his talent and good fortune had raised
him to a position where the public would listen to
him, it was his responsibility to tell them the truth.
There is no incident of his life which illustrates more
clearly his sincerity, his loyalty to his friends, and his
belief in enlightening the public, than his defense of
an old friend in the face of the united opposition of
the San Francisco press.

When Norris arrived in California, he learned that
Dr. William Lawlor, whom he had known from child-
hood, was being victimized in what Norris considered
to be a cowardly attack by unscrupulous politicians.
Lawlor, who had been put in charge of the Glen
Ellen Home for the Feeble-minded by Governor
Henry T. Gage, was singled out for attack during the

primary election by Gage's opponents, who, in the time-honored method of attacking state appointees, were doing their best to present Lawlor to the public as an inhuman monster who resorted to third-degree methods in keeping his charges in order. As the press was united in opposition to Gage, it welcomed an opportunity to publish the distorted reports of Lawlor's cruelty. By the time Norris reached the city, it had aroused public opinion, forcing Lawlor to the wall.

Norris immediately went to Glen Ellen, where he told his sixty-year-old friend that he proposed single-handed to inform the public of the injustice being done. He would investigate the charges himself and tell the people the truth. Lawlor was being deposed for using a "dark room" as a disciplinary measure; Norris wrote an article white with anger in which he affirmed that in the far corner of the room he could read without difficulty the date on a coin held at arm's length. Other charges he had found to be equally ungrounded. As he wrote, he struck with all his force, addressing the enemy as "the conscience-less, heartless bullies, who manage to maintain the presses of San Francisco. A name and reputation that for the term of an entire life have been without reproach are butchered and defiled, so that votes may be won. There is no murder more wanton than this, no assassination more cowardly. It is worse than stabbing in the dark—Caligula was more merciful than this; Torquemada more humane. . . . And all of this is done under the name of virtue, of righteous indignation, and the people, the public, are called upon to assist in the annihilation of a good name, the wrecking and ruining of a career, the condemnation of a man unheard in his own defense."

But when Norris turned to find an organ to publish his defense, he discovered a front united against him. Before he could do a thing the drama came to a climax in a meeting of the board of directors in the Grand Hotel in San Francisco, the second of August. The enemies of Lawlor on the board were resolved to name his successor, while Norris, together with Lawlor's eldest son, was determined to see that he received justice. It was a tense situation. The remarks during the meeting kindled feelings as if they were dry tinder until a heated personal attack by one Colonel Harrington in the peroration of his speech caused young Lawlor to speak his mind. This in turn brought Dr. Lawlor to his feet; he stated that the Colonel had lied in telling the press that the superintendent was quartering his sons on the state. The action which followed was graphically described by Norris: "Then it was that the gentleman from Kentucky drew his revolver upon Dr. Lawlor, drew like a coward who knew the miserable weakness of his position, the puerility of his logic, drew like the hero of a melodrama strutting and posing in the limelight, playing to the gallery, showing off like a little boy with a toy pistol." Before Harrington could shoot, Norris had pinioned his arm to his side—the committee interfered, and the meeting broke up in confusion.

The next morning the newspapers carried headlines telling of the attack upon the life of Dr. Lawlor and giving credit to Norris for his prompt action. That afternoon the San Francisco *Examiner* called him on the phone. The New York *Journal* had wired for a

front-page story of the "shooting-scrape" in which
Frank Norris had saved his friend's life. Norris's
reply was eloquent of his contempt for such publicity.

"You tell the New York *Journal* kindly to go to
hell," said he, and hung up the receiver.

At last Norris succeeded in getting his article
printed in the *Argonaut*, where it appeared as a letter
without editorial support. If the public was anxious
to learn the truth, it gave no indications of it. The
castigated editors refused to reply, and a month later,
after the primary election, Lawlor was finally dis-
missed, formally whitewashed. Whether the incident
shook Norris's faith in democracy will never be
known; however, the article remains a worthy vale-
dictory.

★   ★   ★

IN THE Santa Cruz mountains about one hundred
miles south of San Francisco and fifteen miles north
of Gilroy, Mrs. Robert Louis Stevenson lived upon
a ranch which she called Vanumanutagi, or vale of
the singing birds. Not long after the Norrises reached
California, they made the long, hot, dusty ride from
Gilroy to the secluded valley in order to visit Mrs.
Stevenson and her children, Lloyd Osbourne and
Isobel Strong, who had but recently come out from
New York to spend the winter. During their stay, the
couple were so pleased with the rough hill country
and with its redwoods and canyons that they decided
they would like to live there. Accordingly, Norris
opened negotiations to buy a ten-acre tract of land
on the mountainside back of Vanumanutagi upon
which stood a one-room log cabin. The cabin, which

was reached by a path that wound up a canyon with a stream at the bottom, was backed by redwoods and flanked by a spring; it perched near the edge of a precipitous slope looking down upon one of finest views in the region. *Quien Sabe*, as they named it, was to be used for the moment as a writing retreat, but after their return from the trip around the world, it was to be enlarged and made into a permanent home.

Norris wrote enthusiastically to his friends in New York about his purchase in the wilderness; to Mr. Doubleday he stated that he had a trout stream around the corner, and could shoot bears from his windows, all of which was better than a Harlem flat. He saw great story possibilities in the country and struck up acquaintance with the mountain people living in the vicinity, making extensive plans for novels about them. He was full of ideas. He would complete *The Wolf*—show the triumph of the wheat as it ran through the streets of a famine-stricken city; he would write his trilogy on the Battle of Gettysburg; then he would write stories about the mountain people of the West. Norris felt that he was just getting into his stride.

★   ★   ★

EARLY in September Mrs. Stevenson received a letter which announced a change in plans for the couple who had been waiting in San Francisco to start on their adventure. "This is to tell you that our famous round-the-world trip has been curtailed to a modest excursion Samoa-wards and back, or mebbe we get as far as Sydney. We won't get to France, but will come back to *Quien Sabe* in February—FEBRUARY! We find in figuring up our stubs that we have a whole lot more money than we thought, but the blame stuff has got to be transferred from our New York bank to here, which (because we went about it wrong in the first place) can't be done for another two weeks. We will make the first payment on *Quien Sabe* before October 1st—$250. Will you ask Lloyd to let us know —or I mean to bear us in mind—if he hears of a horse for sale so we could buy the beast when we come up in February? Meanwhile will keep you informed as to 'lightning change' program we are giving these days."[1]

The voyage to the South Seas had been delayed in order that Jeannette Norris, who frequently suffered appendicitis attacks, might undergo an operation. While Mrs. Norris was in the hospital, her husband called at Bruce Porter's studio, haggard and despairing. He told his old friend that his wife had been operated on and was now out of danger, but as they lunched together he seemed unable to shake off the depression which held him. They walked to the hospital together, and outside the door they stood for a moment:

"Bruce, I'm afraid!"

His friend gave him the formal assurance that all was well.

"Yes—but I'm afraid!"

"Afraid of what, Frank?"

"I'm afraid of death!"

He did not tell his fears to his wife, however, but

[1]Printed in *The Life of Mrs. Robert Louis Stevenson* by Nellie Van de Gift Sanchez, N. Y.: Scribners, (1920), p. 275. Quoted by permission of Mrs. Sanchez.

pretended to take the matter lightly, insisting that she had always hoped for the luxury of an operation and had taken this means of satisfying herself. He broke the hospital rules by smuggling in raffia so that she might further amuse herself by making baskets during her convalescence. It was not long before she was up and around once more, and with her recovery the depression was forgotten.

On Monday evening the twentieth of October, a month after his wife had returned to their temporary home at 1921 Broderick Street, Norris complained of an attack of indigestion. When Mrs. Norris suggested that it was appendicitis, he laughed. When the doctor called and agreed with her, Norris refused to take it seriously.

"Jeannette thinks that because she had an operation, everyone should have one. I think that one in the family is enough!"

When Norris felt better the following morning, he was sure that he had been right in opposing the doctor. All of his life he had been having attacks of indigestion, and why should this be more serious than the others? He had made fun of one of these attacks in *Blix*. Condy had sent a note to Blix by special messenger. "'All our fun is spoiled,' he wrote. 'I've got ptomaine poisoning from eating the creamed oysters last night, and am in for a solid fortnight spent in bed. Have passed a miserable night.'" When Blix reached his house with dire forecasts in her mind, she found him sitting on the front steps.

"'I've got eleven dollars!' he announced cheerfully.

"'But I thought it was ptomaine poisoning!' she cried with vexation.

"'Pshaw! that's what the doctor says. He's a flap-
doodle; nothing but a kind of a sort of a pain. It's all
gone now. I'm as fit as a fiddle—and I've got eleven
dollars. Let's go somewhere and do something.'"

Norris's attitude was much the same as he looked
forward to his plans for Wednesday, but at three
o'clock Wednesday morning he was in agony. When
he reached the hospital the doctor operated at once
and found an advanced state of general peritonitis,
with gangrene and perforation of the appendix.
Throughout the next three days, Norris fought for
his life, and, if he had not been too severely handicapped, he might have won the battle. But the fever
attacks of his South African and Cuban adventures,
which had left his system in a weakened condition,
gave the advantage to the enemy. He died Saturday
morning, the twenty-fifth of October, and was buried
the following Monday in the Mountain View Ceme-
tery at Oakland. The nation mourned the loss of a
young man who in his short life of thirty-two years
had written his name indelibly upon American literature.

Index

309

Index

314 Index

Francisco, 125 ff.; joins staff of *Wave*, 127; friendship with staff of the *Lark*, 134 ff.; decline of work on the *Wave*, 144 ff.; courtship of Jeannette Black, 151 ff.; renews activity on the *Wave*, 155 ff.; visits Big Dipper mine, 157–160; joins *McClure* staff in New York, 165 ff.; goes to Cuba during war, 173 ff.; recuperates from fever in San Francisco, 203 ff.; spends disagreeable winter in New York, 208 ff.; collects material for *The Octopus*, 244 ff.; joins Doubleday, Page & Company, 266–267; marries, 267; discovers *Sister Carrie*, 269–270; moves to Roselle, N. J., 270; goes to Chicago, 274 ff.; daughter born to, 278; leaves New York, 296; plans trip around world, 298; lives in San Francisco, 299–304; buys cabin in Santa Cruz Mountains, 304–305; wife's illness, 306; illness and death, 307–308 estate at death, 286 n.

PERSONALITY: appearance, 11, 24, 49, 277; interest in girls and horses, 46 ff.; love for college pranks, 49 ff.; personality at U. C., 59 ff.; college activities, 61–63; early attitude towards poverty, 88; autobiography in *Vandover*, 96; attitude towards life and literature, 102; attitude towards women, 148–149; as Condy Rivers, 154–155; attitude towards "New Bohemia," 207 ff., 279 ff.; friends, 268 ff., 281–282.

WRITINGS: writes *Robert d'Artois*, 41 ff.; writes *Yvernelle*, 47 ff.; writes stories for college papers, 50 ff.; writes stories for S. F. journals, 67 ff.; writes Junior farce, 69 ff.; his illustrations, 70, 71; writes *Lauth*, 73 ff.; starts *McTeague*, 89 ff.; continues *McTeague*, 95; writes *Vandover*, 96; discussion of work on *Wave*, 130 ff.; completes *McTeague*, 157 ff.; writes *Moran*, 160–165;

writes *Blix*, 169 ff.; writes *A Man's Woman*, 212 ff.; conceives *Epic of the Wheat*, 239 ff.; writes *Octopus*, 253 ff.; writes *Pit*, 278 ff., 291 ff.; writes short stories, 286 ff.; writes articles, 288 ff.

READING: interest in Froissart, 33 ff.; preference of Froissart to Zola, 37–38; influenced by Kipling, 67 ff., 76 ff.; influenced by Davis, 72, 73, 76 ff.; attitude towards realism, 78 ff.; influenced by Zola, 81 ff.; adaptation of naturalism, 84, 85; methods of observation, 139; taste in short stories, 145 ff.; attitude towards writing short stories, 157; favorite reading, 282–284.

Norris, Gertrude Doggett (Norris's mother), marriage, 5; parentage, 5, 6; birth in Mendon, Mass., 6; early life in Chicago, 6; stage career, 7; trip abroad, 26; teaches Norris French, 32 ff.; returns to America, 35; meets Norris in New York, 42; separation and divorce, 86 ff.; encourages Norris's writing, 51, 88 f.; moves to Cambridge, 90; injects Norris into society, 149–150; Norris reads *Moran* to, 203 ff.; *Blix* dedicated to, 150; appearance and personality, 8, 11, 13, 14, 44.

Norris, Grace, 10.

Norris, Jeannette Black (Norris's wife), 162, 169, 203, 245, 251, 299, 300; quoted, 286, 291; as *Blix*, 151, 151 n.; meeting with Norris, 151; courted by Norris, 152 ff.; attends school in St. Louis, 157; visited by Norris in St. Louis, 168; ill with mastoid infection, 208–209; marries Norris, 267; daughter born to, 278; illness, 306–307.

Norris, Jeannette, Jr. ("Billy"), 278, 298, 299, 300, 301.

Norris, Kathleen, 286 n.

Norris, Lester, 10, 13, 21, 22 ff., 26, 44.